Advance Praise for *Critical Teaching Behaviors*

"It was a privilege to watch Lauren and Claudia create and test the CTB framework at our institution. Their passion and desire to help faculty provided my colleagues with a much-needed comprehensive, yet personal and practical approach to good teaching. I love how the framework beautifully captures the encompassing nature of reflection. It transformed the way I document and assess my teaching and conduct peer evaluations. I cannot wait to share this book with all colleagues in higher education!"—*Diana Botnaru, Professor and SoTL Commons Conference Chair, Georgia Southern University*

"*Critical Teaching Behaviors* is an in-depth observation tool. The CTB has an extensive list of teaching behavior categories and observable teaching items. The inclusion of different teaching modalities is another exceptional component to this tool. This tool includes a multi-step process of materials review, observation, and debrief, providing a well-rounded opportunity to work together and learn from our own and others' teaching behaviors." —*Erica Bowers, Director of the Faculty Development Center; Gina Harmston, Department of Public Health; and Susan R. Sy, Department of Psychology; California State University, Fullerton*

"The question of what constitutes 'good' teaching is a perennial one in higher education, a reflection not of indecision, but rather a recognition that teaching and learning practices are highly sensitive to context, whether that context is disciplinary, institutional, or geo-political. In *Critical Teaching Behaviors*, Lauren Barbeau and Claudia Cornejo Happel do not provide us with a one-size-fits-all prescription for good teaching, but rather a flexible framework that can be adapted to a multitude of learning environments. Their framework is grounded in the considerable body of evidence-based practice that has emerged from the scholarship of teaching and learning (and related fields), while allowing space to imagine how our practice will evolve in the future."—*Laura Cruz, Associate Research Professor, Schreyer Institute for Teaching Excellence; Penn State University*

"This book offers the rare combination of being timely, useful, helpful, and relevant by offering a means to answer questions about 'what is good teaching?' As faculty work to address the shifting needs of students by modifying their approaches to teaching, the critical teaching behaviors framework provides an iterative, contextualized, reflection tool to guide thoughtful engagement with what it means to be an effective teacher. A must-read for anyone serious about supporting student learning."—*Natasha Jankowski, Coeditor of* Reframing Assessment to Center Equity

"Barbeau and Cornejo Happel's *Critical Teaching Behaviors* offers a comprehensive, practice-based, growth-oriented framework and process for planning, documenting, observing, and improving teaching and learning. It is well grounded in the SoTL literature and incorporates research on Students as Partners (SaP) in a way that I have not seen before in approaches to evaluating teaching. I use their CTB framework in my own teaching practice and have recommended my department adopt it for our peer observation process."—*Trent W. Maurer, Professor of Human Development and Family Science, Georgia Southern University*

"A beautifully written answer to the age-old question of how to assess and document effective teaching. This is a must-read for faculty and educational developers alike."—*Marina G. Smitherman, Director of the Center for Excellence in Teaching and Learning, Dalton State College*

"The critical teaching behaviors framework is evidence-based, well-organized, and user-tested. Its structured approach supports educators and administrators to talk systematically and thoughtfully about teaching while still creating space and flexibility for each educator to find the teaching approaches that work best for their discipline and personal style. Importantly, it is also designed to foster growth as a teacher. However, the best endorsement came from a graduate teaching fellow at my institution: 'This framework slaps!'"—*Carol Subiño Sullivan, Assistant Director, Faculty Teaching and Learning Initiatives, Center for Teaching and Learning, Georgia Tech*

CRITICAL TEACHING BEHAVIORS

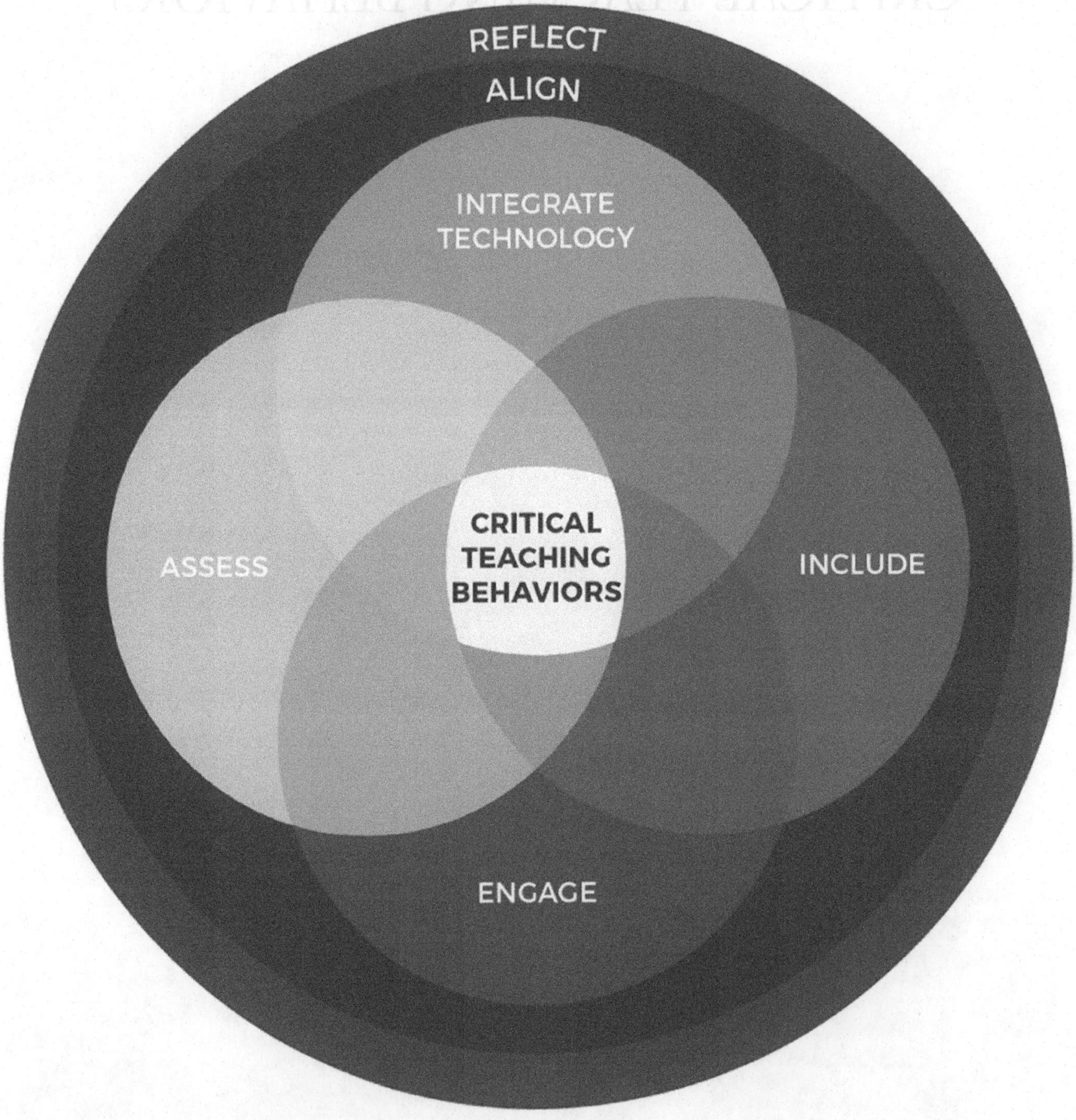
REFLECT
ALIGN
INTEGRATE TECHNOLOGY
ASSESS
CRITICAL TEACHING BEHAVIORS
INCLUDE
ENGAGE

CRITICAL TEACHING BEHAVIORS

Defining, Documenting, and Discussing Good Teaching

Lauren Barbeau and Claudia Cornejo Happel

Foreword by Nancy L. Chick

Routledge
Taylor & Francis Group

NEW YORK AND LONDON

First published in 2023 by Stylus Publishing, LLC.

Published in 2023 by Routledge
605 Third Avenue, New York, NY 10017
4 Park Square, Milton Park, Abingdon, Oxon OX14 4RN

Routledge is an imprint of the Taylor & Francis Group, an informa business.

© 2023 Taylor & Francis Group

Library of Congress Cataloging-in-Publication-Data
Names: Barbeau, Lauren, author. | Cornejo Happel, Claudia A., author.
Title: Critical teaching behaviors : defining, documenting, and discussing good teaching / Lauren Barbeau and Claudia Cornejo Happe ; foreword by Nancy L. Chick.
Description: First edition. | Sterling, Virginia : Stylus, [2023] | Includes bibliographical references and index.

Identifiers: LCCN 2023001056
ISBN 9781642673685 (cloth : acid-free paper) | ISBN 9781642673692 (paperback : acid-free paper)
Subjects: LCSH: Teachers--Rating of--United States. | Teaching--United States--Evaluation. | Teacher effectiveness--United States.
Classification: LCC LB2838 .B27 2023
LC record available at https://lccn.loc.gov/2023001056

ISBN: 9781642673685 (hbk)
ISBN: 9781642673692 (pbk)
ISBN: 9781003443902 (ebk)

DOI: 10.4324/9781003443902

Contents

Foreword

WHEN I WAS COMING up through the tenure track from assistant to associate to full professor, faculty talked about question #17 on the student evaluation form in hushed tones. The prompt on the form read, "Overall, I consider this instructor to be an excellent teacher," but everyone called it the "overall instructor rating," a troublingly exaggerated shorthand. When in the role of evaluator, many faculty invoked question #17—or, more precisely, someone's average score for question #17—as a singular indication of the quality of a peer's teaching. When in the role of the one being evaluated, faculty submitted thick dossiers with 10,000-word self-assessments, course artifacts, grade breakdowns by course type, annotated student work, letters from peers' class observations, department-solicited letters from former students, and more. But no matter how much evidence demonstrated various angles of someone's teaching effectiveness or captured the complexities of different teaching experiences, that single number weighed heavily in campus and departmental deliberations about whether to let someone stay. Or at least it felt that way. But this was nearly a quarter of a century ago.

One of the paradoxes of higher education is that it's focused on transforming people's minds, but the institution itself changes with glacial speed. However, I'm hopeful about some of the trends in higher education in recent history. Slowly, we've been turning toward equity in how we think about students. The G.I. Bill of 1944 opened up the ivory towers to countless returning military veterans who otherwise might not have been able to afford a college degree. The 1960s ushered in the gradual acceptance of students of color at major American universities, and campus protests erupted to make the curriculum reflect the student body. And when it became clear that faculty were still teaching in the same old one-size-fits-all ways, pedagogy began to evolve as well. The assumption that students who don't succeed aren't college material has grown into the quest to understand and improve the complex processes of teaching and learning within different contexts and for different students. It's slow, but it's happening.

Even more recently, we've started to turn toward equity in how we think about faculty, too. Unfortunately, the diversification of faculty on American campuses continues to be painfully unhurried (National Center for Education Statistics, 2022), as seen in the 2020 demographic data: "White faculty are overrepresented any way you cut it" (Matias et al., 2021, para. 6). The #thisiswhataprofessorlookslike Twitter thread (Nadal, 2018) and the chapters in *Picture a Professor: Interrupting Bias About Faculty and Increasing Student Learning* (Neuhaus, 2022) illustrate the current efforts to amplify the problem. Greater attention to job advertisements, cluster and opportunity hires, open field searches, bias training for hiring committees, and other recruitment strategies will hopefully open more doors to faculty offices. Yet retention efforts for a diversified faculty are equally important, parallel to focusing on student access to campus without planning both academic and emotional supports to get them to stay.

Certainly, one of the most important retention strategies is changing how faculty are evaluated. Just as we learned that a one-size-fits-all approach to students no longer supports our understanding of teaching and learning, evaluating faculty according to things like "fit" and other euphemisms for replicating the status quo no longer supports our understanding of our fellow educators. Most of the energy in this movement is concentrated on changing the instrumentation of student evaluations of teaching, particularly by highlighting their role in reinforcing the biases of traditional faculty evaluation practices (e.g., Boring et al., 2016; Esarey & Valdes, 2020). This is an important undertaking. Similarly, there is some work in the sciences to develop systematic methods and tools for classroom observations by peers (e.g., Sawada et al., 2002; Smith et al., 2013). More holistically, centers for teaching, individual campuses, and clusters of institutions or disciplinary groups are developing context-specific approaches to peer evaluation of teaching (e.g., the University of Southern California Center for Excellence in Teaching's [n.d.-b] definition of *excellence teaching* and accompanying checklists [n.d.-a]; the University of Oregon Office of the Provost's [2020] impressive process and outcomes for revising their evaluation of teaching; the NSF-funded TEval project at University Massachusetts, University of Kansas, and University of Colorado).

What Lauren Barbeau and Claudia Cornejo Happel have done in *Critical Teaching Behaviors* is a significant leap forward for the entire project of evaluating faculty—not just for specific campuses or disciplines, but for everyone. Shaped by high-level behaviors that are grounded in research on effective teaching and learning, that can be expressed in myriad ways across contexts, that can be documented in multiple forms of evidence, and that can be seen and assessed by peers, their framework is a gift to the hard work of changing the face of higher education.

I first learned about their framework at a conference in February 2020 (Barbeau & Cornejo Happel, 2020). After their presentation, I told them I couldn't wait to share it with colleagues, and they told me they were working on a book. But 20 days later, we all went home for over a year because of a global pandemic.

It's now late 2022, and here we are. They somehow managed to complete the book during some of the darkest days in our lifetime. (As an aside, this feat suggests to me they should now write about the effectiveness of their collaborative relationship.) I'm counting the days until I can share with colleagues more than a conference pdf of their framework. With publication of this book, Lauren Barbeau and Claudia Cornejo Happel are ushering in a new phase in the gradual evolution of higher education.

Nancy L. Chick
Rollins College
Winter Park, Florida

References

Barbeau, L. M., & Cornejo Happel, C. (2020, February 20). *Critical teaching behaviors: What does "good" teaching look like?"* [Conference session]. SoTL Commons Conference, Georgia Southern University, Savannah, GA, United States. https://digitalcommons.georgiasouthern.edu/sotlcommons/SoTL/2020/34

Boring, A., Ottoboni, K., & Start, P. (2016, January 7). Student evaluations of teaching (mostly) do not measure teaching effectiveness. *ScienceOpen Research*. https://doi.org/10.14293/S2199-1006.1.SOR-EDU.AETBZC.v1

Esarey, J., & Valdes, N. (2020). Unbiased, reliable, and valid student evaluations can still be unfair. *Assessment & Evaluation in Higher Education, 45*(8), 1106–1120. https://doi.org/10.1080/02602938.2020.1724875

Matias, J. N., Lewis, N., & Hope, E. (2021, September). Universities say they want more diverse faculties. So why is academia still so white? *FiveThirtyEight*, 7. https://fivethirtyeight.com/features/universities-say-they-want-more-diverse-faculties-so-why-is-academia-still-so-white/

Nadal, K. L. (2018, March 9). *What does a professor look like?* Psychology Benefits Society. https://psychologybenefits.org/2018/03/09/what-does-a-professor-look-like/

National Center for Education Statistics. (2022). Characteristics of postsecondary faculty. *Condition of Education*. U.S. Department of Education, Institute of Education Sciences. https://nces.ed.gov/programs/coe/indicator/csc

Neuhaus, J. (2022). *Picture a professor: Interrupting bias about faculty and increasing student learning.* West Virginia University Press.

Sawada, D., Piburn, M. D., Judson, E., Turley, J., Falconer, K., Benford, R., & Bloom, I. (2002). Measuring reform practices in science and mathematics classrooms: The reformed teaching observation protocol. *School Science and Mathematics, 102*(6), 245–253.

Smith, M. K., Jones, F. H. M., Gilbert, S. L., & Wieman, C. E. (2013). The classroom observation protocol for undergraduate STEM (COPUS): A new instrument to characterize university STEM classroom practices. *CBE-Life Sciences Education, 12*(4), 618–627.

University of Oregon Office of the Provost. (2020). *Revising UO's teaching evaluations.* https://provost.uoregon.edu/revising-uos-teaching-evaluations

University of Southern California Center for Excellence in Teaching. (n.d.-a). *Peer review and evaluation.* https://cet.usc.edu/resources/instructor-course-evaluation/

University of Southern California Center for Excellence in Teaching. (n.d.-b). *USC definition of excellence in teaching.* https://cet.usc.edu/about/usc-definition-of-excellence-in-teaching/

Acknowledgments

THERE ARE MANY PEOPLE we want to thank for their support and feedback as we developed, tested, and improved the critical teaching behaviors framework and materials and as we wrote, reviewed, and revised this book. Our colleagues at Georgia Southern University were instrumental in making this project a reality; they provided input on the first iterations and made it possible for us to use the CTB tools in practice. We appreciate Georgia Southern faculty and administrators who invited us to present workshops on the CTB framework and used it for documenting teaching; they provided us with encouragement as well as critical feedback that helped us improve the CTB tools in the early stages of this project. We especially thank Debbie Walker and Diana Botnaru, SoTL Commons Conference chair, who have generously supported our work and given us a stage to share it on.

Further, we would like to express our gratitude to our early adoption partners, Janice Dawson (Mesa State Community College) and Erica Bowers and Gina Harmston (California State University, Fullerton), who introduced the CTB to their faculty and developed adaptations of the peer observation protocol for their campuses; their feedback has been invaluable in making final adjustments to the tools and helping us ensure they are easy to use and to adapt based on individual needs. We are excited to share their adaptations as the first items in our adaptation database.

We also want to acknowledge the work of colleagues who have inspired components of this book. Peter Berryman's comprehensive guide, *Designing Online Courses for Web Accessibility and Usability* (Center for Teaching Excellence, Georgia Southern University, 2019) served as the basis for Table 2.3 ("Increasing Accessibility of Digital Course Materials").

Lauren

I feel it most appropriate to start by expressing my gratitude to Claudia, whose unwavering faith in the value and appeal of this project convinced me that the critical teaching behaviors could and should be a book. I appreciate her friendship and collaborative spirit that made this work seem less like, well, work.

To Debbie Walker, I owe thanks for her support in piloting both the observation and student feedback protocols. Laura Reefer's feedback on the peer observation chapter ensured that it speaks equally to online as well as face-to-face observations. Kelly Ford's feedback on the core value activities both broadened and deepened the reflective prompts. My Intro to College Teaching students read several of the chapters in Part One and offered insights that allowed us to clarify some of the more complex concepts.

I'm fortunate to have parents who allowed me to crash at their beach condo periodically so I could have the "room of one's own" to focus on writing as well as the proximity to meet with Claudia in person. I give my deepest love and appreciation to my husband, Michael, who always believed I would write a book and who took on more than his fair share of the domestic responsibilities to give me the time to do it. Finally, I dedicate this to my daughter, Elora, whose pending arrival ensured the completion of this manuscript.

Claudia

I want to start by thanking Lauren for her attention to detail, project management skills, and constant encouragement and friendship throughout this project. I am grateful for my colleagues at Embry-Riddle Aeronautical University who embraced the CTB when I arrived at ERAU in 2019 and have used it in their own practice since. Especially, I want to express my gratitude to CTLE director Lori Mumpower, who has promoted the CTB tools on campus providing opportunities to implement them in different settings and gather data on their effectiveness; to my colleagues Teha Cooks and

Chad Rohrbacher, who have been my collaborators in testing and improving the midterm student feedback tool; and to Carmen Resco and Kimberly Williams, who have been instrumental in helping me understand the data.

I also want to acknowledge that this book would not exist without my family—my children, Asiri and Leandro; my husband, Martin; and my parents, Christa and Hans—who each inspire, motivate, and support me in their own way. I am forever grateful!

Introduction

WHAT DOES "GOOD" TEACHING mean, and how can we know it when we see it? Perhaps you have grappled with these questions at some point in your career, either as an instructor wanting to document or grow your teaching effectiveness or as a peer or administrator trying to provide guidance to or assess the teaching of others. Your search for answers may be what has led you to peruse this book, and if so, you are not alone. These questions motivated us to begin the project you now hold in your hands (or scroll on your screen). In January of 2018, our then institution consolidated with another local university. The two institutions had little in common beyond geographic proximity. Vastly different methods of evaluating teaching for tenure, promotion, and annual review purposes understandably emerged as a chief concern for instructors as departments merged and leadership changed. As educational developers supporting instructors in their teaching, we began fielding an influx of questions related to the documentation and evaluation of teaching from anxious instructors and conscientious administrators. Although we received many variations on the theme, they usually boiled down to two fundamental questions: What is "good" teaching, and how can we identify it for purposes of documentation and evaluation?

To respond to these questions, we began reviewing a myriad of frameworks and resources related to this topic. While each resource had its merits, we found that none of them was flexible enough to accommodate disciplinary and contextual differences while also offering a suite of comprehensive, aligned tools for documenting and discussing teaching. Many of the resources we reviewed functioned more as checklists of qualities or actions that characterize the effective teacher than as guidance that flexibly adapts to the unique teaching styles of individual instructors. Research provides invaluable guidance on effective teaching practices; however, successful implementation of those practices depends on a broad range of variables, including but not limited to instructor persona, students, discipline, class size, modality, and course and institutional context. We believe that good teaching can be learned, but we also believe that there is no "one-size-fits-all" version of good teaching. When it comes to defining good teaching, we realized that no checklist can capture the complex decisions we as individual instructors make about what practices to implement in our courses and how. We needed an instrument that was both flexible enough to accommodate individual expressions of good teaching and comprehensive enough to provide a unifying language and common understanding of the components of good teaching. Thus, the critical teaching behaviors (CTB) framework was born.[1]

As we began to share our work on the CTB, we realized the questions that initially inspired us and challenges we faced in finding the right resource were not unique to our situation. Rather, these issues seemed relevant to others across higher education as well. An increasing number of studies indicate the problematic nature of evaluating instructor performance based exclusively on student evaluations, which have long been a staple means of assessing "good" teaching (Boring, 2017; Kreitzer & Sweet-Cushman, 2022; Mitchell & Martin, 2018).

With the search for alternative documentation and evaluation methods, interest in peer observation and student feedback sessions has risen, as has the need for guidance on how to conduct them and how to use the reports as evidence of teaching effectiveness. Many institutions have also begun to look for means to incorporate more of the instructor's perspective on their own teaching into the evaluation process. Overall, we see a trend toward more holistic means of documenting and assessing teaching effectiveness, one that includes a variety of evidence and perspectives.

The CTB contributes to and advances this movement to holistically document teaching in several ways. First, in developing the CTB, we focused on dynamic behaviors instructors enact rather than innate characteristics they possess. This emphasis on behaviors that can be adopted, adapted, and refined through learning and reflection means that anyone has the potential to become a "good" teacher. It also allows us to provide clear guidance on what instructors and observers can look for as evidence of good teaching while simultaneously leaving space for instructors to flexibly express these behaviors. In reviewing other, more behavior-oriented frameworks, however, we noticed a potential danger of this approach: Concentrating on instructor actions can lead us to privilege what happens in the learning space over the effort an instructor puts into preparation. As we discussed this problem, we frequently found ourselves using an iceberg analogy to understand how good teaching is identified and documented through behaviors. Only about 10% of an iceberg is visible above water; the vast majority of its bulk remains hidden below the surface to the casual observer. When it comes to proving teaching effectiveness, we likewise tend to showcase or review only what is visible in the learning space, whether that space is face-to-face or online. As instructors ourselves and professionals working with teachers to enhance teaching and learning, we can confidently say that what can be seen in the learning space captures only a fraction of the time and effort that goes into effective instruction. Much of the work instructors do to design and deliver quality learning experiences goes unseen and undocumented, especially when we place the focus on behaviors. In keeping with our desire to promote a more holistic approach to the documentation and discussion of teaching effectiveness, we considered what instructors do outside the learning space to engage in good teaching practices and then generated suggested

documentation instructors might provide to capture these otherwise invisible behaviors.

As part of our desire to help instructors present their teaching holistically, we came to understand that documenting good teaching requires more than simple guidance on behaviors to observe and evidence to collect; instructors need to articulate a sense of self to which they can align their artifacts. Without this guiding set of teaching values to drive the curation of artifacts, instructors may cobble together a hodgepodge of materials with little rhyme or reason evident to the reviewer. When materials do not tell a coherent story about our teaching, even the best teachers may be overlooked by reviewers because we fail to communicate our effectiveness in a manner that makes sense to an external audience. Consequently, we began to think more about how we could help instructors produce coherence across their materials so that each selected artifact expands upon the central story they want to tell about their teaching. Instead of thinking of the CTB framework merely as a list of definitions, behaviors, and evidence, we saw that, with a little training, instructors can use it to create a persuasive, cohesive narrative of teaching effectiveness that helps them convey a genuine sense of self as a teacher. Because the voices of peers and students play crucial roles in our materials as well as in our development of a sense of self as teacher, we also developed aligned peer observation and student feedback instruments that make it easier to incorporate their voices while maintaining coherence across selected artifacts. The end result of our reflections is a suite of tools and activities aligned to the CTB framework, designed to help instructors craft a cohesive narrative of teaching effectiveness supported by relevant evidence.

What Is the CTB Framework?

Now that you understand the "why" behind this project, we can turn our attention to the "what." Before moving forward, however, we recommend that you first review the framework in Appendix A, as the following explanation will make much more sense if you have seen the framework. The CTB framework consists of six categories of behaviors that, based on our review of research, encompass the actions effective instructors exhibit when designing and delivering their courses. (*Note:* If you visit the book resources at https://criticalteachingbehaviors.org, you will be able to access the original, full-color version of the framework where each category box is color coded for easy reference because Claudia likes boxes and Lauren likes colors.) Designed for the purpose of helping instructors and administrators define, document, and discuss good teaching, the framework includes category definitions, example behaviors that break the definition into more easily identifiable actions, and a final evidence column that offers suggestions on how to document behaviors in each category. Table I.1 provides the categories and their definitions for ease of reference.

We intentionally chose to title each category and start each set of accompanying behaviors with a verb. This focus on action makes it easier for both instructors and those assessing instructors to recognize and document concrete elements of good teaching. While good teaching means that an instructor will consistently engage in behaviors across all categories, we did not design nor do we intend the CTB to be used as a checklist of behaviors all instructors should enact all the time to be considered effective. Instead, we hope to promote agency by offering a range of behaviors instructors can choose to implement in each category

depending on their contextual needs, as discussed previously.

To build the CTB framework itself, we conducted extensive literature reviews and found two primary phenomena. First, instructors are nearly drowning in a sea of information about good teaching practices. Each year, a proliferation of newly published books seeks to inform instructors of specific, research-based teaching practices. These books offer a deep dive into one aspect of teaching, such as inclusivity or engagement. Sometimes they may even focus on one specific but complex teaching strategy—for example, project-based learning. Second, we noticed a significant uptick in the last decade in the number of models for assessing teaching as individual departments, institutions, and professional organizations have grappled with questions about how to document teaching. These models run the gamut from frameworks to checklists to rubrics to self-assessments and beyond, but with few exceptions, they are at most accompanied by a white paper or published article primarily focusing on the need for and research related to the implementation of the model. Rarely is the goal to produce a thorough review of teaching literature captured in one

TABLE I.1: CTB Categories and Definitions	
Align	Instructors who align components of learning experiences start with clear learning goals. Measurable outcomes, teaching and learning activities, assessment tasks, and feedback build on each other to support student progress toward these goals.
Include	Instructors who create an inclusive learning environment promote equity by using accessibility standards and learner-centered strategies when designing and delivering content. They cultivate an atmosphere in which students see themselves positively represented and experience a sense of belonging conducive to emotional well-being for learning.
Engage	Instructors who engage students purposefully select research-based techniques to ensure that students actively participate in the learning process and take responsibility for their intellectual development.
Assess	Instructors who assess learning develop and facilitate transparent, meaningful tasks to provide students with timely feedback on their learning and to measure achievement of learning outcomes. They frequently review data to improve instruction.
Integrate Technology	Instructors who integrate technology responsibly use tools to design accessible, high-quality instructional materials and engaging learning opportunities beyond traditional barriers of place and time.
Reflect	Instructors who reflect gather feedback on their teaching from self-assessment, peers, and students to regularly identify opportunities for growth. They pursue improvements to their instruction through engagement with professional development and scholarship.

overarching model as well as a suite of instruments aligned to that model. Only a handful of publications have attempted to present a comprehensive overview of research that more generally amasses and defines the necessary elements of good teaching practice. In other words, if you are looking for one resource that summarizes and synthesizes these deep dive books into a comprehensive model of effective teaching practices, you will be hard-pressed to find it. Existing models tend to facilitate instructor self-assessment and base the recognition of effective teaching on self-reported data. They usually focus on only one type of teaching assessment and feedback—evaluative, formative, or self-reflective—whereas assessments in practice often serve more than one purpose. Most models we encountered stand alone; they do not provide aligned guidance or instruments to gather or make effective use of student and peer perspectives on teaching. While they might list behaviors to look for or materials to gather, current models rarely provide guidance on how to connect behaviors with materials in a narrative that makes an argument for teaching effectiveness.

We sought to fill these gaps with the CTB. The six categories that now comprise the framework emerged primarily from a thematic analysis of teaching and learning literature. We began to code prevailing concepts across the research until we had established consistent categories into which they fell. This approach also allowed us to make note of specific strategies and behaviors associated with each category. The chapters in Part One outline research-based practices in each category, providing you an accessible summary of what foundational research as well as the most recent studies reveal about teaching for improved learning. Because our goal is breadth of strategies in these chapters, we cannot provide significant depth on any one strategy, but our references offer excellent resources for deeper dives on particular subjects. Part Two introduces CTB-aligned instruments for collecting self, peer, and student perspectives on your teaching and offers guidance on how to gather these perspectives as well as options for using them for different assessment purposes. Throughout the book, we strive for a practical approach that goes beyond mere summary to explain how you can translate research into behaviors and what documentation you can collect as evidence of those behaviors.

Because we found some degree of simplification and separation necessary for creating a useful tool, CTB categories are artificially neat, and in that regard, they do not reflect the often messy business of teaching. Teaching does not fall nicely into bounded, color-coded boxes. Realistically, a behavior listed in the Assess category might also fall into any of the other categories depending on the purpose behind your implementation of it. We will talk more about this fuzziness and how to deal with it when documenting your teaching in Part Two, specifically in the first and last chapters of that section. To visually capture the blurriness of behaviors across categories, we created the model in Figure I.1. While we jokingly dubbed it the "zygote model" in our brainstorming sessions because it looks like a cell dividing, we like to think that the name captures something important about the way these categories interact. Like a cell dividing, the productive overlap of behaviors in this model leads to growth—in this case, your growth as a teacher. Neither placement nor size in the model indicate greater or lesser importance; all categories are equally important aspects of good teaching. Rather, placement indicates how we conceptualized the interactions among categories.

The four inner categories, Integrate Technology, Include, Engage, and Assess, tend to be the most visible behaviors. Of course we invisibly perform components of these categories outside the learning space, but we can typically see evidence of these behaviors when we perform an observation without having to request additional documentation. Align behaviors can be harder to see in the learning space and often require us to look at additional documents, such as the syllabus, for proof an instructor is engaging in these behaviors. Although not always as visible, alignment holds the four inner categories together by providing purpose and direction to the behaviors we implement in those categories. Reflect behaviors usually require a conversation with the instructor. Because these behaviors can be difficult to document, we include spaces for instructor reflection in both our peer observation and student feedback instruments. Despite its elusiveness when it comes to documentation, reflection encompasses all other behaviors because it allows us to zero in on particular aspects of our teaching to self-assess, document, and grow.

As you learn more about each category, you may find that you conceptualize these interactions differently. You may even develop your own personalized model that reflects how you believe these categories interact to produce your particular way of teaching.

Figure I.1. CTB model of teaching behaviors.

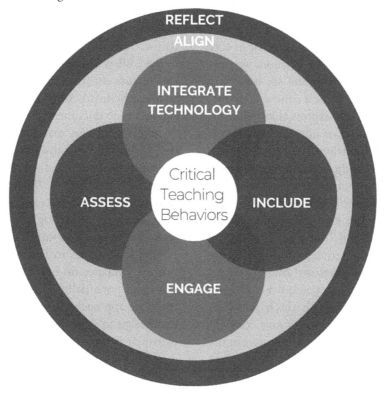

We offer this model not as the definitive depiction of how the components of good teaching interact but as a means of problematizing the artificial order we imposed on the categories to create the framework. As you read about each of the categories in Part One, we encourage you to look for and reflect upon points of overlap across categories. Sometimes we explicitly cross-reference between categories, but if you are attentive, you will certainly find additional areas of overlap.

How Can You Use This Book?

We designed this to be an interactive workbook. While you can choose to read passively, you will get the most value from this book by completing the prompts and activities along the way. Our holistic approach to the documentation of teaching led us to develop reflective methods that encourage you to continue growing even as they help you identify and showcase current achievements. Engaging in this kind of meaningful reflection will take some dedicated time and effort on your part; however, doing so will also empower you

to take charge of your teaching documentation. After responding to the prompts, by the end of this book, you will be able to:

1. Identify behaviors consistent with good teaching.
2. Reflect upon the teaching behaviors you already exhibit.
3. Implement research-based, effective teaching behaviors across each of the six CTB categories.
4. Document your teaching behaviors.
5. Articulate a core value statement that motivates your approach to teaching.
6. Conduct and/or reflect on a peer observation.
7. Collect and/or reflect on midterm student feedback.
8. Use your core value statement to purposefully select and frame evidence of effectiveness in a coherent teaching narrative.

Part One leads you through the first four listed outcomes by defining and expounding upon the CTB categories. Each chapter follows the same format for the sake of consistency. The "What Do We Know?"

section summarizes key research on the category. If you need a quick reference on what research says about a particular category, we recommend you start in this section and dig deeper when necessary using the in-text citations. In the "What Do We Do?" section, we provide a step-by-step breakdown of the six behaviors listed on the framework to provide a concise overview of the different ways you can express that behavior. Remember, these breakdowns are not checkboxes; you need not engage in every behavior to be a good teacher, nor does your expression of the behavior need to look the same as someone else's. Chapters in Part One end with a "What Do We Show?" table that explains the type of documentation you can collect as evidence of behaviors in each category. We explain what the documentation is and offer strategies for collecting it. The table is broken into "Personal Materials" and "Materials From Others" to help you quickly identify the source of the documentation. Each chapter concludes with a set of "Reflection Questions" to help you think more deeply about topics introduced in the chapter and begin to identify behaviors you already engage in related to the category as well as areas for growth.

In Part Two, we explore instruments and activities aligned with the CTB framework that guide you through the last four listed outcomes. This section begins with chapter 7, "Identifying Your Core Value." If your goal in reading this book is to craft a persuasive narrative of teaching effectiveness, you will not want to skip this activity. Subsequent chapters will refer back to your core value to explain how you can use it as a lens to frame other materials you collect as evidence of your teaching effectiveness. The following chapters on "Peer Observation" and "Midterm Student Feedback" sessions introduce CTB-aligned instruments you can use to gather perspectives on your teaching from peers and students. These chapters do double duty, both training you to conduct observations and feedback sessions using CTB tools and explaining how you can reflect upon these reports to productively advance your effectiveness narrative. The final chapter ties it all together by providing instruction on how you can use the CTB to frame a narrative of teaching effectiveness and intentionally select evidence that supports a coherent narrative.

For readers fulfilling an administrative role, you will necessarily approach the content from a different perspective, and we want to give some guidance on how

you can use this book. Consider Part One the foundation for a common language around defining good teaching. The research contained in the "What Do We Know?" sections as well as the breakdown of actions in the "What Do We Do?" sections help you identify and discuss effective teaching practices. You may also be asked by instructors for guidance on evidence they can gather to document their teaching. In addition to the more common materials instructors can collect, the "What Do We Show" sections list items you may not have considered and act as easy references you can share with instructors. If you are seeking information on how to incorporate peer or student voices in the process of evaluating teaching, you will want to read the "Peer Observation" and "Midterm Student Feedback" chapters in Part Two. These chapters will provide guidance on how you can conduct these sessions and potentially allow you to train others to use the same approach. We realize that no perfect instrument exists to meet the needs of every possible context in which it might be used; for this reason, materials we introduce in these chapters are Creative Commons licensed. While we welcome you to use the instruments as designed and according to the protocols we developed, we recognize that you may need to adapt both the instruments and the protocols to suit your needs, and we encourage you to do that. Use the chapters in Part One to add or replace example behaviors on the instruments, narrow the instruments to focus on one or a few categories, alter the protocols, and so on. We wanted to design instruments that give you the freedom (and supporting guidance that gives you the knowledge) to make changes based on your needs. All we ask is that you share your adaptations with us (at criticalteachingbehaviors@gmail.com) and allow us to post them on the "Adaptations" portion of our website so others can benefit from your ideas.

As you prepare to dive into the CTB, we leave you with a word of caution as well as encouragement. You may read some behavior lists and discover you are already implementing many or most of the research-based practices. If so, wonderful! Focus on documenting your efforts in that category. Other times, you may read a behavior list and feel overwhelmed by the number of things you could be doing. The CTB is as comprehensive as we could make it while still maintaining intelligibility and applicability, but this does mean it might feel like an overwhelming amount of information to try to act upon. Should you find yourself in this position while reading, we encourage you to concentrate on being the best teacher you can be without overdoing it. We are all too aware of the many responsibilities instructors bear. Even in the best of circumstances, none of us can do everything all at once. Instead, prioritize the changes you want to make to your teaching or documentation you want to generate. Select one category to work on for a defined period of time or choose a behavior you want to implement and dig deeper into how to do it well. Becoming a better instructor and documenting your effectiveness take time. Do what you can when you can. Incremental efforts add up to a career defined by good teaching.

Note

1. The name *critical teaching behaviors* came from our early research into assessing the impact of professional or educational development training on participants. We were interested in determining whether our pedagogy workshops actually led to improved student learning as a result of changes instructors made to their teaching after attending training. In *Four Levels of Training Evaluation*, Kirkpatrick and Kirkpatrick (2016) identify "behavior" as the third tier of assessment, beyond satisfaction with and learning as a result of training. They explain "critical behaviors" as the "few, key behaviors that the primary group will have to consistently perform on the job to bring about targeted outcomes" (p. 14). For our purposes, we identified the "primary group" as instructors and the "targeted outcome" as student learning. We then set about identifying critical "teaching" behaviors that, when consistently performed by instructors, lead most frequently to student learning according to research. While we eventually set aside this assessment project to focus on this project instead, the name *critical teaching behaviors* stuck.

References

Boring, A. (2017). Gender biases in student evaluations of teaching. *Journal of Public Economics, 145*, 27–41.

Kirkpatrick, J. D., & Kirkpatrick, W. K. (2016). *Four levels of training evaluation*. ATD Press.

Kreitzer, R. J., & Sweet-Cushman, J. (2022). Evaluating student evaluations of teaching: A review of measurement and equity bias in SETs and recommendations for ethical reform. *Journal of Academic Ethics, 20*, 73–84. https://doi.org/10.1007/s10805-021-09400-w

Mitchell, K. M. W., & Martin, J. (2018). Gender bias in student evaluations. *Political Science & Politics, 51*(3), 648–652.

Additional Reading

Advance HE. (n.d.). *UK professional standards framework (PSF)*. https://www.advance-he.ac.uk/guidance/teaching-and-learning/ukpsf

Association of College and University Educators. (2021). *Effective practice framework*. https://acue.org/?acue_courses=acues-effective-practice-framework%2F

Australian Institute for Teaching and School Leadership Education Council. (2011). *Australian professional standards for teachers*. https://www.aitsl.edu.au/docs/default-source/national-policy-framework/australian-professional-standards-for-teachers.pdf?sfvrsn=5800f33c_64

Blumberg, P. (2014). *Assessing and improving your teaching: Strategies and rubrics for faculty growth and student learning*. Jossey-Bass.

Boise State University. (2021). *Implementing a framework for assessing teaching effectiveness (IFATE)*. https://www.boisestate.edu/ctl/initiatives/implementing-a-framework-for-assessing-teaching-effectiveness-ifate/

Cheong, G. (2017). Developing an instrument for self-evaluation of teaching and learning competencies: A review of faculty professional development and the changing higher education landscape in Singapore. *Educational Research and Perspectives, an International Journal, 44*, 1–20.

Devlin, M., & Samarawickrema, G. (2010). The criteria of effective teaching in a changing higher education context. *Higher Education Research & Development, 29*(2), 111–124.

Donlan, A. E., Loughlin, S. M., & Byrne, V. L. (2019). The fearless teaching framework: A model to synthesize foundational education research for university instructors. *To Improve the Academy, 38*(1), 33–39.

Finkelstein, N., Corbo, J. C., Reingholz, D. L., Gammon, M., & Keating, J. (n.d.). *Evaluating teaching in a scholarly manner: A model and call for an evidence-based, departmentally-defined approach to enhance teaching evaluation for CU Boulder* [White paper]. University of Colorado Boulder.

Forstenzer, J. I. (2016). *The Teaching Excellence Framework: What's the purpose?* [Report]. The Crick Center—Center for Engaged Philosophy and the University of Sheffield.

Green, B. P., Calderon, T. G., Gabbin, A. L., & Habegger, J. W. (1999). Perspectives on implementing a framework for evaluating effective teaching. *Journal of Accounting Education, 17*, 71–98.

Keeley, J., Smith, D., & Buskist, W. (2006). The Teacher Behaviors Checklist: Factor analysis of its utility for evaluating teaching. *Teaching of Psychology, 33*(2), 84–91.

Marquitz, M. S. (2019). *Defining and assessing teaching effectiveness in higher education* (Publication No. 13813094) [Doctoral dissertation, Colorado State University]. Proquest Dissertations and Theses.

Miguel, C. V., Moreira, C., Alves, M. A., Campos, J. B. L. M., Glassey, J., Schaer, E., Kockmann, N., Porjazoska Kujundziski, A., Polakovic, M., & Madeira, L. M. (2019). Developing a framework for assessing teaching effectiveness in higher education. *Education for Chemical Engineers, 29*, 21–28.

Richmond, A., Boysen, G. A., & Gurung, R. A. R. (2016). *An evidence-based guide to college and university teaching: Developing the model teacher.* Routledge.

Shao, L. P., Anderson, L. P., & Newsome, M. (2007). Evaluating teaching effectiveness: Where we are and where we should be. *Assessment & Evaluation in Higher Education, 32*(3), 355–371.

Subbaye, R., & Vithal, R. (2016). Teaching criteria that matter in university academic promotions. *Assessment & Evaluation in Higher Education, 42*(1), 37–60.

TEval. (n.d.). *Transforming higher education—Multidimensionalevaluation of teaching.* https://teval.net/index.html

Tieglaar, D. E. H., Dolmans, D. H. J. M., Wolfhagen, I. H. A. P., & Van der Vleuten, C. P. M. (2004). The development and validation of a framework for teaching competencies in higher education. *Higher Education, 48*, 253–268.

University of Oregon Office of the Provost. (n.d.). *Revising UO's teaching evaluations.* https://provost.uoregon.edu/revising-uos-teaching-evaluations#:~:text=There%20are%20three%20important%20inputs,receive%20useful%20and%20constructive%20feedback

Wieman, C., & Gilbert, S. (2017). The teaching practices inventory: A new tool for characterizing college and university teaching in mathematics and science. *CBE—Life Sciences Education, 13*(3). https://doi.org/10.1187/cbe.14-02-0023

CRITICAL TEACHING BEHAVIORS

CHAPTER 1

Align

> **DEFINITION**
>
> Instructors who align components of learning experiences start with clear learning goals. Measurable outcomes, teaching and learning activities, assessment tasks, and feedback build on each other to support student progress toward these goals.

EACH TIME WE ENTER our classrooms—whether physical or virtual—we have goals for student learning: We want our students to be changed by the learning experiences we create for them, to become better versed in the disciplinary knowledge of our fields, to more fluently use skills, to improve their ability to solve problems in new contexts, or, maybe, just to care more deeply about the issues we discuss. Goals—whether stated or unstated—also play a role when we set out to develop, plan, and then teach a course; course goals describe the impact we hope to make on our students' lives. While learning *goals* provide the inspiration and vision for our courses, learning *outcomes* translate them into observable, measurable actions that allow students to demonstrate to us and themselves that they have achieved these goals. Outcomes focus on the things students do rather than think because we cannot read our students' minds. We do not reach these course goals and outcomes by accident. When critical course components work together to ensure students achieve desired learning, we call this *alignment*.

Compare it to planning a trip: Goals and outcomes help us identify the destination and the type of trip we are planning. Once we know where we are going

and the activities that are planned, it is easier to decide what we need to pack and how to prepare for the trip; for example, preparations for a tent camping trip to Anchorage, Alaska, would look very different from those for a trip to an all-inclusive resort on the beaches of the Florida Gulf Coast. As the disciplinary expert, we are familiar with the destination—the knowledge, skills, and values our students need to take away from a course to develop a well-rounded knowledge base and be prepared for future courses and their career—and what it takes to get there; our students, disciplinary novices, rely on us to provide guidance and plan the steps that will help them reach the goal.

Once identified, course goals and outcomes provide guidance for selecting content, planning appropriate instructional activities and assessments, and identifying tools and resources that allow us to help our students reach the intended destination. In other words, we create a map or itinerary to help students navigate the learning journey in our course without getting lost. Depending on our goals and outcomes, there can be room for flexibility on the itinerary—in some instances there is only one right turn that students must take to reach the destination, while in others there are multiple options, and sometimes it's worth taking a detour to see an interesting landmark along the way. To determine the itinerary options, we leverage our expertise to select and align content and resources, plan activities, and identify appropriate milestones and assessments that help students engage with and practice the essential knowledge and skills that will allow them to succeed—in the course, their program, and their chosen careers.

The alignment of learning components matters at various levels: institutional, program, course, unit, and individual assessment (Sridharan et al., 2015). While we focus on aligning components within a course, we recognize the importance of considering alignment with programmatic and institutional goals as well as outcomes and competencies defined by applicable accrediting bodies. John Biggs (1999) observes that

> in aligned teaching, there is maximum consistency throughout the system. The curriculum is stated in the form of clear objectives, which state the level of understanding required rather than a list of topics to be covered. Teaching methods are chosen that are likely to realize those objectives: you get students to do the things that the objectives nominate. Finally, the assessment tasks address the objectives, so that you can test to see if students have learned what the objectives state they should be learning. All components in the system address the same agenda and support each other. (p. 26)

Biggs's description places emphasis on the fact that individual courses as well as programs of study are parts of a larger system with interrelated parts that is aimed at preparing learners for professional careers, citizenship, and personal fulfillment. Like any complex system, the interrelated components of the curriculum will be most effective when they are like well-aligned gears, working in concert with each other.

As part of this bigger curricular system, some of us have limited input when it comes to defining course outcomes, as they may be prescribed (e.g., institutionally defined general education outcomes, outcomes required by disciplinary accrediting bodies). However, even when working with predefined course outcomes, our disciplinary expertise and personal experience help us interpret and integrate these outcomes to design courses and activities that provide students with relevant information as well as opportunities to practice and demonstrate knowledge and skills.

No matter what we hope students will take away from our courses, it is important that we clarify, define, and communicate our expectations in the planning stages of a course to ensure critical components are integrated; in the classroom, we must provide students with a clear understanding of how to work toward achieving the goals we have for them. Establishing learning goals and outcomes increases transparency and supports self-directed learning as it communicates to our students what they should expect to take away from a course and what they can do to be successful. Additionally, directing students' attention to the relevance of course concepts in relation to their program of study or lifelong learning can increase awareness of transferable skills and a deeper understanding of disciplinary networks of knowledge.

What Do We Know?

Alignment is not a new concept or practice when it comes to teaching. In the United States, teacher education began introducing prospective teachers to the idea of instructional alignment in the mid-20th century. Within the context of higher education, a focus on alignment and learning outcomes has gained in prominence since the 1990s as institutions of higher education face an increasing demand for accountability and evidence of effectiveness. This connection may have soured us on the idea of alignment as we may perceive that the call for alignment and specific, measurable learning outcomes negates faculty agency (e.g., Carroll, 2010) and limits instructors' flexibility to respond to emergent needs or explore student and local interests (e.g., Addison, 2014). While we acknowledge these concerns, we encourage you to keep an open mind to the benefits of an outcomes-based approach. In our experience, using learning goals and outcomes as a foundation for a course has the potential to increase faculty agency by prompting us to inquire about and explore the best approaches to teaching in our disciplines. An outcomes-based approach also centers instruction on our aspirational vision for our students—not just content delivery. Using learning outcomes to guide teaching and learning in our courses does not eliminate opportunities for productive detours, as long as we keep the destination in mind; at the same time, outcomes provide faculty and students a focus that makes it easier to avoid unproductive tangents or busywork.

While alignment of learning components is an important precondition for effectively and efficiently gathering data on student achievement, its relevance and impact extend far beyond learning assessment and accountability, offering benefits for faculty and students. Years of research have shown that constructive alignment of course components is associated with a range of benefits to students, as outlined in Table 1.1.

The evidence from Table 1.1 shows that a clear learning destination—as defined by aspirational goals and concrete learning outcomes—plays a central role in designing aligned learning experiences and offers multiple benefits for instructors and students. Learning outcomes are foundational building blocks in the design of an aligned course, and for this reason, we will take a closer look at characteristics of effective outcomes. In the CTB framework, we conceive of learning outcomes as markers and signposts that indicate a specific learning destination and define what

students can do to show they have arrived, based on faculty expertise and experience. For any course, it is useful to think about outcomes at the course level (What will students be able to do at the end of the course?); however, instructors and students also benefit from increasingly specific outcomes that serve as guides for planning course units or modules, teaching and learning activities, and assignments. Breaking down a larger outcome into smaller steps and intermediate milestones increases transparency, helps scaffold learning in our classes, and models expert approaches to problem-solving and other disciplinary tasks for our students, who are still developing knowledge and fluency in our areas of expertise. While course outcomes are generally broadly defined and often allow us to choose from a range of teaching and learning activities that could help our students practice and demonstrate their achievement, outcomes for a learning unit or activity are progressively narrower and more specific.

Let's dig a little deeper into the characteristics of transparent, functional learning outcomes as well as

---

TABLE 1.1: Benefits of Alignment

Increased Perceptions of Competence and Self-Efficacy
If we share our goals/vision and concrete course learning outcomes with students, they are able to identify important learning milestones, valuable skills, as well as the overall course destination. This makes it easier for them to know what they are working toward and helps them prioritize where they spend time and dedicate their attention (Habel, 2012; Rossnagel et al., 2020).

Increased Student Motivation and Effort
Clear awareness of course goals and learning outcomes has been positively associated with student motivation as related to their enjoyment of the course, the effort they invest, and the perceived usefulness of the course and learning activities. Based on their research Rossnagel et al. (2020) even suggest that "good course design alone—in terms of constructive alignment—may boost student motivation, sparing instructors the need to come up with additional 'extrinsic' ways to increase motivation" (p. 10).

Decreased Frustration With Teaching and Learning Activities and Assessment Tasks
Alignment of course components reduces cognitive load and frustrations from learning, as students don't have to stumble in the dark to figure out where they are going. With a clear itinerary and destination in mind students can focus on the learning tasks they need to complete rather than spending time in determining an uncertain goal and then guessing about the best way to get there on their own. Activities and assessments that are explicitly aligned with course outcomes are also less likely to be perceived as busywork as their purpose and benefit is clear to students (Larkin & Richardson, 2013; Rossnagel et al., 2020).

Decreased Rate of Failing Grades and Withdrawals
Research by Gynnild et al. (2021) confirms that aligning summative course assessments with course learning outcomes and providing students with opportunities to practice all types of tasks they will be asked to demonstrate on assessments decreased the rate of failing grades and course withdrawals.

some of the resources available to help us define what our students should *do* to make their learning visible. We advocate for learning outcomes that are learner-centered, action-focused, and measurable:

- Learner-centered outcomes focus on students' rather than instructors' actions or content coverage given that "learning is not something done to students, but rather something students themselves do" (Ambrose et al., 2010, p. 3). For example, a learner-centered outcome might state the following: "You will be able to identify fundamental principles and equations of incompressible flow including vorticity, circulation, and Bernoulli's equation," whereas a content-focused outcome might simply list all concepts covered in the class or unit.
- Action-focused outcomes translate changes in student understanding and attitudes into concrete actions. Researchers in the Harvard Zero Project identified a close connection between understanding and action: "If you understand something properly you act differently" (Biggs, 1996, p. 351). It is up to us to identify the ways in which our students can perform understanding in our classes.
- Measurable outcomes focus on actions that are observable and measurable. While we may want our students to understand fluid dynamics or appreciate the complexity of Foucault's writing, it is hard to tell if they actually achieved this goal; after all, we cannot know their thoughts. Measurable outcomes identify observable actions that students can complete *only* if they understand. These actions then serve as evidence of their learning.

Refer to the example in Table 1.2 to see these principles for designing outcomes in action. The example provides an overview of a potential breakdown of an overarching course outcome into more specific unit outcomes and activities. Notice that the outcomes and aligned activities require students to complete tasks that vary widely in complexity and the type of thinking and skill asked of them.

TABLE 1.2: Example of Aligned Outcomes

From Course Outcomes to Unit Outcomes

Claudia teaches a humanities course focused on art in Latin America. Her goal/vision is that, after taking her course, students will appreciate the role of art in capturing and influencing history in Latin America and will be able to critically evaluate and discuss this interrelation in other contexts.

- An aligned course outcome may state, "At the end of the course, you (the students) will be able to identify and discuss links between art, history, and culture in Latin America."
  - This outcome is student-centered and action-focused as it describes what the students will do as a result of learning in this course.
  - This outcome is measurable because students can demonstrate their ability to identify and discuss these links in class activities and assignments, such as quizzes, discussion boards, presentations, course projects, and so on.
- To support students along the way, this course outcome can be broken down into multiple smaller unit outcomes that are distributed over the course of the semester. These outcomes (and potential aligned activities) may include the following:
  - Students will list the main events leading to the colonization of South America and the Caribbean by Spanish conquistadors. To address this outcome, students complete assigned readings and take a quick quiz.
  - Students will explain syncretism in Andean religious art of the colonial period. To address this outcome the instructor presents a short lecture followed by a small-group exploration of multiple examples of religious art from colonial Latin America where students are asked to identify influences from African, Indigenous, and European cultures.

Various frameworks exist to define and categorize the types of skills and cognitive efforts we ask students to perform in our courses. These frameworks can be great resources to help us think about the type of learning and growth we expect to see from our students over the course of our time with them. In the United States, two frameworks are most frequently used:

1. *Bloom's cognitive taxonomy* (1956) and its more recent revised version developed by Anderson et al. (2001). In addition to the taxonomy focused on the cognitive domain, Bloom also proposed similar taxonomies for the affective and psychomotor domain. Iowa State University's Center for Excellence in Learning and Teaching provides an excellent resource if you are interested in learning more (www.celt.iastate .edu/teaching/effective-teaching-practices/ revised-blooms-taxonomy/).

2. *Fink's taxonomy of significant learning* (2003, 2013), which defines learning more broadly and advocates for instructors to consider additional dimensions beyond disciplinary knowledge and skills—such as learning how to learn and caring—when designing a course. Fink provides a helpful "Self-Directed Guide for Designing Courses for Significant Learning" on his website (https://www .deefinkandassociates.com/index.php/ resources/).

3. Additional frameworks and tools are available to support us as we aim to translate the vision for our students into more concrete, measurable actions they perform to demonstrate what they know and can do, including understanding by design (Wiggins & McTighe, 2005), the 5E model (Bybee et al., 2006), and others. The Poorvu Center for Teaching and Learning at Yale University presents a concise overview of several additional frameworks for those interested in exploring further (see https://poorvucenter .yale.edu/BackwardDesign).

An awareness of multiple dimensions of learning can be a crucial part of good alignment. When students provide feedback indicating that the materials tested on the course exam were never covered in class, this is often an example of misalignment between course learning activities (e.g., lectures focus on conveying factual information that students should *remember*) and assessments (e.g., quiz questions that ask students to *apply* knowledge to solve a problem). If our lectures have prepared students to remember facts but have not provided opportunities for students to analyze and apply the information, students may struggle to solve more complex problems or transfer information to a new context.

What Do We Do?

So far in this chapter, we have explored the benefits of an intentionally aligned course and have examined the characteristics of actionable, learner-centered outcomes as foundational building blocks for alignment in more abstract terms. Now let us unpack some of the concrete steps you can take to align your course components.

More so than any of the other critical teaching behaviors, the work we do to effectively align our courses goes unseen, because most of the effort takes place before we step into the classroom. As we make design decisions and prepare to teach, we need to make sure we have clear learning goals in mind and all course components are aligned and well integrated to help our students achieve these goals. Before the course begins, the overarching, aligned course structure should be in place and should undergo little change for the duration of the semester, although we may still make just-in-time teaching decisions to provide additional practice, review, or expansions of topics that our students struggle with or find particularly interesting.

That said, our work toward intentional alignment is not over once the course starts. We can support student motivation, self-regulation, and learning success through transparent communication of course goals, outcomes, and the work we have done to create alignment between course components. Additionally, drawing explicit connections between course components and relating new ideas and skills to knowledge from previous courses and lived experiences help us facilitate the expansion of networks of knowledge for our students who are still developing disciplinary skills and expert ways of engaging with our discipline. Table 1.3 provides a list of "Align" actions to consider when

TABLE 1.3: Benefits of Alignment

Behaviors	Step by Step
AL.1 Connect course outcomes to program, department, and/or institutional outcomes and accreditation standards as applicable	• Familiarize yourself with program outcomes (whether this is a disciplinary program or part of the general education curriculum) to determine how your course fits within the curriculum. If available, consulting a program map may be helpful to identify how the program curriculum scaffolds knowledge and skills (e.g., by assigning prerequisite or corequisite courses) and which connections exist between courses. • In programs accredited through outside agencies (such as the Accreditation Board for Engineering and Technology or the American Psychological Association to name just a few), identify any accreditation standards students are intended to achieve in your course and make sure to plan instruction, practice, and assessment to document achievement. Consider also how your course may prepare students for accreditation exams. • This can be an opportunity to discuss questions about curriculum with your colleagues at the departmental and/or program level.
AL.2 Define actionable, learner-centered outcomes for your course, learning units (module, lesson, etc.), and assignments	• Use outcome statements that describe what the students (rather than the instructor) will do. • Determine observable actions students will perform to demonstrate learning in each part of the course and/or essential questions students should be able to answer. Whereas course outcomes are often fairly broad, unit/assignment outcomes generally hone in on specific, discrete pieces of information or smaller steps of more complex tasks. • If outcomes provided to you are vague, take some time to translate them into specific actions you would expect a student to be able to perform if they truly understood the course content. • Write outcomes with the student in mind. Keep them clear and simple by using language and terms that are easy to understand for an average student in your course. Be transparent about the things learners should be able to do to help them understand expectations and self-assess their progress.
AL.3 Align content, assessments, and activities with outcomes	• Ensure clear connections between overarching course outcomes and the more detailed outcomes for learning units and assignments. Faculty often find it helpful to create a course map that shows links between course components and outcomes and makes misalignment obvious. A course map provides an at-a-glance overview of the structure of your course and visualizes outcomes, assessments, and activities for each learning unit—it can be set up as a table or a flowchart. • Eliminate misaligned components. These might be content or activities that are not tied to any of the course outcomes; components that don't have a clear purpose are often perceived as busywork by students. Outcomes that are not practiced and assessed are other examples of misalignment. Verify whether an outcome is still relevant to your course (see AL.1). Depending on your findings, either eliminate the outcome or design teaching and learning content and activities that help students practice relevant skills and demonstrate achievement of outcome. • Plan instruction and activities that provide learners with opportunities to practice skills that are assessed in course exams and assignments. For example, if you want students to be able to calculate equations in the exam, provide opportunities for practice in the classroom and/or homework assignments; if you want them to analyze a problem, identify the correct equation to solve it and then calculate it correctly; create opportunities to practice this more complex task.

Behaviors	*Step by Step*
AL.4 State course, module, lesson, and/or assignment outcome(s) at each stage of learning	• Create a syllabus that not only states course learning outcomes but translates and contextualizes them to make them meaningful for students. • Share and discuss outcomes/essential questions at the beginning of the course and each lesson or activity. This helps establish relevance by connecting it to the overarching course goal and provides students with an opportunity to check in on their learning.
AL.5 Emphasize connections of course concepts and skills across learning units (and courses)	• Explicitly address any connections between learning units in your course to help students create and reinforce links in their knowledge network. • Activate prior knowledge from previous courses or life experiences, through intentional reminders, reflection, low-stakes quizzes, and so on.
AL.6 Present content and activities at multiple, appropriate levels of engagement and challenge	• In many classes it is not enough for students to simply be able to recall information; we expect them to do more, whether that includes analyzing data, solving problems, creating designs, communicating information, or the like. As you plan your course and instruction, consider how you want students to engage with and manipulate the content you teach. Frameworks such as Bloom's taxonomy and Fink's dimensions of significant learning (mentioned previously) are helpful tools.

designing and delivering a course as well as step-by-step recommendations for putting these actions into practice.

What Do We Show?

Despite its foundational importance, the effort we invest into designing and delivering well-aligned courses is often invisible to students and even to colleagues who observe our teaching. That leaves us responsible for calling attention to the work we do toward aligning course components and creating integrated learning experiences for our students. While this can mean additional work, it also provides us with an opportunity to tell our story, to show growth, and to highlight successes, not to mention the fact that it renders visible one of the more invisible (and time-intensive) aspects of good teaching. Table 1.4 suggests materials that provide evidence on alignment in our courses and offers guidance on intentionally calling attention to how we implement this critical teaching behavior in our instruction.

Reflection Questions

1. What are your goals for students who successfully complete your course? What should they be able to know/do/care about? As you think about this, you may want to consider both official goals tied to disciplinary outcomes as well as goals you have for students in developing social or learning skills.

2. At what level do students need to be able to use the course content? Is it enough for them to remember information or will they need to apply it to new situations? Use Bloom's cognitive learning taxonomy or Fink's significant learning framework in creating nuanced outcomes at the appropriate level of challenge.

3. How will you communicate learning goals and outcomes to students? Do you need to "translate" some of the official language so they make sense to a general audience? How can you connect goals to skills and knowledge students need to succeed in future courses and their career?

TABLE 1.4: Documenting Alignment

Teaching Materials	
Provide annotations for materials to focus attention on the critical teaching behavior(s) you want to showcase.	
Course map	A course map is a visual representation such as a table or flowchart showing the alignment of course learning outcomes with content, assessments, and activities. Creating a course map helps you demonstrate alignment and identify an itinerary and clear path for your course with the learner in mind.
Course materials and assignments that explicitly show alignment across course components	Course materials reiterating outcomes and demonstrating alignment may include the following: • Module introduction text—What are the outcomes for this learning unit? • Lecture notes—What are the outcomes for this class session? • Assignment prompts—How will the assignment allow students to demonstrate achievement of course or unit outcomes?
Learning outcomes at course, module, lesson, and assignment levels	Clear and specific learning outcomes allow us to communicate to students and peers the purpose and outcome of the learning that is happening in our course. In sharing our outcomes at different levels, we can communicate what matters in our course each step of the way. We can also showcase how all our outcomes build on each other. In your annotations note why you selected outcomes that may be unexpected for your course or go above and beyond disciplinary content and skills, in a way appropriate to the course (e.g., career preparation, teamwork skills, etc.).
Lesson plan	Lesson plans allow us to show a snapshot of aligned course components in a single class period. Often alignment is not apparent from the document alone, but using appropriate annotations can allow us to highlight how each learning activity, from minilectures to simulations, aligns with course learning outcomes.
Syllabus	A course syllabus provides an opportunity to communicate learning outcomes and expectations for students and can provide information on the following: • how they will be able to demonstrate their learning • self-assessment of their progress • knowledge from previous courses they need to refer to/use in this course
Test blueprints	Test blueprints are a simple tool that help us be more intentional about achieving learning outcomes when creating exams. When creating a test blueprint matrix, you start by listing the learning outcomes you want students to demonstrate through the exam and determine the distribution of questions or performance tasks focused on each of the outcomes.
Materials From Others	
Peer feedback and/or observation	Ask your observer to note moments of explicit alignment in your teaching presentation and materials. Instead of—or in addition to—inviting a peer to observe your classroom teaching, you can also ask for a course material review. For these reviews you might ask a peer or teaching expert (e.g., your campus teaching center colleagues) to review specific materials or learning units and provide feedback. Here, too, you may ask your colleague to note moments of explicit alignment in your materials. Be sure to share your course syllabus and other relevant materials to ensure your observer is aware of the outcomes you aim to accomplish.
Student feedback	As stated previously, students benefit from transparent alignment and explicit conversations about learning expectations and outcomes. They can provide targeted feedback on their experience in your class through formal and informal feedback. • *CTB midterm feedback.* The CTB midterm feedback survey includes questions that specifically solicit your students' feedback on alignment in your course. • *Select end-of-term surveys.* Questions related to alignment are part of many—but not all—end-of-term student surveys. If no question related to alignment is included on the survey used in your institution, you may be able to add a custom question or facilitate your own survey.

4. Finally, the big question: How do all of your course components align with each other? You may want to come back to this question after learning more about the other critical teaching behaviors to evaluate how well your course activities align with your learning goals and outcomes. When you do, the following questions may provide guidance on integrating and aligning multiple critical teaching behaviors:

   a. How can you communicate course goals and learning pathways in a way that eliminates unfairness associated with a "hidden curriculum"? (See chapter 2.)

   b. Do the activities you select scaffold student development of skills and knowledge linked to course learning outcomes? Do they provide students with practice at an appropriate level of challenge? (See chapter 3.)

   c. Do the assessment tasks in your class allow you to appropriately evaluate student achievement of learning outcomes at the desired level of challenge? (See chapter 4.)

   d. Do technology tools selected support learning outcomes for your course? (See chapter 5.)

References

Addison, N. (2014). Doubting learning outcomes in higher education contexts: From performativity towards emergence and negotiation. *The International Journal of Art & Design Education*, *33*(3), 313–325. https://doi.org/10.1111/jade.12063

Ambrose, S. A., Bridges, M. W., DiPietro, M., Lovett, M. C., & Norman, M. K. (2010). *How learning works: Seven research-based principles for smart teaching*. Jossey-Bass.

Anderson, L. W., Krathwohl, D. R., & Bloom, B. S. (2001). *A taxonomy for learning, teaching, and assessing: A revision of Bloom's taxonomy of educational objectives*. Longman.

Biggs, J. (1996). Enhancing teaching through constructive alignment. *Higher Education*, *32*(3), 347–364. https://doi.org/10.1007/BF00138871

Biggs, J. (1999). What the student does: Teaching for enhanced learning. *Higher Education Research & Development*, *18*(1), 57–75. https://doi.org/10.1080/0729436990180105

Bloom, B. S. (1956). *Taxonomy of educational objectives: The classification of educational goals*. David McKay.

Bybee, R. W., Taylor, J. A., Gardner, A., Van Scotter, P., Powell, J. C., Westbrook, A., & Landes, N. (2006). *The BSCS 5E instructional model: Origins and effectiveness*. BSCS. https://media.bscs.org/bscsmw/5es/bscs_5e_full_report.pdf

Carroll, J. (2010). The art of education. *Thesis Eleven*, *100*(1), 31–36. https://doi.org/10.1177/0725513609353700

Fink, L. D. (2003). *Creating significant learning experiences: An integrated approach to designing college courses* (1st ed.). Jossey-Bass.

Fink, L. D. (2013). *Creating significant learning experiences: An integrated approach to designing college courses* (2nd ed.). Jossey-Bass.

Gynnild, V., Leira, B. J., Myrhaug, D., Holmedal, L. E., & Mossige, J. C. (2021). From teaching as transmission to constructive alignment: A case study of learning design. *Nordic Journal of STEM Education*, *4*(2), 1–11. https:doi.org/10.5324/njsteme.v4i1.3402

Habel, C. (2012). "I can do it, and how!" Student experience in access and equity pathways to higher education. *Higher Education Research and Development*, *31*(6), 811–825. https://doi.org/10.1080/07294360.2012.659177

Larkin, H., & Richardson, B. (2013). Creating high challenge/high support academic environments through constructive alignment: Student outcomes. *Teaching in Higher Education*, *18*(2), 192–204. https://doi.org/10.1080/13562517.2012.696541

Rossnagel, C. S., Fitzallen, N., & Baido, K. L. (2020). Constructive alignment and the learning experience: Relationships with student motivation and perceived learning demands. *Higher Education Research and Development*, *40*(4). https:doi.org/10.1080/07294360.2020.1787956

Sridharan, B., Leitch, S., & Watty, K. (2015). Evidencing learning outcomes: A multi-level multi-dimensional course alignment model. *Quality in Higher Education*, *21*(2), 171–188. https://doi.org/10.1080/13538322.2015.1051796

Wiggins, G. P., & McTighe, J. (2005). *Understanding by design* (2nd ed.). Association for Supervision and Curriculum Development.

CHAPTER 2

Include

> **DEFINITION**
>
> Instructors who create an inclusive learning environment promote equity by utilizing accessibility standards and learner-centered strategies when designing and delivering content. They cultivate an atmosphere in which students experience a sense of belonging conducive to emotional well-being for learning.

WHAT IF WE TOLD you there are a few simple strategies you can use to boost the success and retention of *all* students? You might think we are exaggerating, but we also hope you would want to know more about these strategies. Institutional assessment data and ongoing higher education research make it clear that, despite our best intentions, we are not currently meeting the needs of all our students. Minoritized student groups consistently face an unequal and unfair uphill battle in their higher education experiences. Some of the challenges these students face are structural and may be beyond what we as individual instructors can accomplish on our own, but we have an opportunity to address many other obstacles by proactively incorporating inclusive teaching strategies and design in our courses. Inclusive teaching encompasses a range of practices and behaviors. What these practices have in common is an overarching aim of creating a learning environment that provides equitable access and opportunities and fosters a sense of belonging for all students. Creating inclusive learning spaces may start with ensuring all learning materials we use are accessible—as required by the Americans with Disabilities Act—but it does not end there. Research suggests that

to foster diversity, equity, and inclusion in the classroom we must, among other things, endeavor to create a sense of belonging for all students, plan multiple pathways for learning using universal design for learning guidelines, decolonize the curriculum, use examples that do not reinforce existing stereotypes and biases, and critically reflect on our own background and experiences to understand how they may shape our preferences, perspectives, and biases and, ultimately, the way we teach and engage with students. Given the sheer sense of being overwhelmed that a list of strategies this long likely produces, we may assume that developing inclusive learning experiences is more than we can handle at the moment and decide to postpone our efforts. A growing body of research on inclusive teaching practices, however, makes one thing clear: All students benefit from our implementation of behaviors in this category, which makes them well worth our time to explore further.

Later in this chapter we will discuss the potentially negative impact of the "hidden curriculum" on student learning and success in higher education, but from our perspective as educators, sometimes it can feel as though inclusive teaching has its own hidden curriculum. Think of the "hidden curriculum" as a collection of unwritten rules, unspoken expectations, and implicit academic, social, and cultural messages that stipulate the "right" way to think, speak, and behave. Those who do not know the "right" way are intentionally or unintentionally relegated to the margins. What does the hidden curriculum of inclusive teaching look like for instructors? First of all, inclusive teaching encompasses an incredibly large set of practices, and because of that, there is a sense that we need a vast knowledge to get it right and to avoid making mistakes. Secondly, many of us may fear "getting it wrong," as mistakes seem to come at a much higher cost in this category than for any other teaching behavior. As a result, we are often more comfortable talking about inclusive teaching than committing to using inclusive, equitable strategies in our classroom, or walking the equity walk (McNair et al., 2020). Our goal in this chapter is to help you decode the hidden curriculum by breaking this immense topic into smaller, more manageable and doable actions. Remember that *any* investment we make into creating a more inclusive learning environment helps us communicate to our students that we believe they are all worth our time and effort, that we trust in their potential to succeed, and that they matter as individuals whose backgrounds and experiences are sources of strength. We all start at different places as we work toward creating increasingly inclusive learning environments that welcome and support the diverse students we encounter in our classrooms, research labs, extracurricular instruction, and mentoring. No matter where we start, however, committing to just one change means we are working toward creating a learning experience where more students are able to succeed.

What Do We Know?

When was the last time you felt entirely out of place in a situation? If you are like most people, you likely remember exactly what you felt in that moment but very little about the details of what was going on around you. The same is true for our students. Students who feel worried, isolated, and out of place can find it difficult to dedicate their full attention to academic success or focus on long-term goals as concerns take up a considerable amount of their available cognitive bandwidth (Verschelden, 2017). Stereotype threat presents a related challenge to success for many minoritized students. Stereotype threat is triggered whenever we are in a situation in which a—usually bad—stereotype associated with our identities could be applied. We know what "people could think" and that "anything we do that fits the stereotype could be taken as confirming it" (Steele, 2011, p. 5), ultimately leading to judgment and poor treatment by others. As a result, when stereotype threat is triggered during a task, such as becoming actively concerned about inadvertently confirming a negative stereotype associated with one's identity (e.g., women are bad at math), performance suffers (Steele, 2011; Steele & Aronson, 1995). These are just a few of the challenges students with minoritized identities encounter in the college classroom on a daily basis. As a result of these and other obstacles, minoritized students in the United States have significantly lower rates of retention after the first year of study and of graduation from both public two-year and four-year institutions, with Black students (26% at two-year institutions and 46% at four-year institutions) and Hispanic students (35% at two-year institutions and 55.7% at four-year institutions) showing the overall lowest six-year graduation rates (Espinosa et al., 2019). Research findings and institutional data show us that we are currently not serving all our students equally well and that it is urgently necessary to invest into inclusive teaching practices.

In this section, we will discuss six practices that are especially relevant for inclusive teaching; specifically, we will share research and implementation ideas to help you accomplish the following:

- build community and relational trust with and between students
- decode pathways to success and connect students with resources
- use learner-centered strategies in course design and delivery
- select content and activities that honor and integrate diverse voices, perspectives, and experiences
- remove or reduce barriers to success
- assess personal biases and take steps to mitigate their potential impact on student learning and success

While all these practices are connected and often interrelated in practice, they do not have to be implemented all at once. If thinking about the whole of inclusive teaching seems overwhelming, we encourage you to select one of these areas to focus on for now and come back for more later.

Build Community and Relational Trust

Creating a learning environment that promotes a sense of community, trust, and belonging is an essential foundation for inclusive teaching. Students who feel a sense of belonging experience a "sense of being accepted, valued, included, and encouraged by others (teachers and peers) in the academic classroom setting and of feeling oneself to be an important part of the life and activity of the class" (Goodenow, 1993, p. 80). Research shows that, for students, a sense of belonging has a significant impact on educational success, persistence, and retention, with this impact being more pronounced for students from minoritized and marginalized groups (e.g., Rainey et al., 2018; Strayhorn, 2018; Yeager et al., 2016). The need to belong, to see oneself connected to others, is a basic human motivation; it affects mental and physical health and, in the context of teaching and learning, has a positive impact on motivation, persistence, and even students' ability to take advantage of opportunities to learn, such as acting on critical feedback (Brown & Campione, 1998; Caprara et al., 2000; Cohen & Steele, 2002; Mahoney & Cairns, 1997; Walton & Cohen, 2007).

Individuals identifying with groups that have been historically excluded and marginalized often suffer a disadvantage. Despite the increased awareness of and attention to creating an inclusive campus environment, students belonging to minoritized groups continue to see few people who look like them represented in academic spaces and curricula. Even before starting their academic experience, these students may hear peers relating stories of feeling excluded and not fitting in on college campuses. On campus and in the classroom, unintentional microaggressions and even overt prejudice can be regular if not daily experiences for students from minoritized groups. While questioning their belonging in higher education, students, especially those who are first-generation college students, might simultaneously begin to feel a sense of alienation from family and friends who view their learning,

growing, and changing with suspicion (Brookfield, 2015; Fuller-Rowell & Doan, 2010). These realities compound feelings of belonging uncertainty and, as a result, students may conclude that "people like me do not belong here" (Walton & Cohen, 2007, p. 83). A sense of alienation and doubts about belonging make it difficult for these students to attend to tasks at hand or take advantage of learning opportunities. We should note that the perception of belonging is context-dependent, and students' performance will be positively impacted in environments where belonging needs are met, and vice versa (Strayhorn, 2018). This means that we, as individuals, have an opportunity and responsibility to create learning environments where each student feels like an important member of the community every single time they enter the learning space.

Research indicates various strategies we can employ to promote community and a sense of belonging. Some of these are as simple as getting to know our students and addressing them by their preferred names and pronouns when interacting with them (Addy et al., 2021; Murdoch et al., 2018). Students who perceive their instructor knows their name feel more valued, invest more in the course and classroom community, and feel more comfortable asking for help (Cooper et al., 2017). The beginning of the term is the best time to set the tone for an inclusive classroom, but it is also important to maintain an inclusive and welcoming environment throughout the semester. The syllabus and first day of class activities can set a positive note in terms of creating an inclusive classroom environment and sense of belonging. Research shows that syllabus tone impacts students' perceptions of a course and their instructor (Denton & Veloso, 2018; Harnish & Bridges, 2011). A course syllabus that contains "deficit-based language, academic jargon, lists of what not to do, and fear-evoking policies . . . can exacerbate stereotype threat, belongingness uncertainty, and imposter syndrome" (Pacansky-Brock, 2021, para. 3). This emphasizes that the tone of our syllabus is an important first clue to students of what to expect in the classroom and their interactions with us as instructors and—as a result—also communicates implicitly whether they are welcome in their uniqueness.

Beyond the syllabus there are other strategies to consider implementing from day 1 or early in the semester to create a classroom and learning environment that communicates to students that they are welcome and that their presence in the learning space matters because others depend on them and the contributions they make. The strategies listed in Table 2.1 allow us to emphasize the learning community in our course and minimize feelings of alienation and disengagement as students have an increased awareness of the fact that they are not the only ones facing challenges and have a clear sense of a support network available to them.

In short, we have an opportunity to promote students' sense of belonging, persistence, and success by being approachable, helpful, and encouraging in our interactions with them. To do so, we should resist making assumptions about student backgrounds and experiences with the awareness that all of us come to the table with different strengths and stories; some students may not yet have identified how their strengths connect to their learning journey. Finding spaces in our courses that allow them to engage in an exploration of their strengths and goals and celebrating the diversity of perspectives students bring to course

discussions, however, may support students in developing a sense of belonging and pride based on their unique identity.

Decode Pathways to Success and Connect Students With Resources

It can be difficult to resist making assumptions about what our students know and do not know when we first meet them. For many of us, academia has been an important part of our lives for quite a while, so we might especially take for granted that our students are already familiar with expectations for "appropriate" academic behavior—such as correctly using titles and greetings in an email—and the skills to navigate the pathway to completing a degree and starting their career—such as identifying appropriate internship experiences or requesting a letter of recommendation. Rather than assuming students are as fluent in these academic skills as we are now, we recommend demystifying expectations for success, which often go beyond completing academic expectations of a degree. In doing

TABLE 2.1: Strategies for Fostering Community and a Sense of Belonging	
Foster classroom community.	Building community can start with providing opportunities for students to learn their classmates' names and get to know each other. This does not have to be limited to the beginning of the semester: George Lakey (2020) reports success with colearning, a strategy that dedicates time each class period for student pairs to share anything that is on their mind; taking this time to connect led not only to a closer connection between student pairs but a stronger class community overall.
Normalize struggles.	In an effort to prevent students developing a global sense that they just do not belong, some social belonging interventions have used "stories from older students to represent academic and social challenges as normal and temporary in the college transition— not as evidence of a global or permanent lack of belonging" (Murphy et al., 2020, para. 1). Normalizing doubts as something temporary and experienced by most students contributed to a significant increase of continuous enrollment for socially disadvantaged students and an increase in GPA that was especially pronounced for students who initially struggled the most (Murphy et al., 2020).
Implement trauma-informed educational practices (TIEP).	A review of research indicates that between "66–94% of college students report exposure to one or more traumatic events" (Carello & Butler, 2015, p. 263), showing that a significant number of students in our classrooms have been or continue to be impacted by trauma and would benefit from teaching practices that are intentionally grounded in the five fundamental principles of TIEP: "ensuring safety, establishing trustworthiness, maximizing choice, maximizing collaboration, and prioritizing empowerment" (p. 265). TIEP principles expand on practices previously mentioned as effective tools for fostering a sense of belonging in their focus on learner choice and empowerment and encourage us to consider opportunities for sharing agency with students.

so, we can draw back the curtain on the hidden curriculum of higher education and explicitly address skills and knowledge we expect students to employ.

The term *hidden curriculum* describes an amorphous collection of unwritten rules, unspoken expectations, and implicit academic, social, and cultural messages, which stipulate the "right" way to think, speak, and behave in the university setting. The assumptions and expectations inherent in the hidden curriculum are not formally established or communicated, yet they often invisibly govern academic achievement: Students who are unaware of the unarticulated values of the hidden curriculum—including first-generation students, students from minoritized groups, as well as international students—are still held to its hidden norms and expectations. As a result, they may struggle academically, feel excluded, or be perceived as lazy or disrespectful in academic spaces when they fail to adhere to rules they do not know exist (Delgado, 2020; Haeger et al., 2018; Hariharan, 2019; Hooker & Brand, 2010; McNutt, 2020; Paradkar, 2019). On the other hand, students who have acquired insights into the hidden curriculum through prior academic experiences or from family and friends (i.e., individuals who bestow academic, cultural, or social capital) find it easier to navigate expectations and leverage opportunities. An initial orientation to a college's social, academic, and physical geographies and expectations is essential for students to feel that they belong (Hurtado & Carter, 1997). Explicitly stating these expectations and clearly explaining requirements, criteria, and the rationale for what we do in our courses and how we do it "can be a critical tool for leveling the academic playing field" (Addy et al., 2021, p. 65). Our effort to communicate transparently will support not only minoritized students but all learners as we provide clear guidance on expectations. Our intentional efforts to demystify college are especially important, however, in supporting students whose life and educational experiences have led them to develop strengths that traditionally might not be valued in academia. When we decode the hidden curriculum, we give students the opportunity to understand how they might bring these strengths to bear while also expanding their knowledge and skills.

Aside from transparently communicating expectations and rationales in our courses, we can also support students by connecting them to available resources on campus. Many universities and colleges provide a range of resources for students, ranging from mental health counseling to tutoring centers and career support, to mention just a few services commonly offered. Yet not all students are aware that these resources exist or the benefits they provide to students who use them. For example, career service centers frequently not only support students who are looking for employment after graduation but they can also help students identify internship opportunities while still in college or facilitate mock interviews with students before their first conversation with a potential employer. Some of the resources available will be located within departments and might not be widely advertised, such as opportunities for students to participate in research projects or discipline-specific mentorship programs. When we have information about programs and resources that would be beneficial to students, we should not assume that students know about them and instead share the information with students; it can be helpful to also include an explanation of why we think students should engage and how it can help them accomplish academic and/or professional goals. Remember, while we may know and take for granted that engagement in undergraduate research can give students an advantage in graduate school applications as well as on the job market, they might not be aware of this connection.

Use Learner-Centered Strategies in Course Design and Delivery

Ideally, when we design our courses, we have a clear idea of what our students will need to know after completing them; with this in mind, we plan a transparent course structure with logically aligned components and teaching strategies as outlined in chapter 1. However, Kimberly Tanner (2013) reminds us that "the aspect of classroom teaching that seems to be consistently underappreciated is the nature of 'whom' we are teaching" (p. 322). The students in our classroom do not come to us like empty vessels waiting to be filled with information. They arrive already shaped by prior experiences that inform their attitudes and motivation related to the subject of our course as well as their confidence in their ability to learn and succeed in that subject and in college more broadly. Learner-centered instructional strategies that (re-)focus attention on the learner experience by centralizing learner engagement, choice, and empowerment allow us to foster more equitable learning spaces where all students are explicitly welcomed into the discussion and have opportunities to participate, all students can see personal connections to the course, and all students have time to think and construct their knowledge (Tanner, 2013). In a learner-centered class, instructors prioritize opportunities for students to actively work on learning tasks while shifting their role from conveying information to facilitating and supporting students in their personal learning journey. As guides and coaches in the classroom, we are then able to check in with students to see how they are learning and what challenges they face with the content or skills in the class (Weimer, 2013). Consequently, we can provide individualized guidance and adjust teaching so that it more effectively promotes learning. Often, using learner-centered strategies that engage students and allow us opportunities to provide just-in-time feedback does not require us to invest a lot of time. A range of active learning options are available, and several ideas are described in chapter 3, "Engage."

While we actively engage students in the learning process and pay attention to student needs when using learner-centered strategies, another important component of the learner-centered classroom is a shift in the balance of power to increase student agency (Dewsbury & Brame, 2019; Freire, 2014; Weimer, 2013). Importantly, we do not transfer power to students wholesale; instructors "still make decisions about learning, just not all of them, and not always without student input" (Weimer, 2013, p. 94). We need to be conscious to redistribute power in amounts proportional to students' preparation and abilities to handle it. Advanced students will be able to make more informed decisions and thus can play a more active role in contributing to teaching and learning decisions than students who are just beginning to study a subject.

Much has been written about approaches that involve students as partners and their impact on student learning. "Students as partners" is defined as a "reciprocal process through which all participants have the opportunity to contribute equally, although not necessarily in the same way, to curricula or pedagogical conceptualization, decision-making, implementation, investigation, or analysis" (Cook-Sather et al., 2014, pp. 6–7). Involving students in this way has been linked to a positive impact on student learning overall, including heightened responsibility and motivation for the learning process, increased student

confidence and self-efficacy, an enhanced sense of belonging, and deepened trust between students and instructor (Cook-Sather et al., 2014; Matthews et al., 2019; Mercer-Mapstone et al., 2017; Werder et al., 2012). Inviting students to collaborate with us on our curricula communicates that their input and experience is valued. De Bie et al. (2021) observe that "partnership affirms students, especially those from equity-seeking groups, as knowers; recognizes students' knowledge gained from diverse backgrounds and experiences; and develops and shares students' knowledge, which can, in turn, facilitate broader change" (p. 27). In short, collaborations with students as partners do not just benefit the students but these partnerships can also motivate personal and professional growth and provide new insights for instructors.

We all have moments in our courses where it would be easy to involve students as partners in big or small ways. We might start to include students as partners by asking them to work together to define classroom behavior expectations or participation policies at the beginning of the semester, to share relevant examples or stories based on personal experience, to provide input on project deadlines or exam dates, or to vote on which four out of six possible topics the course should focus on this semester. Beyond that we might also work with former students or students in other disciplines to improve our course based on their input. Weimer (2013) cautions that students may initially respond with anxiety to this new responsibility; it is essential that the instructor provide feedback and reinforcement—

> if that's provided, they move forward with a bit more confidence. Then one day, seemingly all of a sudden, students get it, or at least a number of them do, and that critical mass generates an energy and enthusiasm that often ignites the rest of the class. (p. 96)

It is easy to start integrating student input in small ways, and for many of us, that will be where we are comfortable working with students as partners. For instructors who are looking for even less hierarchical partnerships, there are also options for involving students in all aspects of a course from identifying a textbook to setting the course calendar, making learning a true cocreation between students and instructors.

Finally, we would be remiss if we did not note that inviting student feedback, not only at the end of the term but throughout the semester, can be an important component of making our courses more learner-centered and sharing agency with students. Especially for low-achieving students and those from lower socioeconomic backgrounds, the opportunity to provide feedback is crucial as it honors their perspectives as active participants in their own learning and provides an opportunity to communicate any learning challenges they encounter (Flutter, 2007; Levin, 2000). Chapter 9 provides tools and a system for gathering midterm student feedback that specifically asks students to reflect on our use of CTB in the classroom. While this is a great option for gathering feedback, it is not the only way we can check in with students. Instructors may include quick anonymous surveys or questionnaires on a regular basis as part of homework or in-class activities. These can be facilitated through the learning management system (LMS), online survey tools, or even as a quick "ticket out the door" written on a notecard or scrap paper at the end of a class meeting. While a quick survey is often the easiest way to check in with students, we might also facilitate focus groups or ask students to keep learning diaries (Hand & Rowe, 2001). Meaningful feedback from students provides valuable opportunities for teacher improvement (Mandouit, 2018) and allows us to center students' learning experience in our course as an impetus for professional growth. While we all have different levels of comfort concerning the extent to which we are willing to put students in control of shaping the learning experience in our courses, intentionally soliciting student input on the choices we have made for our course and keeping an open mind when engaging with their feedback is an essential component of inclusive instruction as it allows us to identify and respond to challenges we could not anticipate.

Select Content and Activities That Honor and Integrate Diverse Voices, Perspectives, and Experiences

Course content, including the selection of readings, examples, and activity types, can impact students' experience of either feeling included or marginalized in our courses. Even when we are invested in creating inclusive learning experiences for our students and are careful to avoid instructional behaviors that might marginalize or discriminate against certain student populations, we are not immune to unintentionally marginalizing individuals or groups of people in subtle and indirect ways. Our selection of activities, course materials, and examples can contribute either positively or negatively to the creation of an inclusive classroom climate "where marginalized perspectives are not only validated when students spontaneously bring them up, but they are intentionally and overtly integrated in the content" (Ambrose et al., 2010, p. 172). Intentionally selecting course materials, examples, and activities allows us to honor and integrate diverse perspectives, create learning environments that centralize diversity as a strength, positively represent the lived experiences of our students, and reduce the perpetration of stereotypes and epistemic, affective, and ontological violences (de Bie et al., 2021) against students belonging to minoritized groups. When we perpetrate epistemic violence, we may criticize or devalue ways of knowing that do not align with what we perceive as the standard; when we perpetrate affective violence we minimize or ridicule feelings and emotions; when we perpetrate ontological violence we dismiss and marginalize others for their identity such as their belonging to minoritized populations. As we plan our curriculum, we have opportunities for selecting content, examples, and applications, as well as learning activities that centralize diversity and inclusion and honor different ways of knowing, feeling, and being. Table 2.2 outlines examples of problematic practices followed by research-based suggestions for planning a more inclusive curriculum.

These examples demonstrate that we must start considering diverse perspectives and strengths as we develop curricula and design learning activities to foster inclusion and equity, both as we develop the course and continuing throughout the semester as we deliver instruction.

Remove Barriers to Success

Everybody brings strengths and weaknesses to learning spaces; sometimes these limitations and challenges are visible or known while others are invisible or private. For example, according to the U.S. Department of Education, in 2015/2016, 19% of undergraduate students and 12% of postbaccalaureate students in the United States reported having a disability; this is a significant increase from 11% of students reporting a disability in 2008 (National Center for Education

TABLE 2.2: Planning an Inclusive Curriculum

Content (i.e., textbooks, written and audiovisual texts, etc.)	Curricular decisions convey values and can send intentional or unintentional messages about who belongs. *For example:* If the intellectuals we choose to include in our curriculum all represent a Western perspective, we implicitly communicate that non-Western perspectives are less valuable, a form of epistemic violence that implies that some knowledge and knowers are legitimate while simultaneously "disqualifying other knowledge and people as subknowers" (de Bie et al., 2021, p. 15). *Inclusive practice:* Whenever possible choose content that reflects a range of races, ethnicities, gender identities, sexualities, abilities, ages, religions, and so on and avoid only including a token marginalized perspective here or there. By selecting inclusive course readings and activities, aim to place multiple perspectives at the center of the course and contextualize them with nuance (Ambrose et al., 2010; Appert et al., 2017).
Examples and Applications (i.e., case studies, visuals, examples from professional practice, text problems, etc.)	Incorporating examples, visuals, case studies, and narratives of relevant professional and personal experiences has the potential to engage students and make abstract ideas more tangible. However, we may unwittingly reinforce stereotypes or feelings of marginalization if examples, visuals, and other course materials selected explicitly or implicitly deny or erase diverse identities and experiences. *For example:* If we default to talking about scientists using male pronouns or using illustrations and examples featuring male scientists and their achievements, we implicitly communicate that individuals with nonmale gender identities cannot or should not be scientists. Similarly, consider the LGBTQ2+ student who remembers, "I took a French class last year, and even though my TA seemed very liberal, as part of getting us to speak in French, she'd ask questions like 'How would you describe your ideal boyfriend?' and 'How would you describe your future plans for marriage and children?' I know it was unintentional, but it felt like my whole existence was erased" (cited in Farrell et al., 2004, p. 1). In this context the heteronormative perspective of the instructor negated the experience and identity of the student and likely compounded feelings of nonbelonging and exclusion. *Inclusive practice:* Use examples that are relatable to people from various socioeconomic statuses, ages, and religions and do not single out a certain culture—either positively or negatively (Oleson, 2020). Additionally, "ground examples in specificity and discuss limitations (for example, 'This study conducted research on white male Ivy League students in the 1970s, which changes the way we apply the findings to higher education classrooms today.') . . . Make sure not to reward students for their similarity to you at the expense of others (for example, chatting warmly with students who are from your hometown, but never asking other students about their backgrounds). Instead, try to draw on resources, materials, humor, and anecdotes that are relevant to the subject, and sensitive to the social and cultural diversity of your students," suggests the Inclusive Teaching Guide developed by Columbia University Center for Teaching and Learning (Appert et al., 2017, p. 20).

(*Continues*)

TABLE 2.2 (*Continued*)

Learning Activities and Structures (i.e., expectations for engagement, types of activities, roles of the teacher and the student, etc.)	The way we learn and make sense of teaching and learning is a result of cultural practices, language, and values in each individual's life. Scholars of culturally responsive/culturally relevant teaching advocate for an increased awareness and integration of differing cultural frameworks into classroom interactions (Gay, 2001; Hutchison & McAlister-Shields, 2020; Ladson-Billings, 1995, 2014). Currently, North American institutes of higher education privilege an individuated cultural framework that assumes and values individual, linear, abstract, mind-based emphases in teaching and learning; integrated cultural frameworks that prioritize interconnected, circular, contextual, and holistic mind/body/spirit/heart-based approaches to teaching and learning are comparatively rare (Chávez & Longerbeam, 2016). However, this preference for one cultural framework privileges populations of learners for whom this cultural framework is familiar while underserving learners who grew up in another.
	For example: Consider protocols of student participation in the classroom. While there has been a trend to adopt more learner-centered methods of instruction in recent years, the traditional lecture continues to be the instructional method of choice for many faculty. The lecturer in this case takes on an active role whereas students experience a passive-receptive style of communication; they are expected to listen quietly unless called upon. However, students whose culture relies on a more communal, participatory communication style can feel out of place in these settings and—when asked to not engage in dialectic communication styles they are familiar with—"may be, in effect, intellectually silenced. Because they are denied use of their natural ways of talking, their thinking, intellectual engagement, and academic efforts are diminished as well" (Gay, 2001, p. 111).
	Inclusive practice: Familiarize yourself with diverse cultural frameworks and incorporate a range of techniques to enrich teaching and learning over time. One set of guidelines to honor approaches to learning that center connectedness, reciprocal relationships, and a sense of place, the *First People Principles of Learning*, was developed by Indigenous elders, scholars, and knowledge keepers of British Columbia (First Nations Education Steering Committee, n.d.). Chávez and Longerbeam in *Teaching Across Cultural Strengths* (2016) present additional ideas for balancing cultural strengths in teaching.

Statistics, 2018). This statistic, however, only captures a segment of the diversity in our classes, as not all disabilities are reported nor are learner variability and the diverse needs of our students limited to disability status alone.

To an extent, creating accessible course materials and learning opportunities is required by law. The Americans with Disabilities Act and the Rehabilitation Act require institutions that receive federal funding to ensure that "no qualified individual with a disability in the United States shall be excluded from, denied the benefits of, or be subjected to discrimination" (U.S. Department of Labor, 1973, para. 1) and that diverse learners have equivalent access to digital course materials including text, media, and learning activities. In fact, these laws require that all materials we share at all times meet accessibility standards, even if none of our students requests specific accommodations. This might seem a big task without significant return on investment if none of our students actually require accommodations; however, accessible materials and media that can be accessed in a variety of ways rather than relying on a single sense or ability (e.g., vision or audio only) benefit everyone. Accessible web pages, documents, and media are easier for everyone to read and navigate; imagine, for example, the commuter students who can listen to the audio narration of the textbook while driving to campus or the student whose first language is not English who can refer to video subtitles or transcripts to increase their comprehension of complex ideas and specialized vocabulary. Table 2.3 summarizes design solutions that increase accessibility and usability of digital materials.

Beyond ensuring we meet these legal requirements, we have options in both the design and delivery of the course to accommodate a wider variety of needs of diverse learners. In doing so, we reduce barriers to learning and increase equitable access and student success. The idea of creating learning opportunities that eliminate barriers is the foundation for universal design for learning (UDL) principles and guidelines. Based on the assumption that learner variability is the norm not the exception and the "average student" is an illusory concept, UDL aims to create learning environments that meet the needs of most if not all learners from the outset. How can that be achieved? Based on scientific insights into how humans learn, CAST—the organization that created the UDL framework and has invested in ongoing research to grow the field of UDL since 1984—provides an outstanding set of guidelines that can be applied to any discipline or domain to ensure that all learners can access and participate in meaningful, challenging learning opportunities.

The underlying principle of these guidelines is the idea that providing multiple means of engagement, representation, and action and expression helps us effectively support the greatest number of diverse learners. In other words, UDL guidelines suggest we provide "multiple ways for getting students motivated and interested (engagement), acquiring information (representation), and demonstrating what they know (action and expression)" (Super et al., 2021, p. 3464). Identifying more than one option in each of these three domains, when possible, allows students to engage and demonstrate learning in ways that leverage their strengths rather than accommodate challenges they may face. Table 2.4 provides a quick breakdown of the main strategies falling into each of the three UDL categories along with examples for implementation; this table draws on the "UDL Progression Rubric" (Novak & Rodríguez, 2018) and the "UDL Implementation Rubric" (Torland & Novak, 2019), which are both excellent resources for anybody interested in exploring further.

Universal design principles challenge us to foster students' agency in leveraging their strengths when working toward personal and professional goals and to provide tools and resources that allow students to act

TABLE 2.3: Increasing Accessibility of Digital Course Materials

Usability Factors	*Design Solution*
Text is structured for readability.	Understand that online users "scan" documents for information. Create documents that use design features such as headings, subheadings, bullets, tables, and so on strategically to help students find the information they need and support screen reader efficiency.
Images are optimized for screen readers.	When using images to convey information (e.g., graphs, charts, etc.), keep in mind that screen readers cannot decipher the content of an image. Instead, they look at the document source code for an alternative text (Alt-text) description of the image. *Using Alt-text for all images used to convey information allows us to meet the requirements of Section 508 of the Rehabilitation Act.*
Audio/video are captioned or include transcripts.	Captions allow students to read on screen what is spoken while watching a presentation or video. Transcripts are especially useful in support of multimedia files when relevant content of a presentation is both spoken and visual—for example, a narrated PowerPoint presentation with embedded diagrams and/or other complex images. *Using captions or transcripts for all audio/video learning materials allows us to meet the requirements of Section 508 of the Rehabilitation Act.*
Organization of content facilitates navigation.	Organize content in a logical format so that students may quickly access information and tools to complete tasks and assignments.

strategically and self-regulate their learning based on transparent and timely information regarding expectations, performance, and effective learning strategies. By planning instruction that provides students with the skills, resources, and structures needed to make informed decisions about their own learning and

empowering them to engage with materials and demonstrate learning through multiple means, we support not only their academic success but also help them develop learning and professional skills.

Despite our best planning, some students might require additional accommodations to succeed in our

TABLE 2.4: Getting Started With Planning UDL Lessons and Activities

Domain	Example
Multiple Means of Engagement *Strategies fostering:* • interest • persistence • self-regulation	**Optimize Individual Choice and Autonomy** For example, offer students choices in what they learn (e.g., choose own topic for a paper), how they engage with content (e.g., present info through books, video, lectures), and how they express what they know (e.g., create a poster or research paper). Tobin and Behling (2018) call this the "Plus One" strategy, as we provide at least two options for students to complete the work in our course.
	Develop Self-Assessment and Reflection and Mastery-Oriented Feedback For example, share tools (e.g., rubrics, examples of student work) that allow students to self-assess and reflect on their learning. Give guidance on how to use these tools effectively (e.g., discuss rubric in class and apply to sample work). Provide feedback that encourages a growth mindset and suggests use of specific supports and strategies in the face of challenge. (See chapter 3 for an explanation of growth mindset.)
Multiple Means of Representation *Strategies clarifying:* • perception • language • comprehension	**Clarify Vocabulary and Symbols** For example, explain idioms, culturally exclusive phrases, disciplinary terminology, symbols, and acronyms. Explicitly teach vocabulary/terminology to students using definitions, visuals, and examples and provide opportunities for students to use the important terminology in authentic and meaningful ways.
	Highlight Patterns, Critical Features, Big Ideas, and Relationships For example, give explicit clues, prompts, or guiding questions to help students recognize the most important information and relationships. Consider teaching students to create and use outlines, graphic organizers, and other organizing tools. Ask students to reflect on practices to identify their own best strategies for recognizing patterns, big ideas, and relationships.
Multiple Means of Action and Expression *Strategies supporting:* • communication • goal-setting • monitoring progress	**Use Multiple Media for Communication** For example, provide multiple options for students to engage with information *and* express their understanding (i.e., assess their learning), for example, through text, audio, video, and so on. Consider letting students reflect on a course outcome or competency and identify authentic and innovative tasks and products that allow them to demonstrate their mastery.
	Support Planning and Strategy Development For example, encourage students to create personalized learning plans that include goals and strategies to optimize personal strengths. Encourage students to reflect on how much time they will need to perform selected tasks and set personal due dates to reach goals. Consider providing tools such as checklists for tasks, due dates, and planning templates and guidance on scaffolding tasks.

course, and it is important that we provide these in a way that does not create additional barriers for students or make them feel unwelcome in our classes. Accommodations are generally verified and communicated through a disability services center (or similar). The EDUCAUSE 2020 Student Technology Report found that

> many students with disabilities do not have positive responses to how their institution supported their need for accessible content and/or technology accommodations. . . . Some respondents cited the difficult and/or lengthy process to apply for accommodations, as well as insufficient or limited resources at their institution's disability services office. Several students discussed challenges related to suitable technology and delays in getting the tech tools they need for their coursework. Meanwhile, of the students who responded to this question (n = 124), half cited difficulties working with their course instructors. These issues were discussed in terms of instructors' (1) lack of awareness or knowledge about following accommodation policy/directions, (2) lack of discretion in maintaining student privacy and confidentiality, and (3) reluctance or refusal to give students their approved accommodations. Many student comments suggest that some instructors are ignorant about the purpose of accommodations or are apathetic to or even disdainful of students who have different learning needs. Such attitudes and behaviors are discriminatory and put additional obstacles in the way of students who have specific needs that institutions are obligated to accommodate. (Gierdowski et al., 2020, Not Making the Grade)

Unfortunately, student responses in this report indicate that potentially half the students who work with the university to be approved for learning accommodations encounter additional barriers in the classroom that are only indirectly related to the teaching strategies or technologies used but directly the result of instructors' attitudes and biases toward these students.

Assess Personal Biases and Mitigate Their Potential Impact on Student Learning and Success

As human beings our identities—both personal and social—are linked to our own lived experiences and histories of privilege and exclusion. As a result, Chávez and Longerbeam (2016) observe that "we bring behavioral interpretations and judgments with us into collegiate learning environments, which affects how

we design learning activities [and] how we feel about students" (p. 5). Those behaviors and judgments can negatively impact our students' learning, achievements, and persistence, as well as sense of belonging (Ambrose et al., 2010; Carrell et al., 2010; Fairlie et al., 2014; Oleson, 2020). Specifically, Ambrose et al. (2010) caution us that

> it is common for instructors to assume that students share our background and frames of reference (for example, historical or literary references). It is equally common to make assumptions about students' ability (for example, Asian students will do better in math), identity and viewpoint (for example, students share your sexual orientation or political affiliation), and attributions (for example, tentative language indicates intellectual weakness). These assumptions can result in behaviors that are unintentionally alienating and can affect climate and students developing a sense of identity. (p. 182)

In our efforts to create an inclusive and fair teaching and learning environment, it is therefore important we explore our identities and how they may influence our pedagogical decisions and shape our assumptions about students. Unless we do this often uncomfortable work to uncover and sometimes challenge our assumptions and biases, it may be difficult to acknowledge that unconscious and largely unintentional stereotypes and attitudes influence our interactions with students in small ways (e.g., whether or not we respond to their email; Milkman et al., 2015) and big ways (e.g., whether or not we prepare a high-quality lesson; Jacoby-Senghor et al., 2016).

As well as an intentional effort to develop cultural self-awareness and understanding, self-reflection on our own identities and implicit biases can help us mitigate their impact (both positive and negative) on interactions with our students; in fact, we may "cultivate the ability to reinterpret others' cultural norms as strengths and redesign our teaching and courses to engage these strengths" (Chávez & Longerbeam, 2016, p. 5). More importantly, we need to be open to learning more about what we do not know we do not know as we cannot change behaviors or attitudes we are unaware of. To do this, it can be helpful to invite feedback from students and peers who may point out any blind spots or hidden biases we hold. Although these conversations can be difficult for both the person providing feedback and the person receiving it, it is essential that we receive any feedback provided with gratitude and with an open mind. The Implicit Association Tests (https://implicit.harvard.edu/implicit/takeatest.html) developed at Harvard University are another useful resource for learning more on assumptions we make about people based on their identity. Chapter 6 ("Reflect") provides some ideas for getting started with intentional reflection on classroom practices and interactions.

Neither reflecting on and acknowledging our biases nor creating inclusive learning spaces are easy tasks. Both have the potential to leave us with more questions than answers and leave us open to criticism and self-doubt. Concerning this, bell hooks (1994) reminds us the inclusive, holistic classroom can be a place "where teachers grow, and are empowered by the process. That empowerment cannot happen if we refuse to be vulnerable while encouraging students to take risks" (p. 21). In the inclusive learning space, we have the opportunity to grow as instructors and to learn from and with our students; being vulnerable and open can be an asset even as it feels uncomfortable. If we take risks in creating an inclusive learning space, these will ultimately allow us to better serve our students.

What Do We Do?

Efforts to create inclusive learning spaces are vitally important but complex considerations in teaching. Our knowledge and understanding of practices that promote equity and inclusion in the classroom continue to evolve. The CTB framework aims to provide a concise overview of what we currently know about inclusive strategies with a focus on the strategies research indicates as especially important to student learning and success. Table 2.5 summarizes "Include" behaviors and suggests step-by-step actions we can take to make the learning environment and experience more inclusive and welcoming. We hope that these practices provide you with a starting point for expanding your inclusive teaching practice and encourage you to keep exploring the topic on your own as new research and insights become available every day.

TABLE 2.5:   Include: Critical Teaching Behaviors in Practice

Behavior	Step by Step
IN.1 Build community and relational trust between students–instructor and students–students	• Get to know your students and allow them to get to know you as a person (that does not mean you have to share every detail about your life). ○ Learn student names and use them in interactions with students. ○ At the beginning of the semester/first day of class, plan an activity (e.g., in-class discussion, survey) to allow students to communicate their goals and any concerns they may have, to share about themselves, but also to let you know about any other specific needs they may have. • Invest in relationships with intention, especially across difference. Honor stories. Practice empathetic listening (Liberatory Design, n.d.). • Encourage students to engage in professional relationships with their instructors (including office hours, open-door policy, mentoring, etc.). • Teach the whole student. ○ Avoid making quick judgments about students who may not meet your expectations. Instead reach out to students and understand any challenges they may be facing. ○ Demonstrate consideration for student learning, well-being, and long-term success. ○ Be appropriately flexible in accommodating students' needs. • Normalize struggle (e.g., you may share about your own failures and challenges or invite students from previous semesters to visit your class or record a video).

Behavior	Step by Step
IN.2 Decode pathways to success and connect students with resources (e.g., career and internship services, research and mentorship opportunities, learning support, etc.)	• Make a list of your personal expectations for students, including behaviors, attitudes, and so on as well as expectations your discipline has for students who are successful in the field (e.g., "hidden curriculum"); plan for explicitly communicating these expectations to your students to increase equity. • Get to know resources available for students on your campus and in your department so you can refer students to relevant resources and opportunities. ○ Include an overview of resources on your syllabus and/or course page on your LMS. ○ Reference resources where relevant (e.g., encourage students to take advantage of the on-campus writing center or tutoring services when preparing a project for your course).
IN.3 Use learner-centered strategies in course design and delivery	• Remember that we are teaching students, not content; thinking about whom we are teaching helps us tailor our strategies to best support students' learning experience. • Engage students as partners on select pedagogical decisions such as setting ground rules for interactions in the learning space. • Whenever possible promote student agency and voice by allowing them to make choices for their own learning (e.g., topic selection for a research paper, option to retake quizzes and exams for a better grade, etc.). • Solicit student feedback to gain a better understanding of how the course is going and of any challenges they may be facing.
IN.4 Select content and activities that honor and integrate diverse voices, perspectives, and experiences	• Review materials and examples you include in your course to evaluate whether they include perspectives from multiple cultural groups and positively represent a range of experiences. • Plan a variety of activities that allow students to engage in different ways, ranging from verbal to written, individual to group, and so on. • Honor approaches to learning that center connectedness, reciprocal relationships, and a sense of place. *First People Principles of Learning* published by the First Nations Education Steering Committee (n.d.) is a great resource (www.fnesc.ca/first-peoples-principles-of-learning/).
IN.5 Remove barriers to success by designing activities and materials with equitable access and representation in mind	• Design activities and materials with equitable access in mind. Federal regulations require that we meet minimum standards for accessibility in materials shared with students, but designing materials with these guidelines in mind allows us to increase access for all learners. • Use UDL principles to develop courses that prioritize access for all learners from the beginning. Consider how you can provide learners with multiple means for engagement, representation, and expression. • Support students who receive learning accommodations through the institutional disability services office (or similar).
IN.6 Assess personal biases and mitigate their potential impact on student learning and success	• Solicit feedback and reflect on your interactions with students. Are there differences in how you engage with male versus female students? Are you using examples that assume a shared knowledge of specific religious or cultural practices even though not all students may actually share that knowledge? These reflections and conversations can be uncomfortable, but it is important to keep an open mind. • Take one or more Implicit Association Tests to explore whether you have biases you might be unaware of (see https://implicit.harvard.edu/implicit/takeatest.html).

What Do We Show?

Inclusive practices can inform all aspects of a course from the design of course materials to communication with our students. How and why some of these documents represent our efforts to create inclusive and welcoming learning spaces is not always apparent to an outside observer. The documentation ideas included in Table 2.6 are all examples of materials that can manifest our efforts, but only through our annotations will we be able to call attention to how they demonstrate inclusive teaching. Annotations also provide us with an opportunity to tell our story, to discuss growth over time, and to highlight successes.

TABLE 2.6: Documenting Inclusive Teaching

Teaching Materials *Provide short annotations for materials to focus attention on the critical teaching behavior(s) you want to showcase.*	
Ground rules for interaction in course learning spaces	You may include your students in the development of ground rules, but even if you do not, having ground rules for productive and respectful interactions in the course learning spaces can be an important part of creating a welcoming environment. Ground rules for interaction should include information about what students can expect from you (e.g., how fast you will respond to emails, what type of feedback you will provide on their work, when and where you are available to meet if they have questions, etc.).
Instructor-created accessible digital materials	Throughout a course we may produce quite a few instructional materials to support student learning. These may include instructional videos, interactive webpages or documents, just-in-time teaching materials in response to a concept students are struggling with, and many more. We are required by law to ensure these materials meet minimum accessibility standards, but many instructors go above and beyond to ensure that materials are accessible and inclusive. Make sure to annotate your materials to show how their creation was informed by a desire for inclusivity.
Lesson plan	A lesson plan represents the activities and content we use in the learning space on any given day. Classroom activities as well as content can promote an inclusive environment and community. Point out how you are leveraging content (e.g., readings representing multiple perspectives on a situation, examples that allow students to see themselves in a positive way, etc.) and activities (e.g., group work and community-building activities, activities that give students choice in how they complete them, etc.) to increase relevance of the course to all students.
Mentorship agreement and products of mentorship	Seeking mentors is one of the areas and activities that can fall into the bucket of the "hidden curriculum"—especially students from minoritized groups may not know how to reach out to instructors for support and mentorship, may not understand the benefits associated with having a mentor, or may not have access to an instructor or other staff member whom they feel can relate to their situation. Efforts to provide mentorship to students and discussing with students the benefits of having a mentor and pathways to create a network of mentors can increase equitable access to this opportunity for all students.
Syllabus	A course syllabus can support transparent communication with students and can help us set the tone for a welcoming and inclusive learning environment. In your annotations you may want to highlight and emphasize the following: • accessibility statement—describe what you do to make sure your course and materials are accessible to all students and that other resources are also available to students • diversity statement, student-centered • inclusive language in the phrasing of the syllabus • inclusive policies regarding, for example, office hours, attendance, make-up policies, and so on. Annotate the syllabus to emphasize how you are integrating and honoring diverse perspectives and people in your course curriculum.

Diversity statement	A diversity statement demonstrates your experiences and/or willingness to contribute to a culture of diversity, equity, and inclusion through your work in general, and in this context, your teaching more specifically. Some instructors also choose to include a diversity statement on their syllabus to signal a commitment to creating an inclusive and supportive climate for all students. The Carnegie Mellon University Eberly Center provides a quick introduction to diversity statements that can provide you with a place to start writing your own (www.cmu.edu/teaching/designteach/syllabus/checklist/diversitystatement.html).
Materials From Others	
Learning materials cocreated with students	Include examples of course materials you cocreated with your students. These may include the following: • ground rules for interaction—asking your students to contribute to the creation of ground rules can be a great activity for the beginning of the semester • assessment rubrics • reading lists • study guides and exam questions—asking students to collaboratively create a study guide or create a few relevant exam questions at the end of each lesson or unit encourages self-regulation, student agency, and can ease your workload
Peer feedback and/or observation	Ask your observer to note examples of inclusive teaching behaviors in your teaching presentation and materials. Instead of—or in addition to—inviting a peer to observe your classroom teaching you can also ask for a course material review. For these reviews you might ask a peer or teaching expert (e.g., your campus teaching center colleagues) to review specific materials or learning units and provide feedback. Here, too, you may ask your colleague to note moments of explicit alignment in your materials. Be sure to share your course syllabus and other relevant materials to ensure your observer is aware of the outcomes you aim to accomplish and the inclusive strategies you are employing across modalities and course components.
Student feedback	As stated previously, gathering student feedback gives you an opportunity to ensure that your efforts are in fact supporting students' learning. They can provide targeted feedback on their experience in your class through formal and informal feedback. • *CTB midterm feedback.* The CTB midterm feedback survey includes questions that specifically solicit your students' feedback on inclusivity in your course. • *Select end-of-term surveys.* Questions related to your efforts to create inclusive learning environments are part of many—but not all—end-of-term student surveys. If no question related to inclusivity is included on the survey used in your institution, you may be able to add a custom question or facilitate your own survey.

Reflection Questions

1. How does your curriculum—content and activities—demonstrate to all students that they have a place in your class and in your discipline? How do your communications invite students to be a part of the learning community in your course?

2. What assumptions do you make about knowledge, skills, and behaviors all college students should be able to perform? What are some of the unwritten expectations of your institution, your discipline, and your class ("hidden curriculum")? What can you do to make these unstated expectations explicit?

3. What concrete steps can you take to reduce and remove barriers to success in your design of course materials and activities?

4. What biases do you hold and how might they impact your interactions with students?

References

Addy, T. M., Dube, D., Mitchell, K. A., SoRelle, M. E., Longmire-Avital, B., & Felten, P. (2021). *What inclusive instructors do: Principles and practices for excellence in college teaching.* Stylus.

Ambrose, S. A., Bridges, M. W., DiPietro, M., Lovett, M. C., & Norman, M. K. (2010). *How learning works: Seven research-based principles for smart teaching.* Jossey-Bass.

Appert, L., Bean, C. S., Irvin, A., Jungels, A. M., Klaf, S., & Phillipson, M. (2017). *Inclusive teaching guide.* Columbia Center for Teaching and Learning, Columbia University. https://ctl.columbia.edu/resources-and-technology/resources/inclusive-teaching-guide/

Brookfield, S. (2015). *The skillful teacher: On technique, trust, and responsiveness in the classroom* (3rd ed.). Jossey-Bass.

Brown, A. L., & Campione, J. C. (1998). Designing a community of young learners: Theoretical and practical lessons. In N. M. Lambert (Ed.), *How students learn: Reforming schools through learner-centered education* (pp. 153–186). American Psychological Association.

Caprara, G. V., Barbaranelli, C., Pastorelli, C., Bandura, A., & Zimbardo, P. G. (2000). Prosocial foundations of children's academic achievement. *Psychological Science, 11*(4), 302. https://doi.org/10.1111/1467-9280.00260

Carrell, S. E., Page, M. E., & West, J. E. (2010). Sex and science: How professor gender perpetuates the gender gap. *Quarterly Journal of Economics, 125*(3), 1101–1144. https://doi.org/10.1162/qjec.2010.125.3.1101

Carello, J., & Butler, L. D. (2015). Practicing what we teach: Trauma informed educational practice. *Journal of Teaching in Social Work, 35*(3), 262–278. https://doi.org/10.1080/08841233.2015.1030059

Chávez, A. F., & Longerbeam, S. D. (2016). *Teaching across cultural strengths.* Stylus.

Cohen, G. L., & Steele, C. M. (2002). A barrier of mistrust: How negative stereotypes affect cross-race mentoring. In J. Aronson (Ed.), *Improving academic achievement* (pp. 303–327). Academic Press.

Cook-Sather, A., Bovill, C., & Felten, P. (2014). *Engaging students as partners in learning and teaching: A guide for faculty.* Jossey-Bass.

Cooper, K. M., Haney, B., Krieg, A., & Brownell, S. E. (2017). What's in a name? The importance of students perceiving that an instructor knows their names in a high-enrollment biology classroom. *CBE Life Sciences Education, 16*(1), Article 8. https://doi.org/10.1187/cbe.16-08-0265

De Bie, A., Marquis, E., Cook-Sather, A., & Luqueño, L. P. (2021). *Promoting equity and justice through pedagogical partnership.* Stylus.

Delgado, V. (2020, September 23). Decoding the hidden curriculum: Latino/a first-generation college students' influence on younger siblings' educational trajectory. *Journal of Latinos and Education.* Advance online publication. https://doi.org/10.1080/15348431.2020.1801439

Denton, A. W., & Veloso, J. (2018). Changes in syllabus tone affect warmth (but not competence) ratings of both male and female instructors. *Social Psychology of Education: An International Journal, 21*(1), 173–187. https://doi.org/10.1007/s11218-017-9409-7

Dewsbury, B., & Brame, C. J. (2019). Inclusive teaching. *Life Science Education, 18*(2), 1–5. https://doi.org/10.1187/cbe.19-01-0021

Espinosa, L. L., Turk, J. M., Taylor, M., & Chessman, H. M. (2019). *Race and ethnicity in higher education: A status report.* American Council on Education. https://1xfsu31b52d33idlp13twtos-wpengine.netdna-ssl.com/wp-content/uploads/2019/02/Race-and-Ethnicity-in-Higher-Education.pdf

Fairlie, R. W., Hoffmann, F., & Oreopoulos, P. (2014). A community college instructor like me: Race and ethnicity interactions in the classroom. *The American Economic Review, 104*(8), 2567–2591. https://doi.org/10.1257/aer.104.8.2567

Farrell, K., Gupta, N., & Queen, M. (2004). *Interrupting heteronormativity: Lesbian, gay, bisexual, and transgender pedagogy and responsible teaching at Syracuse University.* The Graduate School of Syracuse University. https://surface.syr.edu/books/14

First Nations Education Steering Committee. (n.d.). *First Peoples principles of learning.* https://www.fnesc.ca/first-peoples-principles-of-learning/

Flutter, J. (2007). Teacher development and pupil voice. *The Curriculum Journal, 18*(3), 343–354. https://doi.org/10.1080/09585170701589983

Freire, P. (2014). *Pedagogy of the oppressed.* Bloomsbury.

Fuller-Rowell, T. E., & Doan, S. N. (2010). The social costs of academic success across ethnic groups. *Child Development, 81*(6), 1696–1713. https://doi.org/10.1111/j.1467-8624.2010.01504.x

Gay, G. (2001). Preparing for culturally responsive teaching. *Journal of Teacher Education, 53*(2), 106–116.

Gierdowski, D. C., Brooks, D. C., & Galanek, J. D. (2020). *EDUCAUSE 2020 student technology report: Supporting the whole student.* EDUCAUSE Research. https://www.educause.edu/ecar/research-publications/student-technology-report-supporting-the-whole-student/2020/accessibility-and-accommodations

Goodenow, C. (1993). The psychological sense of school membership among adolescents: Scale development and educational correlates. *Psychology in the Schools, 30*(1), 79–90. https://doi.org/10.1002/

1520-6807(199301)30:1<79::AID-PITS2310300113>3.0.CO;2-X

Haeger, H., Fresquez, C., Banks, J. E., & Smith, C. (2018). Navigating the academic landscape: How mentored research experiences can shed light on the hidden curriculum. *Scholarship and Practice of Undergraduate Research*, *2*(1), 15–23. https://doi.org/10.18833/spur/2/1/7

Hand, L., & Rowe, M. (2001). Evaluation of student feedback. *Accounting Education*, *10*(2), 147–160. https://doi.org/10.1080/09639280110081651

Hariharan, J. (2019). Uncovering the hidden curriculum. *Science*, *364*(6441), 702. https://doi.org/10.1126/science.364.6441.702

Harnish, R. J., & Bridges, K. R. (2011). Effect of syllabus tone: Students' perceptions of instructor and course. *Social Psychology of Education: An International Journal*, *14*(3), 319–330. https://doi-org.ezproxy.libproxy.db.erau.edu/10.1007/s11218-011-9152-4

Hooker, S., & Brand, B. (2010). College knowledge: A critical component of college and career readiness. In N. Letgers & R. Balfanz (Eds.), *Putting All Students on the Graduation Path* (New Directions for Youth Development, no. 127, pp. 75–85). Wiley. https://doi.org/10.1002/yd.364

hooks, b. (1994). *Teaching to transgress.* Routledge.

Hurtado, S., & Carter, D. F. (1997). Effects of college transition and perceptions of the campus racial climate on Latino college students' sense of belonging. *Sociology of Education*, *70*(4), 324–345. https://doi.org/10.2307/2673270

Hutchison, L., & McAlister-Shields, L. (2020). Culturally responsive teaching: Its application in higher education environments. *Education Sciences*, *10*(5), 124. https://doi.org/10.3390/educsci10050124

Jacoby-Senghor, D. S., Sinclair, S., & Shelton, J. N. (2016). A lesson in bias: The relationship between implicit racial bias and performance in pedagogical contexts. *Journal of Experimental Social Psychology*, *63*, 50–55. https://doi.org/10.1016/j.jesp.2015.10.010

Ladson-Billings, G. (1995). But that's just good teaching! The case for culturally relevant pedagogy. *Theory Into Practice*, *34*(3), 159–165.

Ladson Billings, G. (2014). Culturally relevant pedagogy 2.0: a.k.a. the remix. *Harvard Educational Review, 84*(1), 74–84.

Lakey, G. (2020). *Facilitating group learning.* PM Press.

Levin, B. (2000). Putting students at the centre in education reform. *Journal of Educational Change, 1*(2), 155–172. https://doi.org/10.1023/A:1010024225888

Liberatory Design. (n.d.). *What is liberatory design?* https://www.liberatorydesign.com

Mahoney, J. L., & Cairns, R. B. (1997). Do extracurricular activities protect against early school dropout? *Developmental Psychology, 33*(2), 241–253. https://doi.org/10.1037/0012-1649.33.2.241

Mandouit, L. (2018). Using student feedback to improve teaching. *Educational Action Research, 26*(5), 755–769. https://doi.org/10.1080/09650792.2018.1426470

Matthews, K. E., Mercer-Mapstone, L., Dvorakova, S. L., Acai, A., Cook-Sather, A., Felten, P., Healey, M., Healey, R. L., & Marquis, E. (2019). Enhancing outcomes and reducing inhibitors to the engagement of students and staff in learning and teaching partnerships: Implications for academic development. *International Journal for Academic Development, 24*(3), 246–259. https://doi.org/10.1080/1360144X.2018.1545233

McNair, T., Bensimon, E. S., & Malcolm-Piqueux, L. (2020). *From equity talk to equity walk.* Jossey-Bass.

McNutt, C. (2020, August 11). *Liberatory learning: Dismantling the hidden curriculum.* Human Restoration Project. https://medium.com/human-restoration-project/liberatory-learning-dismantling-the-hidden-curriculum-3e65b7a9e3ed

Mercer-Mapstone, L., Dvorakova, S. L., Matthews, K. E., Abbot, S., Cheng, B., Felten, P., Knorr, K., Marquis, E., Shammas, R., & Swaim, K. (2017). A systematic literature review of students as partners in higher education. *International Journal for Students as Partners, 1*(1), Article 1. https://doi.org/10.15173/ijsap.v1i1.3119

Milkman, K. L., Akinola, M., & Chugh, D. (2015). What happens before? A field experiment exploring how pay and representation differentially shape bias on the pathway into organizations. *Journal of Applied Psychology, 100*(6), 1678–1712. https://doi.org/10.1037/apl0000022

Murdoch, Y. D., Hyejung, L., & Kang, A. (2018). Learning students' given names benefits EMI classes. *English in Education, 52*(3), 225–247. https://doi.org/10.1080/04250494.2018.1509673

Murphy, M. C., Gopalan, M., Carter, E. R., Emerson, K. T. U., Bottoms, B. L., & Walton, G. M. (2020). A customized belonging intervention improves retention of socially disadvantaged students at a broad-access university. *Science Advances, 6*(29), eaba4677–eaba4677. https://doi.org/10.1126/sciadv.aba4677

National Center for Education Statistics. (2018). *Students with disabilities.* Institute of Education Sciences. https://nces.ed.gov/fastfacts/display.asp?id=60

Novak, K., & Rodríguez, K. (2018). *UDL progression rubric.* Novak Education. https://info.novakeducation.com/udl-progression-rubric

Oleson, K. C. (2020). *Promoting inclusive classroom dynamics in higher education: A research-based pedagogical guide for faculty.* Stylus.

Pacansky-Brock, M. (2021, Spring/Summer). The liquid syllabus: An anti-racist teaching element. *C2C Digital*

Magazine. https://scalar.usc.edu/works/c2c-digital-maga zine-spring--summer-2021/the-liquid-syllabus-anti-racist

Paradkar, S. (2019, September 14). "Your name is too difficult." What a school's hidden curriculum is telling students. *Toronto Star.* https://www.thestar.com/news/atkinsonseries/2019/09/14/your-name-is-too-difficult-what-a-schools-hidden-curriculum-is-telling-students.html

Rainey, K., Dancy, M., Mickelson, R., Stearns, E., & Moller, S. (2018). Race and gender differences in how sense of belonging influences decisions to major in STEM. *International Journal of STEM Education, 5*(1), Article 10. https://doi.org/10.1186/s40594-018-0115-6

Steele, C. M. (2011). *Whistling Vivaldi: How stereotypes affect us and what we can do.* W.W. Norton.

Steele, C. M., & Aronson, J. (1995). Stereotype threat and the intellectual test performance of African Americans. *Journal of Personality and Social Psychology, 69*(5), 797–811. https://doi.org/10.1037/0022-3514.69.5.797

Strayhorn, T. L. (2018). *College students' sense of belonging: A key to educational success for all students* (2nd ed.). Routledge.

Super, L., Hofman, A., Leung, C., Ho, M., Harrower, E., Adreak, N., & Manesh, Z. R. (2021). Fostering equity, diversity, and inclusion in large, first-year classes: Using reflective practice questions to promote universal design for learning in ecology and evolution lessons. *Ecology and Evolution, 11,* 3464–3472. https://doi.org/10.1002/ece3.6960

Tanner, K. D. (2013). Structure matters: Twenty-one teaching strategies to promote student engagement and cultivate classroom equity. *CBE Life Sciences Education, 12*(3), 322–331. https://doi.org/10.1187/cbe.13-06-0115

Tobin, T. J., & Behling, K. T. (2018). *Reach everyone, teach everyone: Universal design for learning in higher education.* West Virginia University Press.

Torland, M., & Novak, K. (2019). *UDL implementation rubric.* Novak Education. https://www.novakeducation.com/blog/udl-implementation-rubric

U.S. Department of Labor. (1973). Section 504, Rehabilitation Act of 1973. https://www.dol.gov/agencies/oasam/centers-offices/civil-rights-center/statutes/section-504-rehabilitation-act-of-1973

Verschelden, C. (2017). *Bandwidth recovery: Helping students reclaim cognitive resources lost to poverty, racism, and social marginalization.* Stylus.

Walton, G. M., & Cohen, G. L. (2007). A question of belonging: Race, social fit, and achievement. *Journal of Personality and Social Psychology, 92*(1), 82–96. https://doi.org/10.1037/0022-3514.92.1.82

Weimer, M. (2013). *Learner-centered teaching: Five key changes to practice.* Wiley.

Werder, C., Thibou, S., & Kaufer, B. (2012). Students as co-inquirers: A requisite threshold concept in educational development? *The Journal of Faculty Development, 26*(3), 34–38.

Yeager, D. S., Walton, G. M., Brady, S. T., Akcinar, E. K., Paunesku, D., Keane, L., Kamentz, D., Ritter, G., Duckworth, A. I., Urstein, R., Gomez, E. M., Markus, H. R., Cohen, G. I., & Dweck, C. S. (2016). Teaching a lay theory before college narrows achievement gaps at scale. *Proceedings of the National Academy of Sciences of the United States of America, 113*(24). https://doi.org/10.1073/pnas.1524360113

CHAPTER 3

Engage

DEFINITION

Instructors who engage students purposefully select research-based techniques to ensure that students actively participate in the learning process and take responsibility for their intellectual development.

STUDENT ENGAGEMENT CAN TAKE many forms. When we imagine our ideal version of engaged student learning, we might imagine an active class debate where students critically engage with each other's contributions, a fascinating lab experiment where students contribute and gain new insights as they observe what is happening, a collaborative project where online students work together as a team to create a presentation on a course topic, or a range of many other possibilities. All these various possibilities require the instructor to step back and make space for students to take an active role in their learning; to do so we need to build the foundation for productive engagement through careful planning. If we do not invest time up front to create conditions for engagement, we may be discouraged by students' lack of excitement for a subject we are passionate about or frustrated by their lack of preparation, in-class distraction, and sometimes their failure to show up at all. Engagement is a component of teaching and learning that we cannot control unilaterally; teachers and students share responsibility. Fortunately, research offers many strategies we can employ to set the stage for engagement that both instructors and students alike find rewarding.

As instructors, we have the opportunity and responsibility to create the conditions for student success by actively guiding them in analyzing and applying the content and practicing the skills we hope they will develop in our courses. Our efforts to engage students and provide them with relevant, hands-on opportunities and timely feedback make showing up for class worthwhile for learners who manage competing demands on their time. We can create engaging learning environments that add value beyond any information a textbook or instructional video can provide, but if time in the classroom is dedicated solely to presenting information that is easily accessible elsewhere, students may choose instead to engage with that information on their own time through other channels. To be clear, the doing and thinking associated with engaged learning comes in many different forms, ranging from a quiet focus on active note-taking and synthesis of ideas during a lecture to complex and sometimes messy project-based learning activities that engage students in hands-on activities. Engaged learning is not just about being active; an engaged student does not simply "do" but also "actively examines, questions, and relates new ideas to old, thereby achieving the kind of deep learning that lasts" (Barkley, 2010, p. 17). As we consider engagement in our courses, ideally we select a range of different activities to promote students taking an active role in both the thinking and the doing. This chapter will provide an overview of the range of strategies and activities you can select and implement as an instructor to influence students' motivation and actions in becoming engaged participants in the learning experience and the research that supports the effectiveness of these approaches.

What Do We Know?

Activities that require student participation not only enhance the learning experience but also allow us to foster deeper student learning overall. Research shows that student engagement in their own learning is positively related to gains in student motivation, persistence and retention, and success, as measured in gains in abilities, critical thinking, and grades (Cho & Cho, 2014; Pike & Kuh, 2005). Student academic engagement includes both behavioral and emotional engagement components; behavioral engagement encompasses students' effort, attention to and concentration on the content, and involvement in the class, whereas emotional engagement refers to students' enthusiasm, interest, enjoyment, vitality, and zest with regard to the class (Skinner et al., 2008). Generally, we expect learning to go beyond the recall of facts—we want our students to use the information to solve problems, communicate clearly, and think critically and creatively, to name only a few of the expectations and goals we have for successful students. This kind of deep learning, however, only happens when students actively engage with information and can connect it to what they already know, when they see examples of how others have successfully completed a task, and when they practice over and over again. Some students are prepared to independently identify and engage in relevant practice and growth opportunities, but most need support and guidance to identify and take advantage of productive opportunities that will allow them to advance in their academic, professional, and personal growth.

In the following section we explore the multiple components that contribute to student engagement in the learning experience and how they impact learning. They include things we do in the learning space—whether physical or virtual, the decisions we make in planning our class, and the way we communicate with our students. More specifically, we will focus on the following areas as contributors to and examples of student engagement:

- communicating regularly, openly, and transparently
- designing course activities to intentionally promote student–instructor, student–content, and student–student engagement
- using varied instructional methods to engage all students
- fostering self-regulated learning
- relating course content to relevant examples and applications
- incorporating current research and promoting student participation in disciplinary research

For each of these areas, we will present an overview of research insights and introduce select examples of how a principle might be implemented in practice.

Communicating Regularly, Openly, and Transparently

The way we communicate with our students plays an important role in encouraging or discouraging student engagement in class activities and in all other aspects of the learning experience we create in our courses, such as completion of homework and assignments, collaboration with peers, and even attendance. We must communicate regularly in a way that is open and transparent and conveys our enthusiasm for the course and our availability to help them succeed. To communicate in a manner that promotes student engagement, we need to think beyond what we say directly to students in the classroom or through emails and announcements; we must expand our understanding of communication to encompass the course syllabus, assignments, and any other materials we share with students. Consistency and intentionality in the manner and tone of our communication with students allows us not only to engage students more effectively but to establish a consistent persona aligned to our teaching values, a concept we will discuss more in Part Two.

As we establish our teaching persona, we must remember that we send messages through both verbal and nonverbal actions when we communicate with our students; the messages we send can be positive or negative. Research has found that increased immediacy (nonverbal communication such as movement in the classroom, eye contact, smiles, etc.) and other communicative actions that send positive messages of liking and closeness positively affect student motivation and engagement, student interest, and perceived learning (Fallah, 2014; McCroskey et al., 1996; McCroskey & Sallinen, 1996; Roberts & Friedman, 2013). While much research has focused on understanding the impact of communicative action in the physical classroom, immediacy behaviors also play an important role in the virtual learning space. Immediacy behaviors in the online environment include instructor responsiveness to student questions, visible presence in collaborative forums, and prompt media-rich feedback, but they also include less obvious aspects such as the design of the course with color and multimedia elements as well as the use of emoticons in communications (Dixson et al., 2017). These behaviors are often described as an instructor's "social presence" in an online course, or the "ability to project one's self through media and to establish personal and meaningful relationships" (Ice et al., 2017, p. 77). Just as positive communication in the physical classroom is associated with increased student interest and engagement, increased social presence in the online environment also has a positive impact on student learning, engagement, and satisfaction with the course (Gunawardena, 1995; Kehrwald, 2008; Richardson & Swan, 2003). Regular, positive communication with students and timely responses to their questions also demonstrates that we are available and invested in students' learning success, encouraging them to stay engaged with us in- and outside the classroom as they encounter challenges or questions.

Research further suggests that early impressions students glean about us and our class matter more than we might think (Cavanagh, 2016). Our communications with students on the first day of classes, and even before through the sharing of content online, set the tone for the course. Are we using these acts of communication effectively to convey enthusiasm for the course, confidence in our knowledge, and caring for our students? It pays to consider how we can effectively communicate our enthusiasm about our subject and our investment in helping students learn, as this can increase student engagement throughout the semester (Cavanagh, 2016, 2019; Harrington, 2021; Imlach, 2021).

Finally, open and transparent communication with students is an important contributor to creating a classroom environment conducive to student engagement. As Linda Nilson (2016) states in *Teaching at Its Best*, our students "value communication, information, and caring, and they respond well when we explain why we use the teaching and assessment methods we do" (p. 37). We increasingly encounter students who want to know our purpose for assigning tasks and materials and how activities and assessments will help them learn. Getting students excited and helping them see the "why" behind our pedagogical decisions can boost engagement and motivation. For example, one student describes how her instructor's explanation of the reasons that motivated their choice of course texts and enthusiasm for each book assigned allowed the students to look forward to reading them: "Professor Birge described with excitement the unique properties of the books as well as her reason for teaching them. . . . Her enthusiasm for the books fueled classroom discussion" (Gundhus, 2021, p. 22). Transparently sharing our reasons for certain course activities and assignments as well as our expectations, hopes, and goals for our students' learning allows us to convey our excitement for course content and, by doing so, capture students' attention.

When it comes to completing assignments, students, especially minoritized student populations, also benefit from transparent assignment prompts that communicate the purpose of the task, outline the steps needed to complete it, and clearly define expectations and evaluation criteria for a task completed to satisfaction (Winkelmes et al., 2016). Known as "transparency in learning and teaching" (TiLT), this strategy for clearly communicating the expectations for an assessment and the process to achieve success has been shown to increase student efficacy—or their perceived ability to complete the task, which consequently encourages them to earnestly engage with the task at hand rather than disengaging or relying on outside resources for its completion. We discuss TiLT in more detail in chapter 4, "Assess," but for now, we want to emphasize that this strategy is one of several we can use to promote consistent, positive, and transparent approaches to communication. Each of these methods is important for student engagement as they help us create a classroom environment conducive to student participation, encourage students to reach out for support, and foster students' confidence in their ability to complete learning tasks.

Designing Course Activities to Intentionally Promote Student–Content, Student–Instructor, and Student–Student Engagement

While relevant in all instructional modalities, scholars in the context of distance and online learning have extensively inquired into different types of learning space interactions and the role they play in the learning process and student success. The types of interactions most relevant to education and student engagement have been identified as student interactions with course content, student interactions with instructors, student interactions with each other, and student interactions with technology (Anderson, 2003; Nilson & Goodson, 2018). While the following sections address each of these different types of interaction and engagement separately, in practice, they overlap as, for example, discussing ideas with the instructor or peers can help students engage more deeply with the content and consider different perspectives on a topic or problem. The relationship between students and technology is addressed in more detail in chapter 5 ("Integrate Technology").

Student Engagement With Content

Productive interaction with content is essential to successful learning (Anderson, 2003; Liu & Kaye, 2015; Sadik & Reisman, 2004). To foster productive engagement with content, we must be selective about the amount and complexity of materials and information we require students to engage with. Preferably, we choose materials that are relevant, accurate, and well suited to support the learning outcomes while also keeping in mind that less can be more as it allows more time for students to meaningfully interact with resources (Nilson & Goodson, 2018). Creating and communicating a clear path to access the content and sharing it in a way that is accessible to all students removes barriers to students' interaction with the materials we have selected (see chapter 2 for an overview of criteria for accessible materials). Often, even providing relevant and accessible content is not

enough, as we cannot take for granted that students know how to engage effectively with the content we share for academic purposes. As instructors, we can support students in learning how to learn by providing guidance that helps them identify essential information and by clearly linking materials to the course learning goals. Further, we can integrate examples, illustrations, and interactive components such as quizzes or reflection prompts to promote student focus and understanding (Cavanagh, 2016; Nilson & Goodson, 2018). Beyond supporting students in the initial step of engaging with content in order to identify and recall important facts, engaged learning also allows us to foster learning that goes beyond memorization. For example, we can promote academic challenge and deep learning by emphasizing connections between classroom learning and students' professional and personal lives and requiring student engagement in activities such as critical analysis of information and application of ideas to a new context.

Student Engagement With Instructors

Student–instructor engagement has been shown to have multiple benefits, and research indicates that this type of interaction matters more than interaction with either content or peers (Cho & Cho, 2014; Nilson & Goodson, 2018). If we find ourselves with limited resources, investing in developing opportunities for student–instructor engagement might give us the most bang for our buck. For example, students who perceived a connection with their instructor valued learning tasks more highly, reported increased self-efficacy (the belief that they can succeed in the course), and were more satisfied with the course overall (Mullen & Tallent-Runnels, 2006; Yang et al., 2006). In their analysis of engagement factors based on multiple years of National Survey of Student Engagement (NSSE) data, Pike and Kuh (2005) connect "a great deal of interaction with faculty inside and outside the classroom" (p. 202) with intellectually stimulating engagement.

While fostering student–instructor relations is important in all instructional modalities, creating an instructor presence is especially important in modalities with high percentages of virtual learning. To establish instructor presence that is perceived as positive and helpful in virtual settings, ensure interactions have a clear purpose and hold value for students. Interactions can range from video introductions at the beginning of the course that help students get to know you and weekly announcements providing updates for the course to instructor contributions to class discussions and formative feedback on students' work (Nilson & Goodson, 2018). As stated previously, careful attention to tone and immediacy behaviors can help us create a learning environment conducive to student engagement and success.

Student Engagement With Peers

Based on his research into student distractions and strategies that allow us to promote focused attention, James Lang observes that attention and community are closely linked. "We are built to pay attention to other human beings," he claims, to the extent that we unconsciously synchronize thoughts and behaviors (Lang, 2020, pp. 98–99). In this context, knowing and using each other's names can be a powerful tool in building classroom community and in keeping students attentive to each other (in larger classes this may be supported by using name tents). As students develop a sense of belonging with their peers and classroom community, they are more likely to be engaged, active participants and contributors to the learning that happens in the course. Even small cues of social connectedness can enhance students' motivation to achieve learning goals (Walton et al., 2012). Furthermore, in a community, students are called upon to work together in pursuit of shared goals and interest, but more importantly, they have responsibilities to each other and to the group as a whole (Barkley, 2010; Brophy, 2004). Promoting peer learning where students pool their expertise to solve problems and identify misperceptions and implementing cooperative learning activities where students rely on each other to complete a task can improve peer relationships and student performance, especially among minoritized learners (Aronson, 2004, as cited in Walton et al., 2012). Some instructional approaches integrate student–student interactions more formally, including, for example, collaborative learning, team-based learning, and peer instruction. We provide a brief overview of each engagement strategy in Table 3.1.

This brief introduction and overview of a few collaborative learning techniques provides only a glimpse into the many options available for fostering students' engagement with peers. The variety of collaborative activities and approaches ensures that options are available for instructors in all disciplines and teaching modalities.

Using Varied Instructional Strategies to Engage All Students

As a graduate teaching assistant, Claudia read *How Learning Works* (Ambrose et al., 2010). This seminal text on teaching and learning opens with a quote by Nobel laureate Herbert A. Simon. One of the founders in the field of cognitive science, Simon states, "Learning results from what the student does and thinks and only from what the student does and thinks. The teacher can advance learning only by influencing what the student does to learn" (as cited in Ambrose et al., 2010, p. 1). Reading this quote was eye-opening at the time, even though the idea seems common sense now; after all, who has ever learned how to play the piano or write a persuasive essay only by listening to a lecture on the topic? A fundamental characteristic of active learning and for engaging students cognitively, emotionally, and physically is that "students must connect what is learned to what is already known" (Barkley, 2010, p. 39). This means that engagement will be experienced differently from student to student relative to the prior knowledge and experiences they bring into the classroom, which makes it crucial we use a variety of ways to challenge and support students: "[Engaged] students must do more than just listen: They must read, write, discuss, or be engaged in solving problems. Most important, to be actively involved, students must engage in such higher-order thinking tasks as analysis, synthesis, and evaluation" (Bonwell & Eison, 1991, p. iii). That said, active learning does not have to include physical movement, or even students talking; it can be internal and include, for example, thinking through reflection prompts, responding to guided questions, or self-quizzing. There are many options for implementing active learning, some of which we discussed previously when we introduced collaborative learning strategies. Other options range from quick activities that take only a few minutes to complete in the classroom to instructional approaches that prioritize active learning over lecture. Courses centered on active learning generally dedicate most of the class meeting time to learner-centered activities, and lectures are eliminated entirely or delivered virtually outside the class meeting time. Whether you are aiming for more dynamic interactive lectures that integrate quick active learning moments

TABLE 3.1: Instructional Strategies Promoting Student–Student Engagement

Collaborative learning	Collaborative learning includes instructional approaches that "involve joint intellectual effort by students, or students and teachers together. In most collaborative learning situations students are working in groups of two or more, mutually searching for understanding [or] creating a product" (Smith & MacGregor, 1992, p. 11). It is important that group activities are intentionally designed to provide students with meaningful tasks that engage all group members in actively working together toward stated outcomes and coconstruction of knowledge (Barkley et al., 2014; Scager et al., 2016; Volet et al., 2009). Extensive research has been conducted on the benefits of collaborative learning, indicating that students who learn in small groups demonstrate higher achievement than students in traditional instruction settings (Romero, 2009; Springer et al., 1999).
Team-based learning	This approach to collaborative learning uses "a specific sequence of individual work, group work, and immediate feedback to create a motivational framework in which students increasingly hold each other accountable for coming to class prepared and contributing to discussion" (Sweet, 2010, cited in Sibley et al., 2014, p. 6). While team-based learning can hold great benefits for students, such as increased depth of understanding, increased performance, more consistent attendance and participation, and an appreciation for working in teams, this collaborative learning approach requires significant planning up front (Michaelsen & Sweet, 2008, 2011).
Peer instruction	This specific instance of collaborative learning was pioneered by Eric Mazur, professor of physics at Harvard University. Using the peer instruction approach, instructors intersperse lectures with conceptual questions; to solve the problem presented in the question, students first formulate their own answers and then discuss their answers in groups of three to four, attempting to reach consensus on the correct answer (Mazur, n.d.). Using the peer instruction method, students achieve significant gains in their conceptual understanding and problem-solving abilities (Fagen et al., 2002; Lasry et al., 2008; Mazur, n.d.; Zhang et al., 2017). Studies also suggest that this instruction might especially benefit female students in STEM fields (Zhang et al., 2017).

or are committed to more complex active learning strategies, such as project-based learning, research on active learning says your efforts to engage students will positively impact their chances to succeed.

A meta-analysis of 225 studies on active learning showed that "average examination scores improved by about 6% in active learning sections and that students in traditional lectures were 1.5 times more likely to fail than were students in classes with active learning" (Freeman et al., 2014, p. 8410). Moreover, the same analysis showed that students in active learning sections increased their scores on concept inventories—validated tests used to assess students' conceptual understanding in a subject area—even more than on course examinations. Many of us would consider this outcome a desirable indicator of deeper conceptual understanding of course content.

Similarly, Bevan et al. (2014) found a significant shift in students' approaches to learning between first-year students enrolled in active learning and lecture-based sections of the same course; while all students started the semester with a preference for deep learning approaches, by the end of the semester, students who were enrolled in the lecture-based class had shifted to more surface learning approaches, whereas students in the active learning sections maintained their preference for deep learning. This indicates that our efforts to implement active learning (or not) may impact students' learning beyond the time they spend with us.

Interactive Lecturing

For centuries, lectures have been a primary strategy for teaching in higher education, and for many of us, it is a strategy with which we feel comfortable. Starting in the 1990s, scholars of teaching and learning began advocating for a move away from lecturing toward more active learning. However, this does not mean we have to abandon lecturing entirely. While research notes that traditional lectures alone are ineffective, lectures that integrate active learning methods to achieve learning outcomes can be an effective teaching strategy (Barkley & Major, 2018; Freeman et al., 2014; Harrington, 2017). Lectures are an especially useful tool to provide necessary background knowledge that will allow students to engage in related active and collaborative tasks more effectively and with less frustration (Kirschner et al., 2006).

Productive active learning activities can be integrated at the beginning, middle, and end of a lecture. At the beginning of the lecture, we might start with a brief (ungraded) homework quiz that allows us to identify any information that is unclear and should be reinforced prior to sharing new information. This practice is sometimes called just-in-time teaching. Or we might start class with a brief discussion that allows students to share what they already know (or think they know) about a topic and how it applies to their field, career goals, or life to activate prior knowledge and emphasize relevance. During the lecture, we might ask students to follow along by completing guided notes on the lecture. Guided notes might require students to fill in blanks, answer simple questions, or solve problems. Whenever we integrate a question or problem into our guided notes, we need to make sure to build in a brief lecture break to give students enough time to respond. Alternatively, a range of presentation tools now allows us to integrate quick multiple-choice or open-ended questions into our lectures to check students' understanding and clarify misconceptions or remaining questions as needed. Sometimes just taking a quick break to have students compare notes with a neighbor allows us to ensure they take a more active role in the learning process. At the end of the lecture, the brief and popular "muddiest point" reflection can help students summarize their learning by asking them to identify one idea or concept that remains unclear; instructors then use this information to provide additional resources, such as a video explanation, readings shared through the course LMS, or a brief recap at the beginning of the next class meeting.

In addition to engaging students and checking in on their learning, the integration of activities and pauses into a lecture also allows us to reduce the cognitive load for our students. Cognitive load theory describes the reality that our working memory has limited capacity to process new information. In the context of teaching and learning, both the complexity of materials taught and the instructional procedures used for instructions are factors contributing to the load on our working memory (Sweller, 2010). In the classroom or in instructional videos, the more complex the information shared, the more often our brain needs a break to process new knowledge. Integration of application activities, quick reflection opportunities, or even a quick quiz question can provide this break.

Inquiry and Project-Based Learning

Inquiry-based learning and project-based learning (PBL) engage students through the act of questioning and use of critical thinking skills; learning is driven by curiosity, questions, and problem-solving (Laverick, 2018; Leat, 2017). Instructors implementing this instructional method do so with a range of goals in mind; primarily they want students to acquire and/or apply discipline- or topic-specific knowledge at a deeper level and to develop research and professional skills (Aditomo et al., 2013). Unfortunately, little to no conclusive evidence is available regarding the impact of inquiry-based learning and PBL as most available studies do not involve random allocation of participants to control and experimental groups, and as a result, a causal link between PBL instruction and positive student outcomes cannot be established with certainty (Helle et al., 2006; Kokotsaki et al., 2016). Both approaches focus on a project or question, which is often defined by the student. Projects are generally related to "real-world" issues and interdisciplinary in nature, allowing students to apply knowledge as well as develop problem-solving abilities and a capacity for independent work. PBL relies on student initiative; instructors are involved as guides and mentors rather than taking an authoritarian role (Helle et al., 2006). Nevertheless, instructors play an important role in developing and guiding learning as "the successful implementation of PBL in the classroom relies on the teacher's ability to effectively scaffold students' learning, motivate, support and guide them along the way" (Kokotsaki et al., 2016, p. 272). Inquiry-based learning and PBL are frequently used in capstone experience courses for students across disciplines, but at a smaller scale and with careful planning, these pedagogies can also be integrated into any other course.

We have only scratched the surface, introducing but a few of the many active learning methods and strategies available. Readers looking for specific active learning strategies to address different learning outcomes at various levels of complexity should look at the series of handbooks by Elizabeth Barkley and colleagues for excellent guidance to identify activities that can be easily implemented into any classroom, regardless of discipline or instructional modality. The handbooks introduce a wide range of activities along with examples of implementation and practical suggestions for adapting activities for different classroom contexts. Visit https://criticalteachingbehaviors.org for a recommended reading list.

Foster Self-Regulated Learning

Preparing students to be lifelong learners who can independently seek out, acquire, and use new knowledge on their own is a stated or unstated outcome for many academic programs (AAC&U, 2007; Wirth, 2008). Yet research indicates that students frequently perceive learning as something that is happening to them, unaware that their actions and attitudes play an important role in their learning (Nilson, 2013). Promoting and fostering academic self-regulation allows us to help our students become aware of their agency and identify strategies they can employ to become more successful learners. Self-regulated learning requires attention, self-awareness, and acceptance of responsibility for one's learning. That said, self-regulation is not a single trait or behavior; rather, "it involves the selective use of specific processes that must be personally adapted to each learning task" (Zimmerman, 2002, p. 66). This means that self-regulated learning encompasses multiple component skills that students might develop and adopt at varying levels; component skills include goal setting, learning strategies, self-assessment, time management, metacognition, growth mindset, and forward looking planning. Meta-analytical inquiry into multiple studies on self-regulated learning in face-to-face classrooms and online instruction indicate that the self-regulated learning strategies with the highest potential for a positive impact on students' achievement include metacognition or reflecting on learning methods in relation to performance, effort regulation or persistence in the face of challenges, time management, and critical thinking (Broadbent & Poon, 2015;

Richardson et al., 2012). Panadero et al. (2017) also found that self-assessment (addressed in chapter 4) can have a positive impact on self-regulated learning.

Some students may have developed self-regulated learning skills by the time we meet them in our classes, but many will not be prepared to use these strategies to support their learning, as they may not be familiar with them or only use them haphazardly. However, all students can benefit from knowing effective and efficient strategies for monitoring their learning and accessing their knowledge (Dembo & Seli, 2013). To support students in becoming self-regulated learners, consider implementing practices that foster the development and intentional use of these skills: students who improved self-regulated learning activities as a result of an in-class intervention also showed increases in learning achievement as a direct result of these interventions (Jansen et al., 2019). For some practical ideas on promoting self-regulated learning, see Table 3.2.

Self-regulated learners have access to and use a range of resources and skills that help control various factors influencing their learning, including effective reading and study strategies, time management, and self-assessment skills; these skills assist learners in acquiring and retaining knowledge in a structured and methodological way, both in- and outside of structured learning environments such as a college classroom, and, therefore, promote and support lifelong learning.

Student Engagement and Motivation

Motivation is another important component of self-regulated learning and engagement. Elizabeth Barkley (2010) describes student engagement as starting "at the intersection of motivation and active learning, but these two work synergistically and build intensity" (p. 8). While Barkley reiterates the important role of active learning, she also indicates that the best planned activity might fail to engage students unless they, too, show up and invest time and energy into the learning process. Their commitment is often closely linked to their motivation. Student motivation is complex; whether students are motivated to engage in learning sometimes depends on realities and events beyond our control, but there are also components of motivation tied to the design and delivery of instruction that we can control. The question of how we can foster

	TABLE 3.2: Practical Ideas for Fostering Self-Regulated Learning
Metacognition	Metacognition is the process of "thinking about thinking," or reflecting on personal habits, knowledge, and approaches to learning. Tasks on a metacognitive level allow us to check whether we understand information or find the information we need (Ambrose et al., 2010; Poorvu Center for Teaching and Learning, n.d.; Vos & de Graaff, 2004). There are activities that can help us foster metacognition at various stages of a project or task: <ul><li>Assign a task analysis prior to starting an assignment. Students consider, for example, what kind of a task is this? What is my goal? How will I know I have reached it? What do I already know about the topic? What additional information, if any, will I need? What strengths can I bring to the task? (Nilson, 2013)</li><li>Use cognitive wrappers. After an assessment or activity, ask students to reflect on their preparation for this assignment and to make plans by asking questions: Which study habits or strategies were least effective for my learning? Which study habits were most effective for my learning? What content and concepts did I know best, and how/when did I study for them? What content/concepts am I still struggling with? What worked/did not work? What would I do differently? (Harriet W. Sheridan Center for Teaching and Learning, n.d.; Poorvu Center for Teaching and Learning, n.d.)</li></ul>
Growth Mindset	Growth mindset describes a way of viewing challenges and setbacks. People who have a growth mindset believe that even if they struggle with certain skills, they can improve over time as a result of the effort they invest (Dweck, 2007). To foster a growth mindset: <ul><li>Incorporate tasks that allow for practice and cognitive risk-taking without penalizing mistakes. Mistakes are considered opportunities for learning.</li><li>Provide students with multiple opportunities to improve their performance that can foster a growth mindset as it encourages students to think of work as an iterative process (Sahagun et al., 2021).</li><li>Set high standards for tasks and communicate how the student can achieve them; then provide feedback recognizing effort, and identify specific suggestions for improvement and support available to students. Communicate your belief that the student has the ability to achieve the goal (Cohen et al., 1999).</li></ul>

motivation in educational as well as professional settings has been asked and explored for over a century, and responses have evolved over time. Recent scholarship convincingly argues that motivation to perform a task is a function of expectancy and value associated with said task (Ambrose et al., 2010; Barkley, 2010; Rosenzweig et al., 2019). Expectancy describes our expectation that we are able to (or not) perform the task successfully, whereas value describes the degree to which we value the reward associated with the task or the opportunity to perform the task itself. If either expectancy or value is missing, we have low or no motivation to expend effort on a task. Table 3.3 shows examples of how we can use this research to increase student motivation in our courses by fostering positive expectancy and value through teaching decisions and behaviors.

Obviously, student motivation to engage in our class depends on more than just these two variables, but keeping expectancy and value in mind as we select examples, introduce tasks, and interact with our students can help us move the needle toward increased student motivation, engagement, and self-regulation. As Rosenzweig et al. (2019) observe, "having higher task values and expectancies also relates positively to students using self-regulated learning strategies and negatively to students' academic anxiety" (p. 626), outcomes that can further support students in achieving the often unstated goal of becoming lifelong learners who take responsibility for their own learning.

TABLE 3.3: Fostering Expectancy and Value Through Teaching Decisions and Behaviors

Expectancy	To increase expectancy or students' expectation that they will be able to complete a task successfully, we might do the following: • Consider what prior knowledge we can realistically expect our students to bring to our course and determine learning outcomes and expectations as well as the scaffolding and support we provide based on this information. This helps us ensure students have the necessary information and resources to successfully complete tasks with an appropriate level of additional learning and guidance. • Give feedback that clearly provides specific and realistic guidance and actionable suggestions for achieving learning goals of a task or the course more broadly; feedback should emphasize strengths in students' work so students know what they should continue doing as well as specific areas for improvement and, when possible, action steps they can take to make these improvements.
Value	To increase value or students' perception that learning activities meaningfully relate to their goals and interests, we might do the following: • Choose materials, examples, and activities that show how the course content and goals connect to our students' interests and/or professional goals. • Clearly communicate the purpose of a task and how it will help students achieve learning outcomes and/or develop transferable, professional skills. • Conduct reflection activities asking students to think about the ways that the lessons they are learning in a course relate to their lives and/or other academic courses.

Relate Course Content to Relevant Examples and Applications

"Why do I have to know this? I will never have to use this again!" is likely something we have heard from students at least once (we might have even thought it ourselves in situations where we were the learner). It can be hard for students to see connections between theoretical concepts discussed in class and their application in the real world. Demonstrations, simulations, stories, examples, and even memes and other multimedia content can help us illustrate these connections for our students and make abstract ideas more tangible. We provide a brief elaboration on each of these strategies in Table 3.4.

All these approaches allow us to enrich our instruction and engage students in different ways, making information and concepts more tangible and relatable. Ideally, we use a range of these strategies, as each will resonate with students in different ways. Considering both our learning goals and the needs and preferences of the students in our current course, as well as our own teaching strengths and limitations, can provide useful guidance when deciding on which strategy to use when.

Incorporate Current Research and Promoting Student Participation in Disciplinary Research

While different methods of presenting information and modeling allow us to make abstract information more concrete and engage students in different ways, they also provide opportunities for introducing students to research insights from our discipline. Especially in introductory-level courses, we are often so focused on ensuring that students learn the foundations that we do not take advantage of the opportunity to share and discuss exciting new research and findings in our discipline. Some of the students enrolled in our course will be our future colleagues and, as upcoming professionals in our field, will benefit from an awareness of recent trends, controversies, and insights. We might even share one of the projects we are currently working on and discuss both the exciting results as well as failures we had to overcome in the process and adjustments we had to make; this allows us to not only introduce something we are passionate about but also demonstrate the importance of keeping a growth mindset that allows us to see failures and setbacks as learning opportunities.

TABLE 3.4: Strategies for Illustrating Application and Relevance of Course Content	
Demonstrations	Demonstrations allow instructors to illustrate how to complete a task while explaining each step they are working through; this practice is associated with higher levels of student engagement and achievement—especially for low-motivated students—as they help students see the value and relevance of learning tasks (Balch, 2014; Harrington, 2021; Kim, 2015). With increasingly easy access to recording technology, we also have the option of recording demonstrations so students have access to review the task step by step multiple times as necessary. Additionally, access to a range of free video materials on the internet makes it easier to show how abstract concepts apply in realistic contexts by playing a quick video in class or asking students to watch and later discuss the video online.
Simulation/Gaming	In education, simulations and games uniquely allow us to (a) teach students about the behavior of complex social systems and (b) train students how to execute different roles in real systems (Arcos & Lahneman, 2019). Simulations and games are especially useful in contexts where we want students to engage with complex problems and come to a holistic and nuanced understanding of the situation (Kaneda, 2021). Frequently, simulations and games such as those published by the Reacting to the Past Consortium (reacting.barnard.org) require learners to step into the role of another person and inhabit their reality for a while. Research indicates that these types of learning activities have the potential to not only increase student engagement and preparation for a course but also their sense of belonging and empathy for self and others (Hagood et al., 2017; Weidenfeld & Fernandez, 2017).
Storytelling	Storytelling might be one of the oldest approaches to teaching and has been shown to be an effective way of capturing and maintaining students' attention, resulting in increased new knowledge (Hernández-Serrano & Stefanou, 2009). Stories place events in narrative contexts and by doing so assign them meaning, allowing students to develop deeper relationships with others and the ideas or concepts narrated (Alterio & McDrury, 2003). To make course concepts more relevant, we might consider telling stories from our own research and professional experience or invite guest speakers to talk to our students.
Multimedia Integration	Multimedia learning allows us to increase learning by providing a relatable reference (visual, audio, video, etc.) to the new information and building mental representations through words and pictures (Harrington, 2017; Mayer & Fiorella, 2021). Presentations that are enhanced with multimedia materials allow students to encode information through multiple channels, which can facilitate retrieval of information (Mayer & Fiorella, 2021). Before animating our PowerPoint slides with all the bells and whistles, however, it is important to remember that there is a limit to the amount of information that each channel can process at any one time (Roberts, 2018).

Depending on our position and institutional context, we may have the opportunity to invite students to engage in undergraduate research experiences with us, either by including them in ongoing research projects and laboratories or by offering "course-based undergraduate research experiences" (CURE), where students conduct research as part of the course curriculum. In both contexts instructors (or other personnel such as postdocs or graduate students) provide mentoring to the student researcher; successful mentoring supports undergraduates in deepening their understanding of science and guiding them to develop a scientific identity (Linn et al., 2015). Engaging in undergraduate research is identified as a "high-impact practice" (HIP), an experience that increases student retention and success (Kuh, 2008). As such, the goals of CURE are to "involve students with actively contested questions, empirical observation, cutting-edge technologies, and the sense of excitement that comes from working to answer important questions" (AAC&U, n.d., para. 11). Research confirms that engaging in undergraduate research increases students' research skills, problem-solving abilities, critical thinking skills, and intercultural effectiveness (Crowe & Brakke, 2019; Kilgo et al., 2015; Linn et al., 2015; Lopatto, 2010). Providing opportunities for undergraduate research holds great benefits for participants. To ensure equitable access to this opportunity, however, it may be necessary to invest in expanding access and resources at the institutional level.

Engaging students in the learning process can increase motivation, lead to learning gains, and promote self-regulated learning, but it is also an important tool that allows students to practice using skills and knowledge introduced in the course in preparation for course assessment, and in doing so, they gain a better understanding of how they are progressing in their learning journey. Active learning and student engagement therefore is closely connected to assessment, which is discussed in the next chapter.

What Do We Do?

When we discuss student engagement, we often think first about active learning tasks. However, active learning—such as discussion, case studies, group work, and many more—is only one component contributing to student engagement. Our approach to communications and efforts to create a classroom community where students engage not only with the instructor but also with each other play a role in fostering student participation. Our own excitement about a topic, the way in which we present and illustrate content, and our efforts to bring alive abstract ideas through stories or discussion of practical applications are determining factors in student motivation. Fortunately, there are so many options to engage students that every instructor should be able to find ideas that work for their specific teaching context and persona. Table 3.5 summarizes "Engage" behaviors and suggests step-by-step actions we can take to engage students in multiple ways.

TABLE 3.5: Engage: Critical Teaching Behaviors in Practice

Behavior	Step by Step

EN.1 Establish regular and open communication	• Communicate frequently and openly. Regular, clear, and positive communication with students can keep students on task and motivated. We generally communicate with students in multiple ways, including the following:
	  ○ syllabus
	  ○ announcements and reminders delivered through the LMS
	  ○ personal emails
	  ○ feedback on assessments
	• Pay attention to tone and immediacy behaviors; they play an important role in establishing a positive and welcoming environment conducive to student engagement in the classroom as well as their likelihood to reach out to us with any questions they have about the course.

EN.2 Design course activities to intentionally promote student–instructor, student–content, and student–student engagement	• Create opportunities for students to engage with course topics in multiple contexts. Classes that plan for student interactions with course material, instructors, and peers allow students to approach content from different angles and gain different perspectives on ideas and concepts. • Promote engagement with peers and instructors to create a supportive environment where students have access to multiple sources of help should they need it.

Behavior	Step by Step

EN.3 Encourage participation of all students by using varied instructional strategies	• Plan for active learning. Active learning is a useful tool to encourage students to take an active role in their learning, provide opportunities for practice and application, and give students a chance to test their knowledge. Many options are available to us for integrating active learning into our courses. These include the following:
	  ○ interactive lectures
	  ○ discussions (in person or online)
	  ○ reflective and metacognitive activities
	  ○ collaborative learning and team activities
	  ○ project- and inquiry-based learning
	  ○ simulations
	• While we may prefer certain types of activities when teaching it pays to implement a variety of different activities over time to provide students with multiple options for engagement over the course of the semester or term. Not all students are ready to engage in the same way, so planning for a variety of activities ensures that more students find an opportunity to productively contribute.

EN.4 Foster self-regulated learning	• Address effective learning strategies. One of the skills we want students to develop is effective approaches to learning; to foster self-directed, independent learning we can provide a set of learning tools or discuss effective strategies with students. • Foster a growth mindset. Students with a growth mindset believe that their investment in learning will lead to learning gains (e.g., intelligence is *not* fixed but can be developed and expanded with effort). We can foster a growth mindset by, for example, encouraging students to complete multiple iterations of a project and providing growth-oriented feedback. • Ask students to think about their thinking. Metacognitive reflections ask students to consider how they learn and what strategies have been successful as well as what they might do in the future to improve their learning. Through metacognitive reflections, we can foster self-directed learning and self-efficacy as students are asked to take ownership over their learning behaviors.

EN.5 Relate course content to relevant examples and applications	• Make course content tangible. Some course content can be abstract or—as novice learners—students may fail to see how information and skills apply to their chosen career path. Relating content to concrete relevant examples and bringing abstract ideas alive can help us increase student motivation and understanding of complex topics. We can do this by incorporating, for example, the following:
	  ○ illustrations
	  ○ demonstrations—live or on video
	  ○ storytelling
	  ○ guest speakers
	  ○ hands-on experience (e.g., labs, service learning)
	  ○ simulations

(Continues)

TABLE 3.5 (*Continued*)

Behavior	Step by Step
EN.6 Incorporate current research in the field to stimulate discipline-specific critical thinking and promote student participation in disciplinary research	• Share your excitement about your discipline. Our own excitement can be "contagious" to students. One way to share our interest and passion for our field is to talk about current developments in the field and interesting research insights. We can even share our own research or invite guest speakers to talk to students about both the exciting achievements and the failures we inevitably experience. In sharing recent research trends and our own efforts, we also encourage a better understanding of the problems we try to solve, the processes we employ to do so, and the discourse strategies that allow us to talk about them. • Encourage undergraduate research. Undergraduate research experiences are considered a HIP; instructors who have a chance to engage students in research opportunities—whether big or small—can provide students with a formative experience.

What Do We Show?

We have access to a wide variety of options to engage students, and the options we choose should be closely tied to our learning outcomes and instructional context, as well as our disciplinary practices. Table 3.6 presents an overview of materials we can use to document how we engage students in our courses. Because engagement is highly context-dependent, a practice we use to engage students in one class may be questioned by a colleague teaching in a different field or modality. As such, it is important to provide annotations that explain our rationale on materials we choose to demonstrate our efforts to engage students.

TABLE 3.6: Documenting Student Engagement

Teaching Materials	
Provide short annotations for materials to focus attention on the critical teaching behavior(s) you want to showcase.	
Activity instructions/prompts	Assignment prompts allow you to demonstrate different ways in which you engage students in the classroom. Clear instructions also foster engagement as they are helpful in setting up successful activities that can be more easily managed in the classroom. They are also essential for any activities completed online as students will rely on them heavily or exclusively to complete the assignment.
Communications to students	Communications can engage students in multiple ways: They can serve as nudges or reminders, share information or updates, and update or congratulate students on progress. The tone of communications is essential to creating a positive classroom environment where students are comfortable participating.
Lesson plan	A lesson plan represents the activities and content we use in the learning space on any given day and therefore will serve as a great representation of the types of activities you use to engage students in your classroom and how you distribute time between instructor presentations and student engagement.

Online module	Engagement does not only happen in the face-to-face classroom but is an important component of effective online instruction in fully online as well as blended courses and even in face-to-face courses that integrate online learning components. An online module may include a combination of content presentation and activities that promote student engagement with these materials. When including a module, you may want to address how this module fits into your course. Do online activities help prepare students to be more engaged in the classroom? Does your fully online course scaffold activities from short quizzes to more involved application activities? Use annotations to point the attention specifically to how you engage students in this module.
Presentation slides	Many of us prepare presentation slides for each lesson we teach. They are great for creating a shareable record of the content discussed on a given day and can help us stay focused and on track when presenting a lecture. Additionally, they can serve as a record of how we engage students during interactive lectures or the guidance we provide on in-class tasks. To engage students, we may embed activities such as the following: • short quizzes • discussion or reflection questions • discussion board activities • instructions for group activities • short videos or films When including presentation slides to document engagement, make sure to provide a quick overview of the strategies you want your audience to see.
Syllabus	A course syllabus provides an opportunity to communicate to students how they can expect to engage in your class. Are you planning a discussion-based class? Will they have to prepare materials online to be prepared for in-class activities? Will there be a lab associated with the course? These are just a few of the examples of engagement you may want to discuss in the syllabus. A syllabus also provides information on any points or grades associated with student participation and engagement in the class.
Video recording of classroom teaching/video lecture	A video recording of your teaching allows viewers to see you in action. We may expect that our efforts to engage learners in this context might be obvious. Regardless, create annotations to guide the attention to specific examples of engagement you want your audience to notice when watching the video.
Materials From Others	
Student work samples	Student work, such as samples of work students created during an in-class activity or transcripts of an online discussion board, can serve to illustrate the outcomes and effectiveness of specific engagement activities you have planned for your course. Here it is especially important to use annotations to provide a context that explains how the activity was implemented and the learning outcomes it was designed to achieve.

(Continues)

TABLE 3.6 (*Continued*)

Materials From Others	
Peer feedback and/or observation	Ask your observer to note examples of engagement in your teaching presentation and materials. Instead of—or in addition to—inviting a peer to observe your classroom teaching, you can also ask for a review of course materials. For these reviews, you might ask a peer or teaching expert (e.g., your campus teaching center colleagues) to review specific materials or learning units and provide feedback. To receive feedback specifically focused on your efforts at engaging students, you may ask your colleague to comment, for example, on the following: • evidence of engagement activities in your online course components • the integration of examples, illustrations, stories, and so on • resources supporting students in developing effective learning strategies Be sure to share your course syllabus and other relevant materials to ensure your observer is aware of the intended outcomes.
Student feedback	Whether or not they feel engaged in a course may be the component of instruction that is most apparent to students. They can provide targeted feedback on their experience in your class through formal and informal feedback, including the following: • *CTB midterm feedback.* The CTB midterm feedback survey includes questions that specifically solicit your students' feedback on engagement in your course. • *Select end-of-term surveys.* Questions related to engagement are part of many—but not all—end-of-term student surveys. If no question related to engagement is included on the survey used in your institution, you may be able to add a custom question or facilitate your own survey.

Reflection Questions

1. Do your students currently have opportunities for engagement with the content, the instructor, and their peers? In what ways can you foster these types of engagement?

2. What active learning strategies are you already using in your course? Which would you like to try? Especially when we try something new, it is important to set a manageable goal. When it comes to incorporating more active learning, what is your short-term or immediate goal? What is your long-term goal?

3. How can you convey your own excitement and passion for the subject matter to your students? What resources, such as guest speakers, videos, stories from your own experience, and so on, are available to you to make the course content more tangible and relevant?

4. What do you consider the value of promoting self-regulated learning? What strategy are you ready to try to promote self-regulated learning in your course?

References

Aditomo, A., Goodyear, P., Bliuc, A.-M., & Ellis, R. A. (2013). Inquiry-based learning in higher education: Principal forms, educational objectives, and disciplinary variations. *Studies in Higher Education*, *38*(9), 1239–1258. https://doi.org/10.1080/03075079.2011.616584

Alterio, M., & McDrury, J. (2003). *Learning through storytelling in higher education: Using reflection and experience to improve learning.* Taylor & Francis. http://ebookcentral .proquest.com/lib/erau/detail.action?docID=198432

Ambrose, S. A., Bridges, M. W., DiPietro, M., Lovett, M. C., Norman, M. K., & Mayer, R. E. (2010). *How learning works: Seven research-based principles for smart teaching.* Wiley.

American Association of Colleges and Universities. (n.d.). *High-impact practices: Undergraduate research.* https://www.aacu.org/trending-topics/high-impact

American Association of Colleges and Universities. (2007). *College learning for the new global century.* https://secure.aacu.org/AACU/PDF/GlobalCentury_ExecSum_3.pdf

Anderson, T. (2003). Getting the mix right again: An updated and theoretical rationale for interaction. *International Review of Research in Open and Distance Learning, 4*(2). https://doi.org/10.19173/irrodl.v4i2.149

Arcos, R., & Lahneman, W. J. (2019). *The art of intelligence: More simulations, exercises, and games.* Rowman & Littlefield.

Balch, W. R. (2014). A referential communication demonstration versus a lecture-only control: Learning benefits. *Teaching of Psychology, 41*(3), 213–219. https://doi.org/10.1177/0098628314537970

Barkley, E. F. (2010). *Student engagement techniques: A handbook for college faculty.* Jossey-Bass.

Barkley, E. F., & Major, C. H. (2018). *Interactive lecturing: A handbook for college faculty.* Jossey-Bass.

Barkley, E. F., Major, C. H., & Cross, K. P. (2014). *Collaborative learning techniques: A handbook for college faculty* (2nd ed.). Jossey-Bass.

Bevan, S. J., Chan, C. W. L., & Tanner, J. A. (2014). Diverse assessment and active student engagement sustain deep learning: A comparative study of outcomes in two parallel introductory biochemistry courses. *Biochemistry and Molecular Biology Education, 42*(6), 474–479. https://doi.org/10.1002/bmb.20824

Bonwell, C. C., & Eison, J. A. (1991). *Active learning: Creating excitement in the classroom* (1991 ASHE-ERIC Higher Education Reports). ERIC Clearinghouse on Higher Education, The George Washington University. https://eric.ed.gov/?id=ED336049

Broadbent, J., & Poon, W. L. (2015). Self-regulated learning strategies and academic achievement in online higher education learning environments: A systematic review. *The Internet and Higher Education, 27,* 1–13. https://doi.org/10.1016/j.iheduc.2015.04.007

Brophy, J. E. (2004). *Motivating students to learn* (2nd ed.). Erlbaum.

Cavanagh, S. R. (2016). *The spark of learning: Energizing the college classroom with the science of emotion.* West Virginia University Press.

Cavanagh, S. R. (2019, March 11). How to make your teaching more engaging. *The Chronicle of Higher Education.* http://www.chronicle.com/article/how-to-make-your-teaching-more-engaging/

Cho, M.-H., & Cho, Y. (2014). Instructor scaffolding for interaction and students' academic engagement in online learning: Mediating role of perceived online class goal structures. *The Internet and Higher Education, 21,* 25–30. https://doi.org/10.1016/j.iheduc.2013.10.008

Cohen, G. L., Steele, C. M., & Ross, L. D. (1999). The mentor's dilemma: Providing critical feedback across the racial divide. *Personality and Social Psychology Bulletin, 25*(10), 1302–1318. https://doi.org/10.1177/0146167299258011

Crowe, M., & Brakke, D. (2019). Assessing undergraduate research experiences: An annotative bibliography. *Scholarship and Practice of Undergraduate Research, 3*(2), 21–30. https://doi.org/10.18833/spur/3/2/3

Dembo, M. H., & Seli, H. (2013). *Motivation and learning strategies for college success: A focus on self-regulated learning* (4th ed.). Routledge. https://doi.org/10.4324/9780203813836

Dixson, M. D., Greenwell, M. R., Rogers-Stacy, C., Weister, T., & Lauer, S. (2017). Nonverbal immediacy behaviors and online student engagement: Bringing past instructional research into the present virtual classroom. *Communication Education, 66*(1), 37–53. https://doi.org/10.1080/03634523.2016.1209222

Dweck, C. S. (2007). *Mindset: The new psychology of success* (Updated ed.). Ballantine Books.

Fagen, A. P., Crouch, C. H., & Mazur, E. (2002). Peer instruction: Results from a range of classrooms. *The Physics Teacher, 40*(4), 206–209. https://doi.org/10.1119/1.1474140

Fallah, N. (2014). Willingness to communicate in English, communication self-confidence, motivation, shyness and teacher immediacy among Iranian English-major undergraduates: A structural equation modeling approach. *Learning and Individual Differences, 30,* 140–147. https://doi.org/10.1016/j.lindif.2013.12.006

Freeman, S., Eddy, S. L., McDonough, M., Smith, M. K., Okoroafor, N., Jordt, H., & Wenderoth, M. P. (2014). Active learning increases student performance in science, engineering, and mathematics. *Proceedings of the National Academy of Sciences, 111*(23), 8410–8415. https://doi.org/10.1073/pnas.1319030111

Gunawardena, C. N. (1995). Social presence theory and implications for interaction and collaborative learning in computer conferences. *International Journal of Educational Telecommunications, 1,* 147–166.

Gundhus, K. (2021). Explaining the why behind textbook selections. In C. Harrington (Ed.), *Keeping us engaged: Student perspectives (and research-based strategies) on what works and why* (p. 22). Stylus. http://ebookcentral.proquest.com/lib/erau/detail.action?docID=6465696

Hagood, T. C., Norman, N. J., Park, H., & Williams, B. M. (2017). Playing with learning and teaching in higher education: How does reacting to the past empower students and faculty? In C. E. Watson & T. C. Hagood (Eds.),

Playing to learn with reacting to the past (pp. 159–192). Springer.

Harriet W. Sheridan Center for Teaching and Learning. (n.d.). *Promoting metacognition.* Brown University. https://www.brown.edu/sheridan/teaching-learning-resources/teaching-resources/classroom-practices/promoting-metacognition

Harrington, C. (2017). *Dynamic lecturing: Research-based strategies to enhance lecture effectiveness.* Stylus.

Harrington, C. (2021). *Keeping us engaged: Student perspectives (and research-based strategies) on what works and why.* Stylus.

Helle, L., Tynjala, P., & Olkinuora, E. (2006). Project-based learning in post-secondary education—Theory, practice and rubber sling shots. *Higher Education, 51*(2), 287–315. https://doi.org/10.1007/s10734-004-6386-5

Hernández-Serrano, J., & Stefanou, S. E. (2009). Knowledge at work: Learning and transferring expert reasoning through storytelling. *Education, Knowledge & Economy, 3*(1), 55–80. https://doi.org/10.1080/174968909028 87743

Ice, P., Layne, M., & Boston, W. (2017). Social presence and student success. In A. L. Whiteside, A. Garrett Dikkers, K. Swan, & C. N. Gunawardena (Eds.), *Social presence in online learning: Multiple perspectives on practice and research* (pp. 77–85). Stylus.

Imlach, E. (2021). Sharing your enthusiasm and passion. In C. Harrington (Ed.), *Keeping us engaged: Student perspectives (and research-based strategies) on what works and why* (p. 19). Stylus. http://ebookcentral.proquest.com/lib/erau/detail.action?docID=6465696

Jansen, R. S., van Leeuwen, A., Janssen, J., Jak, S., & Kester, L. (2019). Self-regulated learning partially mediates the effect of self-regulated learning interventions on achievement in higher education: A meta-analysis. *Educational Research Review, 28,* Article 100292. https://doi.org/10.1016/j.edurev.2019.100292

Kaneda, T. (2021). Simulation and gaming as instrument for social design. In T. Kaneda, R. Hamada, & T. Kumazawa (Eds.), *Simulation and gaming for social design* (pp. 3–25). Springer Nature. https://doi.org/10.1007/978-981-16-2011-9_1

Kehrwald, B. (2008). Understanding social presence in text-based online learning environments. *Distance Education, 29*(1), 89–106. https://doi.org/10.1080/015879 10802004860

Kilgo, C. A., Ezell Sheets, J. K., & Pascarella, E. T. (2015). The link between high-impact practices and student learning: Some longitudinal evidence. *Higher Education, 69*(4), 509–525. https://doi.org/10.1007/s10734-014-9788-z

Kim, Y. (2015). Learning statics through in-class demonstration, assignment and evaluation. *International Journal of Mechanical Engineering Education, 43*(1), 23–37. https://doi.org/10.1177/0306419015574643

Kim, N., McVay, M. W., & Srinivasa, A. R. (2017, June 24). *Impact of classroom demonstrations and surveys on higher-level learning* [Paper presentation]. 2017 ASEE Annual Conference & Exposition, Columbus, OH, United States. https://peer.asee.org/impact-of-classroom-demonstrations-and-surveys-on-higher-level-learning

Kirschner, P. A., Sweller, J., & Clark, R. E. (2006). Why minimal guidance during instruction does not work: An analysis of the failure of constructivist, discovery, problem-based, experiential, and inquiry-based teaching. *Educational Psychologist, 41*(2), 75–86. https://doi.org/10.1207/s15326985ep4102_1

Kokotsaki, D., Menzies, V., & Wiggins, A. (2016). Project-based learning: A review of the literature. *Improving Schools, 19*(3), 267–277. https://doi.org/10.1177/13654 80216659733

Kuh, G. (2008). *High-impact educational practices: What they are, who has access to them, and why they matter.* Association of American Colleges and Universities. https://www.aacu.org/publication/high-impact-educational-practices-what-they-are-who-has-access-to-them-and-why-they-matter

Lang, J. M. (2020). *Distracted: Why students can't focus and what you can do about it.* Basic Books.

Lasry, N., Mazur, E., & Watkins, J. (2008). Peer instruction: From Harvard to the two-year college. *American Journal of Physics, 76*(11), 1066–1069. https://doi.org/10.1119/1.2978182

Laverick, E. K. (2018). *Project-based learning.* TESOL Press.

Leat, D. (2017). *Enquiry and project based learning: Students, school and society* (Vol. 1). Routledge. https://doi.org/10.4324/9781315763309

Linn, M. C., Palmer, E., Baranger, A., Gerard, E., & Stone, E. (2015). Undergraduate research experiences: Impacts and opportunities. *Science, 347*(6222), Article 1261757. https://doi.org/10.1126/science.1261757

Liu, J., & Kaye, E. (2015). Preparing online learning readiness with learner-content interaction: Design for scaffolding self-regulated learning. In L. Kyei-Blankson, J. Blankson, & C. Agyeman (Eds.), *Handbook of research on strategic management of interaction, presence, and participation in online courses* (pp. 216–243). IGI Global.

Lopatto, D. (2010). Undergraduate research as a high-impact student experience. *Peer Review, 12*(2), 27–30.

Mayer, R. E., & Fiorella, L. (2021). Introduction to multimedia learning. In L. Fiorella & R. E. Mayer (Eds.), *The Cambridge handbook of multimedia learning* (3rd ed.; pp. 3–16). Cambridge University Press. https://doi.org/10.1017/9781108894333.003

Mazur, E. (n.d.). *Peer instruction.* https://mazur.harvard.edu/research-areas/peer-instruction

McCroskey, J. C., Fayer, J. M., Richmond, V. P., Sallinen, A., & Barraclough, R. A. (1996). A multi-cultural examination of the relationship between nonverbal immediacy and affective learning. *Communication Quarterly, 44*(3), 297. https://doi.org/10.1080/01463379609370019

McCroskey, J. C., & Sallinen, A. (1996). Nonverbal immediacy and cognitive learning: A cross-cultural investigation. *Communication Education, 45*(3), 200. https://doi.org/10.1080/03634529609379049

Michaelsen, L. K., & Sweet, M. (2008). The essential elements of team-based learning. In L. K. Michaelsen & L. D. Fink (Eds.), *Team-Based Learning: Small Group Learning's Next Big Step* (New Directions for Teaching and Learning, no. 116, pp. 7–27). Wiley. https://doi.org/10.1002/tl.330

Michaelsen, L. K., & Sweet, M. (2011). Team-based learning. In W. Buskist & J. E. Groccia (Eds.), *Evidence-Based Teaching* (New Directions for Teaching and Learning, no. 128, pp. 41–51). Wiley. https://doi.org/10.1002/tl.467

Mullen, G. E., & Tallent-Runnels, M. K. (2006). Student outcomes and perceptions of instructors' demands and support in online and traditional classrooms. *The Internet and Higher Education, 9*(4), 257–266. https://doi.org/10.1016/j.iheduc.2006.08.005

Nilson, L. B. (2013). *Creating self-regulated learners: Strategies to strengthen students' self-awareness and learning skills.* Stylus.

Nilson, L. B. (2016). *Teaching at its best: A research-based resource for college instructors.* Wiley.

Nilson, L. B., & Goodson, L. A. (2018). *Online teaching at its best: Merging instructional design with teaching and learning research.* Jossey-Bass.

Panadero, E., Jonsson, A., & Botella, J. (2017). Effects of self-assessment on self-regulated learning and self-efficacy: Four meta-analyses. *Educational Research Review, 22,* 74–98. https://doi.org/10.1016/j.edurev.2017.08.004

Pike, G. R., & Kuh, G. D. (2005). A typology of student engagement for American colleges and universities. *Research in Higher Education, 46*(2), 185–209. https://doi-org.ezproxy.libproxy.db.erau.edu/10.1007/s11162-004-1599-0

Poorvu Center for Teaching and Learning. (n.d.). *Encouraging metacognition in the classroom.* Yale University. https://poorvucenter.yale.edu/MetacognitioninClassrooms

Richardson, J. C., & Swan, K. (2003). Examining social presence in online courses in relation to students' perceived learning and satisfaction. *Journal of Asynchronous Learning Networks, 7*(1), 68–89. https://doi.org/10.24059/olj.v7i1.1864

Richardson, M., Abraham, C., & Bond, R. (2012). Psychological correlates of university students' academic performance: A systematic review and meta-analysis. *Psychological Bulletin, 138*(2), 353–387. https://doi.org/10.1037/a0026838

Roberts, A., & Friedman, D. (2013). The impact of teacher immediacy on student participation: An objective cross-disciplinary examination. *International Journal of Teaching and Learning in Higher Education, 25*(1), 38–46. https://eric.ed.gov/?id=EJ1016418

Roberts, D. (2018). The engagement agenda, multimedia learning and the use of images in higher education lecturing: Or, how to end death by PowerPoint. *Journal of Further and Higher Education, 42*(7), 969–985. https://doi.org/10.1080/0309877X.2017.1332356

Romero, C. C. (2009). *Cooperative learning instruction and science achievement for secondary and early post-secondary students: A systematic review* [Doctoral dissertation, Colorado State University]. Proquest. http://www.proquest.com/docview/304862896/abstract/4D5F750ACAA149B8PQ/1

Rosenzweig, E. Q., Wigfield, A., & Eccles, J. S. (2019). Expectancy-value theory and its relevance for student motivation and learning. In K. A. Renninger & S. E. Hidi (Eds.), *The Cambridge handbook of motivation and learning* (pp. 617–644). Cambridge University Press. https://doi.org/10.1017/9781316823279.026

Sadik, A., & Reisman, S. (2004). Design and implementation of a web-based learning environment: Lessons learned. *Quarterly Review of Distance Education, 5*(3), 157–171, 228.

Sahagun, M. A., Moser, R., Shomaker, J., & Fortier, J. (2021). Developing a growth-mindset pedagogy for higher education and testing its efficacy. *Social Sciences & Humanities Open, 4*(1), Article 100168. https://doi.org/10.1016/j.ssaho.2021.100168

Scager, K., Boonstra, J., Peeters, T., Vulperhorst, J., & Wiegant, F. (2016). Collaborative learning in higher education: Evoking positive interdependence. *CBE Life Sciences Education, 15*(4), Article ar69. https://doi.org/10.1187/cbe.16-07-0219

Sibley, J., Ostafichuk, P., Michaelsen, L. K., Roberson, B., Franchini, B., & Kubitz, K. (2014). *Getting started with team-based learning.* Stylus.

Skinner, E., Furrer, C., Marchand, G., & Kindermann, T. (2008). Engagement and disaffection in the classroom: Part of a larger motivational dynamic? *Journal of Educational Psychology, 100*(4), 765–781. https://doi.org/10.1037/a0012840

Smith, B. L., & MacGregor, J. T. (1992). What is collaborative learning? In A. S. Goodsell, M. R. Maher, V. Tinto, B. L. Smith, & J. MacGregor (Eds.), *Collaborative learning: A sourcebook for higher education* (pp. 10–30). https://eric.ed.gov/?id=ED357705

Springer, L., Stanne, M. E., & Donovan, S. S. (1999). Effects of small-group learning on undergraduates in science, mathematics, engineering, and technology: A meta-analysis. *Review of Educational Research*, *69*(1), 21–51. https://doi.org/10.2307/1170643

Sweller, J. (2010). Element interactivity and intrinsic, extraneous, and germane cognitive load. *Educational Psychology Review*, *22*(2), 123–138. https://doi.org/10.1007/s10648-010-9128-5

Volet, S., Summers, M., & Thurman, J. (2009). High-level co-regulation in collaborative learning: How does it emerge and how is it sustained? *Learning and Instruction*, *19*(2), 128–143. https://doi.org/10.1016/j.learninstruc.2008.03.001

Vos, H., & de Graaff, E. (2004). Developing metacognition: A basis for active learning. *European Journal of Engineering Education*, *29*(4), 543–548. https://doi.org/10.1080/03043790410001716257

Walton, G. M., Cohen, G. L., Cwir, D., & Spencer, S. J. (2012). Mere belonging: The power of social connections. *Journal of Personality and Social Psychology*, *102*(3), 513–532. https://doi.org/10.1037/a0025731

Weidenfeld, M. C., & Fernandez, K. E. (2017). Does reacting to the past increase student engagement? An empirical evaluation of the use of historical simulations in teaching political theory. *Journal of Political Science Education*, *13*(1), 46–61. https://doi.org/10.1080/15512169.2016.1175948

Winkelmes, M.-A., Bernacki, M., Butler, J., Zochowski, M., Golanics, J., & Weavil, K. H. (2016). A teaching intervention that increases underserved college students' success. *Peer Review*, *18*(1/2), 31–36.

Wirth, K. (2008). *Learning about thinking and thinking about learning: Metacognitive knowledge and skills for intentional learners*. Carleton College. https://serc.carleton.edu/NAGTWorkshops/metacognition/workshop08/participants/wirth.html

Yang, C.-C., Tsai, I.-C., Kim, B., Cho, M.-H., & Laffey, J. M. (2006). Exploring the relationships between students' academic motivation and social ability in online learning environments. *The Internet and Higher Education*, *9*(4), 277–286. https://doi.org/10.1016/j.iheduc.2006.08.002

Zhang, P., Ding, L., & Mazur, E. (2017). Peer instruction in introductory physics: A method to bring about positive changes in students' attitudes and beliefs. *Physical Review Physics Education Research*, *13*(1). https://doi.org/10.1103/PhysRevPhysEducRes.13.010104

Zimmerman, B. J. (2002). Becoming a self-regulated learner: An overview. *Theory Into Practice*, *41*(2), 64–71. https://doi.org/10.1207/s15430421tip4102_2

CHAPTER 4

Assess

DEFINITION

Instructors who assess learning develop and facilitate transparent, meaningful tasks to provide students with timely feedback on their learning and to measure achievement of learning outcomes. They frequently review data to improve instruction.

AFTER INVESTING HOURS, DAYS, weeks, or even more time into planning a course and creating inclusive and engaging learning environments, you probably want to know if your work paid off and accomplished the desired goals and outcomes. Walvoord and Banta (2010) remind us that "assessment is a natural, inescapable, human, and scholarly act" (p. 2), and as scholars who invest significant time and effort into teaching, it is rewarding to know that the learning materials and activities we designed and implemented had a positive impact on our students' knowledge, skills, and attitudes. While as teachers and scholars we are likely invested in gathering evidence of our students' learning, students, too, have a vested interest in assessment, which remains one of the main motivators for student learning (Wanner & Palmer, 2018). Assessment is not a mere add-on to teaching and learning; done effectively, assessment and learning are almost inseparable, a fact represented in assessment trends in recent years. While traditional forms of assessment, such as midterm and final exams or papers, are still widely practiced and an important source of data at many institutions,

progressively, we see a movement away from assessment *of* learning that focuses on evaluating and, to an extent, certifying students' knowledge and achievement at a specific point in time. Instead, assessment *for* learning and assessment *as* learning approaches are increasingly implemented. To assess *for* learning, instructors assign tasks with the intention of deepening students' understanding of course information and skills through formative and scaffolded assessments that provide students with practice and actionable feedback. Assessment *as* learning approaches additionally integrate self-evaluation and reflection as integral parts of the learning process. These types of rich assessments not only allow us to understand what our students learned and where they are still struggling but they also benefit our students by providing them with an opportunity to deepen their learning, receive constructive feedback, and develop their self-assessment skills. As a result, effective assessment can increase students' learning and retention of information as well as their motivation to engage with our courses. In short, assessment is a necessary component of learning, but whether we can maximize its benefits beyond gathering data on our students' learning depends on how we design and manage assessments in our courses. This chapter will provide an overview of research-based practices that help us and our students make the most of assessment.

What Do We Know?

Assessment has the potential to promote and support student motivation, self-regulation, and "deep learning." Over the last decades, research on assessment has provided a wealth of insights on effective practices. In this section—and in the CTB framework—we focus on introducing some of the foundational elements of effective assessment practices and the research that supports them. Specifically, we will address how we can do the following:

- align assessments with course learning goals and class activities
- schedule regular summative assessments to measure student progress toward learning outcomes
- embed formative assessments and opportunities for self-assessment in instruction and scaffold projects to support learning
- communicate purpose, task, and criteria for assessments
- provide timely, constructive, and actionable feedback to students
- review assessment data to make informed decisions about course content, structure, and activities

Aligning Assessments With Course Learning Goals and Class Activities

Assessment provides an opportunity for students to demonstrate whether they have achieved a certain level of knowledge and mastery of skills—in other words, course or program learning outcomes—that will allow them to succeed in the next course in a series, to earn a professional certification, or to effectively use their learning in their career, among other things. That said, not all assessments are created equal and not all accomplish what they set out to do—namely, to assess student achievement of agreed upon learning outcomes. Vaguely defined outcomes and poor alignment

negatively impact the quality of assessments as both are critical elements of teaching, if you recall the discussion in chapter 1, "Align." In circumstances where outcomes are unclear or unstated, it is difficult, if not impossible, to identify concrete criteria and minimum standards our students should meet and, consequently, to design exams, projects, or other assessment tasks that allow students to demonstrate their learning; both instructors and students are left to muddle through the learning journey without a clear sense of what they intend to achieve or what strategies will help them get "there"—wherever "there" is.

To help you understand the crucial nature of alignment between assessments and outcomes, consider the following metaphor: Imagine spending multiple days trying to figure out the best route for a road trip from point A to point B. You determine the routes to take, the places to stop, and the sights to see. Then, on the day you plan to leave, you are told that you must complete the trip by train. You have 60 minutes to figure it out. Now you feel stressed and frustrated. Moreover, you likely feel distracted by all these emotions as you try to develop a new game plan. All your preparation was in vain. That road map you carefully studied to determine your plans proves to be a worthless guide as you search for train timetables. Given the short time to prepare, your emotional distraction, and your ineffective planning materials, your travel plan turns out to be less than efficient, and consequently, you end up wasting precious travel time with long layovers in the middle of nowhere. You may not even reach your intended destination.

What does this travel metaphor have to do with assessment in our courses? Poorly aligned assessments are like this in the sense that students prepare for an assessment based on the information we share, the stated learning outcomes, and the activities completed in class. These materials make up their "road map" toward the intended destination. If the assessment task presents them with an unexpected twist, we have suddenly rendered those materials as worthless as a road map when planning a train trip. Because this kind of misalignment happens most frequently during high-stakes, timed assessments, students can feel like the train they were supposed to get on has already left the station and there is no way to catch up or seek an alternative route to the intended destination and learning success. This kind of twist causes stress and frustration for all students, but it can disproportionately impact students with mental health concerns and underrepresented minorities who may take their feelings as confirmatory evidence that they do not belong in our courses. Unfortunately, this scenario is fairly common in higher education. Consider, for instance, a course that aims to support students in developing their ability to critically evaluate a range of variables and solve complex problems; class activities have focused on discussing big picture conceptual problems, but the exam unexpectedly asks students to recall and describe minute details from readings instead. Yes, these details can be important, but if they are, students should have had an opportunity to practice recalling them before the exam. Conversely, imagine a class that focuses on solving simple math problems in class demonstrations and homework activities. The exam, on the other hand, presents students with complex problems that require them to combine multiple skills in new and unpracticed ways. Yes, transferring skills to new contexts is an outcome we desire to achieve, but it is unfair to expect students will be able to do so without practice, especially during high-stakes and high-stress situations. Earlier in this book we discussed alignment as a critical teaching behavior that informs all components of teaching and learning. When it comes to assessments, especially high-stakes assessments, alignment is even more foundational as it ensures that we give our students a fair chance to succeed.

Summative and Formative Assessments—A Short Introduction

Traditionally, higher education has relied almost exclusively on high-stakes assessments such as exams or term papers to evaluate students' accomplishments and to certify that they have achieved a minimum level of knowledge and skills at a specific point in time, often the end of a learning unit or course. As you might guess, there is more to effective assessment. However, before we delve further into the research on assessment practices, let us take a moment to discuss and unpack essential terminology—namely, the difference between summative and formative assessment approaches. Many of us are most familiar with high-stakes assessments that take the form of a midterm or final exam, capstone project, or research paper, to name a few; these types of assignments are also known as summative assessments as they evaluate the sum of knowledge and skills students have acquired at a specific point in time. On the other hand, the main

goal of formative assessments is to provide students with opportunities to practice a skill or apply knowledge and receive feedback so they can learn from it. These types of assessments also allow instructors to gain insight into how well students really understand a concept or skill in time to provide additional support and correction (Bridglall, 2001). To understand the relationship between summative and formative assessment, pedagogy literature frequently uses the metaphor of a meal in a fine restaurant: Formative assessment happens when the chef tastes the soup to adjust seasoning; summative assessment happens when the diner tastes the soup. Without formative assessment, we might be served a bland, overly salty, or even spoiled meal, and on the off chance that any meal turns out perfectly without taste-testing, we must attribute success to chance and luck rather than the efforts of the chef. Similarly, if we never check in with students before the exam or the assignment due date, we will not know if our teaching has set them on the right track to successfully complete the tasks we assign them or if there is a risk of derailment due to miscommunication. While formative assessments are crucial to improving our teaching and helping students succeed, we do not mean to suggest they take the place of summative assessments entirely. Continuing our metaphor, without summative assessment, we never get to taste the final version of the dish, meaning that we might never know whether our students reached the course outcomes. In the past few years, an increasing amount of research has demonstrated the benefit of providing opportunities for formative assessment alongside the summative exams or projects, and for quality assessment, both are needed. In the next section, we will explore some aspects of summative evaluation of learning before digging deeper into what we know about formative assessment.

Schedule Regular Summative Assessments to Measure Student Progress Toward Learning Outcomes

Exams, projects, and research papers are familiar go-to tools used to assess student learning in many of our courses. These assessments are intended to get a glimpse into our students' knowledge and skills at a particular moment in time. Do they remember the formula to calculate the area of a circle? Can they discuss the complex historical events that led to the French Revolution? Generally, we expect that students who perform well on the assessment tasks we provide have developed sufficient fluency with the course content and skills to prepare them for what comes next, whether that is another course in a sequence or a career. Summative assessments, therefore, are not only used to check in with our students but also, to a certain extent, to promote rigor in higher education and to certify the quality of their learning. We might remember that research shows that high standards can promote student motivation and deep-learning (Cohen et al., 1999; Driscoll & Wood, 2007; Kickert et al., 2019) and assume that rigorous assessment is the way to go. And it might be, but it's important to get it right.

Rigor has been defined in vastly different ways—some approaches have the potential to promote student learning and motivation while others run the risk of creating barriers to success. Traditionally, there have been two main approaches to conceptualizing rigor as a function of either workload or cognitive challenge. Recent research supports that cognitive challenge has a greater positive impact on student learning—in particular, the development of critical thinking and lifelong learning indicators—while the association of rigor with greater quantity of work can create barriers to success for students, especially students from minoritized populations, students who work part or full time or serve as caretakers, and students who are completing college work in a language they did not grow up speaking (Culver et al., 2019, 2021).

How then do we create rigorous assessments "that challenge students to engage in higher order thinking" (Culver et al., 2019, p. 614)? Research suggests we prioritize questions and projects that require higher order thinking rather than testing them on their knowledge of facts. Instead of simply memorizing and recalling information, higher order questions and tasks ask students to, for example, compare and contrast course content, synthesize information from various sources, apply ideas and skills to novel problems and contexts, or identify strengths and weaknesses of an argument. As you create exams and projects that challenge students to engage in higher order cognitive tasks, you may find it useful to consult Bloom's cognitive taxonomy (1956) and its more recent revised version developed by Anderson et al. (2001), which we introduced in chapter 1, "Align." Multiple free online resources and tools built on these taxonomies

are available to serve as inspiration for tasks and questions that challenge students to go beyond recalling information.

However, it is important to be aware that even when we prioritize cognitive challenge, we can unwittingly promote an exclusionary system unless we also provide the scaffolding and support needed to ensure all students can succeed (see the following section on formative assessment to learn more about scaffolding). In our effort to create rigorous assessments and set high expectations, we are often reluctant to "do the work for our students" or to provide excessive "hand holding." As Jack and Sathy (2021) observe, however, if we assign "rigorous" tasks without scaffolded support, we "privilege students who already have high academic literacy or who are already adept at managing higher education's unofficial rules, routines, and structures—also known as the hidden curriculum" (para. 5). For students who arrive at college and in our classroom without an understanding of the innumerable unstated expectations of college, it can be nearly impossible to decipher what we expect them to do when we ask them to engage in, for example, "deep analysis" or "creative problem-solving" unless we show them what it looks like in our discipline and in our course. As you assign work, take a moment to consider what knowledge, terminology, and skills you take for granted and explicitly state them either in the assignment instructions or in the classroom or provide examples and illustrations to support students in deciphering expectations.

At this point, it will come as no surprise that traditional assessment practices and tools are not always well suited to prepare students for success in their professions, as "content knowledge without understanding the process of 'becoming' a professional creates a divide between learning 'something' and understanding how to engage with that learning within their professional or trade context" (Bourke, 2018, p. 828). Closing this divide between academia and professions is one of the motivations for embracing a range of assessment practices beyond these traditional tools, including authentic assessment approaches. Authentic assessment focuses on "real-world" contexts and challenges students are likely to encounter in their future careers; they allow students to engage with practical problems in order to gain not only an intellectual understanding but to practice using their knowledge and skills in realistic situations (Darling-Hammond &

Snyder, 2000; Wiewiora & Kowalkiewicz, 2019). Authentic assessments are one way to promote students' ability to achieve more complex, higher order learning outcomes (e.g., designing a functioning model of a remote-controlled rover, creating a marketing portfolio for a nonprofit organization, etc.).

Authentic assessments as well as other projects can provide students with the opportunity to show their learning in multiple ways. Offering more than one equivalent (not identical) option for students to demonstrate learning communicates to our students implicitly that assessment is about more than just grades. Providing students with options that allow them to leverage their strengths to showcase their learning builds on the principles of UDL introduced in chapter 2, "Include," to enhance fairness and inclusiveness of assessment. Some even argue that a range of assessment methods *must* be used to create a valid picture of student achievement of learning outcomes (Bourke, 2018). After all, as Gower (2021) reminds us,

> we have all had students who learned, yet performed poorly on multiple choice tests or essay tests, due to test anxiety. If these are the only form of assessing student performance, the punitive and reductive nature of assigning grades is self-evident. (p. 151)

That said, traditional exams and research papers still have an important role in the context of assessment. During a time where we are all asked to do more with less, exams and quizzes provide a streamlined tool for assessing student learning and can ease the grading load. Autograded quizzes and online tasks can also serve a useful role in providing students with opportunities to review and self-assess prior to completing the summative exam. To increase the effectiveness and fairness of assessment, however, high-stakes exams should not be the only tool in our toolbox.

Embed Formative Assessments and Opportunities for Self-Assessment in Instruction and Scaffolding of Projects to Support Learning

Formative assessments are an important addition to the assessment toolbox. The main purpose of formative assessments is not to grade students' work but to support their learning and ultimately their ability to self-assess the quality of their work—an important transferable, professional skill (Hortigüela Alcalá et al., 2019; López-Pastor, 2011). As a result,

formative assignments are generally low-stakes tasks that provide students with opportunities to revise and improve their thinking, help them see their own progress, and allow feedback that prompts them to make adjustments to how they engage with and use information learned in our courses (Fletcher, 2016; Vye et al., 1998). The idea is that these assignments completed in a low-pressure context (e.g., they are worth only a small part of the overall course grade and sometimes are not graded at all) allow students to take risks, explore ideas, or admit confusion. On the other hand, they can also provide students with an opportunity to build confidence by allowing them—if successful—to gain an early "win" that can increase confidence and self-efficacy (Meer & Chapman, 2014; Persellin & Daniels, 2015; Reid & Barrington, 1994). Provided formative assessments are again well aligned with course outcomes and summative assessment tasks, they are signposts of what is important to learn in a course and can help clarify success criteria early on (Fletcher, 2016).

In addition to serving as indicators of learning achievements, low-stakes assessments can play an important role in deepening learning and retention of course materials. Cognitive science shows that learning can not only be assessed but enhanced through testing or recalling information—a phenomenon called the "testing effect" (Brown et al., 2014; Dobson & Linderholm, 2015; Karpicke, 2012). Brown et al. (2014) observe that "repeated recall appears to help memory consolidate into a cohesive representation in the brain and to strengthen and multiply the neural routes by which the knowledge can later be retrieved" (p. 28). Providing multiple opportunities for students to retrieve knowledge and intentionally reflect on what they have learned thus can lead to long-term gains in knowledge retention. Even though traditional methods of study, such as reviewing notes and rereading materials, might lead to higher scores in the short term, learners who use testing and retrieval practice show significantly higher levels of mid- to long-term retention (Roediger & Karpicke, 2006). Research further indicates that testing, compared to rereading, can even increase students' ability to transfer knowledge to new contexts and problems (Brown et al., 2014). Recall activities, including tests as well as assignments that ask students to synthesize information or reflect on course content, promote long-term retention and understanding.

Finally, formative tasks can support student learning by serving as scaffolds to more complex summative assignments. For example, we might ask students to progressively complete smaller sections of a longer project and provide feedback along the way leading up to a final project that requires students to fit together the smaller components they completed, ideally with revisions based on feedback provided by the instructor and/or peers. We may also ask students to solve a complex mathematical problem step-by-step first, before challenging them to work through a similar problem without checking in at each step. In short, "well-designed scaffolding supports learners by incrementally building in complexity toward the desired learning outcome" (Frost et al., 2021, p. 228). Starting with easier tasks allows us to check in with our students and provide individualized feedback, support, and clarifications as needed throughout the process rather than waiting until students submit the final version of a project when any feedback we may provide at that point may be seen as a mere justification of the grade earned rather than guidance on future submissions.

Communicate Purpose, Task, and Criteria for Assessments to Help Motivate Students and Engage With Expectations in a Productive Way

Regardless of the task we ask students to complete, it is important to clearly communicate our expectations to ensure they have the tools and knowledge to complete the task successfully. Transparent assignments should provide information about an assignment's purpose, task, and criteria, suggests the TiLT framework developed by Mary-Ann Winkelmes. In collaboration with the AAC&U, Winkelmes conducted studies at several institutions to assess the benefit of transparent assignments. Her research confirmed that increased transparency resulted in increased academic confidence and sense of belonging, as well as long-term retention in degree programs; these benefits were especially significant for first-generation, low-income, and underrepresented students (Winkelmes et al., 2016). Elements of transparent assignments include the following:

- *Purpose.* Explicitly explaining the purpose of an assessment and its link to the intended learning outcomes of a course (see chapter 1) can contribute to students' understanding of the task and its relevance to their learning; it can also reduce instances of miscommunication

between faculty and students. Too often we take for granted that our students can identify the goals and benefits, including transferable skills, of an assignment as easily as we can. As novices in the discipline, however, students are still building professional competence and a disciplinary network of knowledge. While they do, opening each assignment prompt with a purpose statement allows us to not only increase student motivation for the assignment but also present an insight into how an activity can help them in their career, which they might otherwise overlook (Bishop et al., 2020). It is important to note that clarifying the purpose does not only apply to larger course projects or authentic assignments, however; adding a short purpose statement is equally important and meaningful on exams and helps students see the bigger picture.

- *Task.* A description of the task is the part of an assignment prompt that we are likely most familiar with. It generally includes information about the nuts and bolts of the assignment such as minimum word counts, font size, and other information about what students should do. It can be helpful to ask a student or colleague in a different discipline for feedback on clarity as terms can vary in their meanings in different contexts and we may inadvertently skip important steps that have become second nature in our own practice but are important to include for novices working through a task for the first time.

- *Criteria.* Communicating assessment criteria and taking the time to unpack the terminology and language we use to define expectations help us clarify the qualities we look for in students' work and help them understand what they must do to attain expected or required standards. This can positively impact student learning as it increases student confidence in their ability to complete the work and be evaluated fairly. Transparent communications about expectations and grading criteria can also allow students to self-assess or, with guidance, work with peers to provide in-process peer feedback to each other (Shepard, 2000).

When writing transparent prompts, it is important to consider, however, that simply giving students more information is not the best way to increase transparency. Meer and Chapman (2014) point out that for students who may struggle with information overload,

> the solution is not to give them more information but to help them engage with the information they already have and present it in a format that gradually introduces them to academic language, as the discourse itself can be a significant barrier. (p. 189)

Creating assignment instructions that are more transparent takes little time but has the potential to positively impact learning for all students, and especially for minoritized student populations. Additionally, increased transparency has the potential to reduce the unintentional impact of bias when evaluating student work as it reduces ambiguity in grading, a context in which biases are more likely to come into play (Darley & Gross, 1983; Dovidio et al., 2016; Oleson, 2020).

Having noted the three essential elements of transparent assignments, let us briefly focus our attention on rubrics as a means of increasing transparency in communicating assessment criteria. Rubrics come in many formats, ranging from simple checklists to detailed analytic rubrics. While checklists generally only assess the presence or absence of a criterion, an analytic rubric lists various levels of performance for each category; more detailed analytic rubrics often contain descriptions of what each criterion looks like for each level of performance (Brookhart, 2013; DePaul University Teaching Commons, n.d.). While rubrics can be an important component of increasing transparency, multiple studies suggest that rubrics alone may be insufficient in conveying clear expectations and suggest instructors take time to discuss and explain rubrics or maybe even involve students in their cocreation (Bearman & Ajjawi, 2021; Cockett & Jackson, 2018; Deeley et al., 2019). Additionally, providing samples of exemplary student work can enhance transparency and support students' understanding of expectations (TiLT Higher Ed, n.d.). Whenever rubrics are used it is important that they be available to students before the assignment is due rather than serving merely as a convenient tool to provide feedback.

Provide Timely, Constructive, and Actionable Feedback to Students

Feedback on tasks and assignments plays an important role in the learning process, as without it, students would have difficulty identifying and learning from mistakes or resolving misconceptions. In addition to instructor feedback, peer feedback and even self-assessment guided by an informed understanding of assignment expectations and performance criteria can support student learning. Providing feedback is a process adapted from information technology (IT) and according to its original definition, providing constructive input and suggestions is not sufficient; feedback has not occurred until it has resulted in observable change. Feedback, then, is an iterative process, rather than a one-time event (Boud, 2015; Boud & Molloy, 2013), and as such, must involve learners in the process as active agents who are seeking and using information for improvement. Indeed, research suggests that when it comes to instructor feedback, students suggest that quality feedback is "part of a dialogic guidance *process* rather than a summative *event*" (Beaumont et al., 2011, p. 671). In addition to providing concrete feedback to the learner regarding their task performance and process, teachers can help students gain a better understanding for the criteria and standards applied and help learners build the capacity to calibrate their own judgment as part of this guidance process (Boud, 2015). Importantly, assessment that requires both students and teachers to be jointly involved in the evaluation and feedback process is considered an important tool to help students develop professional skills that will allow them to assess their work performance more accurately in academic as well as professional contexts (Brown & Pickford, 2006; Hortigüela Alacalá et al., 2019). Constructive, forward-looking feedback from instructors helps students identify not only areas for improvement but also provides insights into disciplinary discourse and standards that support student self-regulation.

Thinking about feedback as a dialogue may seem foreign and overwhelming, but it does not have to be. Beaumont et al. (2011) propose a feedback cycle that identifies opportunities for dialogue at multiple stages: Even before students start the assignment we can provide preparatory guidance on the assignment and assessment criteria by creating transparent assignment prompts, as discussed previously; then we give in-task guidance by scaffolding tasks and including opportunities for peer and self-assessment; finally, we provide performance feedback through evaluative grading combined with feedback that allows students to identify concrete actions that will help them improve their work in the future. This supports the call for thinking of feedback as a dialogic or even collaborative process that starts even before students begin working on a task and continues throughout their progress, ending with a final grade on their submission.

Even as we determine the best process for providing feedback, we may also be uncertain about the most effective elements of feedback and how to share it with students in an efficient way, as both instructors and students can struggle with assessment and feedback literacy (Bourke, 2018; Boyle et al., 2020). Surveys from the United States and the United Kingdom indicate that, overall, students are unsatisfied with the guidance and feedback they receive on assignments, focusing a primary concern on lack of transparency, consistency, and fairness in grading (Bourke, 2018; Cockett & Jackson, 2018; Deeley et al., 2019). In terms of feedback transparency, student concerns related to their ability to understand feedback provided, along with the lack of a clear opportunity to apply feedback to either revisions or future assignments, have been shown to have negative impacts on students' motivation to engage with feedback (Boyle et al., 2020). To provide transparent and actionable feedback we must remember that "students' knowledge of the subject being learned is by definition partial. Hence any feedback must be expressed by the teacher in language that is *already known and understood* by the learner" (Sadler, 1998, p. 82). Working with students—during class or in individual meetings—on interpreting feedback may be important to help them understand what they can learn from it about the strengths and weaknesses of the work they have already submitted as well as how they may apply this feedback to improve their future work. Ideally, any feedback provided has the potential to open a door to dialogue with the instructor that allows students to clarify remaining questions, increase their understanding not only of the assigned task but also of academic discourse more broadly, and ultimately demonstrate growth as a result of the feedback they received (Beaumont et al., 2011; Deeley et al., 2019).

Peer Assessment

As stated earlier, not all feedback needs to come from the instructor; peer feedback as well as reflective self-assessment can play an important role in the feedback process. Peer assessment allows one to check their work against another's work and receive feedback through multiple channels beyond the instructor. Students who receive peer feedback can benefit from receiving not only timely but also varied feedback on their work, a practice that can support learners in "calibrat[ing] their own judgments and create for themselves the expertise needed for further study and performance" (Boud, 2015, p. 4). Additionally, peer feedback provides an opportunity for students to practice giving as well as receiving feedback, a means by which they can gain a better understanding of the target performance (Boud & Molloy, 2013). A meta-analysis of research on the impact of peer assessment indicates that students who participate in peer feedback significantly improved their performance on writing tasks over students who did not receive feedback and slightly improved their performance in comparison with students who self-assessed their work against evaluation criteria (Huisman et al., 2019). You may see peer assessment promoted as a way to save teachers time, but it is important to know that while we may spend less time providing feedback on student work, peer feedback activities require us to invest time into carefully planning and preparing for peer feedback activities to ensure students understand expectations and are able to give each other useful feedback (Gibbs, 2020) and to support students throughout the process. Students who are trained to provide effective peer feedback, however, develop transferable skills, take a more active role in the learning process, and gain a better understanding of the standards and criteria of the task they are completing (Adachi et al., 2018; Huisman et al., 2019). Even though peer feedback may not reduce our workload, the available research makes a strong case for the benefits of peer assessment as a way to improve performance and develop professional skills, making it worth the consideration to incorporate it as an activity into our assessment practices.

Self-Assessment

In addition to peer assessment, student self-assessment of learning can be an important tool in our assessment toolbox and an important source of feedback for students. Additionally, the integration of self-assessment can support students in developing the skills that will allow them to self-assess their ongoing learning and performance not only in our classroom but in their future academic and professional careers. Panadero et al. (2016) define student self-assessment of learning as a "wide variety of mechanisms and techniques through which students describe (i.e., assess) and possibly assign merit or worth (i.e., evaluate) the qualities of their own learning process and products" (p. 804). Student self-assessment can lead to increased learning and performance, foster use of self-regulated learning strategies, enhance student self-efficacy—or the belief in their ability to succeed—and promote student ownership of the learning process (Brown & Harris, 2013; Panadero et al., 2016, 2017). However, here too, these potential positive impacts on student learning depend largely on how we implement self-assessment tasks. Recent research advocates for moving away from simpler forms of self-assessment, specifically tasks that only ask students to assign a grade to their own work and self-assessment tasks that do not provide students with clear criteria or expectations against which to compare their work (Panadero et al., 2016, 2017). Promoting reflection on both process and product and encouraging students to describe the qualities of their work in terms of strengths and weaknesses can help students examine their own learning in order to identify and internalize a pathway to improvement (Bourke, 2018; Meer & Chapman, 2014; Panadero et al., 2016).

A frequent concern with student self-assessment relates to a lack of accuracy in students' assessment of their own work; research confirms that students who lack expertise in the area assessed tend to overestimate their achievements, but self-assessment accuracy increases with expertise in the content area and practice in assessing their own work (Bourke, 2018; Panadero et al., 2016). To promote realistic self-assessment, research suggests we design opportunities for self-assessment that incorporate the following:

- communication of concrete, specific, and well-understood criteria or reference points (e.g., rubrics, checklists, etc.) and/or student involvement in identifying standards and criteria to apply to their work (e.g., collaboratively identify criteria of a successful project by reviewing and discussing sample work, etc.)

- training on how to approach self-assessment (e.g., scripts including prompts, collaborative assessment of sample assignment using established criteria, etc.)
- instructor feedback on self-assessment accuracy (not just on completed task)

While self-assessment often occurs prior to submitting an assignment as part of a formative assessment process, it may also take the form of a reflective activity after students submit and receive feedback on an assignment, an activity that prompts them to think about their performance in light of the feedback received and determine how it can support them in future tasks and their career.

Alternative Grading Models and Ungrading
In recent years, a range of alternative assessment approaches have been introduced with the goal of increasing fairness and promoting student self-regulation and intrinsic motivation for learning. Alternative assessment models range from specification grading (Nilson, 2014) to labor-based contract grading (Inoue, 2019) and ungrading (Blum, 2020b). More recently, *ungrading* has stuck as an umbrella term that is used to refer to a range of assessment models including contract and specification grading approaches. One thing they all have in common is their criticism of conventional grading systems and a call for increased student agency in the assessment process. According to Blum, a decade of research shows that grades—beyond pass and fail designations—have been inconsistent from the start and, therefore, fail to consistently and conclusively communicate information about students' knowledge and skills (Blum, 2020b). Additionally, the hyperfocus on grades comes at the expense of deep learning, as students just want to pass the exam or course; intrinsic motivation to learn, explore, and take risks; and even students' mental health (Blum, 2020b; Eyler, 2022; Inoue, 2019; Nilson, 2014). The different models each suggest a slightly different alternative for engaging students in the assessment process and providing them with agency over their learning. For example, many ungrading approaches aim to deemphasize grades and rely more heavily on student self-assessment of learning and assessment that moves away from letter grades toward pass and fail designations (Blum, 2020a; Stommel, 2020; Supiano, 2022); contract and specification grading models focus more

on giving students a voice in choosing their own learning goals and level of engagement (Gibbs, 2020; Inoue, 2019; Katopodis & Davidson, 2020; Nilson, 2014). All models advocate for ongoing formative and individualized feedback on student work from faculty and/or peers to support student learning and help students meet course outcomes as well as personal learning goals. Unfortunately, at this time there is limited research available to support the effectiveness of these models in practice and some questions have been raised. On one hand, there is concern for potential student confusion as they grapple with a new way of assessment and feedback on their learning, which may unfairly impact instructors, especially those belonging to minoritized identity groups (Pittman & Tobin, 2022). On the other hand, some faculty report that the workload associated with models prioritizing flexibility and extensive and iterative feedback on students' work may not be sustainable (Masland, 2022). Despite the fact that there are still open questions, ungrading approaches present some interesting and promising responses to the shortcomings of traditional assessment models without giving up on high expectations for student work.

Review Assessment Data to Make Informed Decisions About Course Content, Structure, and Activities

So far, this chapter has focused on how assessment relates to student learning, but we would be remiss in not at least touching upon the important role of assessment in helping us—the instructors—learn as well. Effective assessment not only helps our students take informed action to improve their performance but also allows the use of data gathered through assessment to determine actions we can take to improve student learning. The practice of assessment is often described as a cycle with multiple steps, including the definition of goals (e.g., determining desired outcomes and planning aligned assessment tasks); the gathering and interpretation of information and data (e.g., student performance on assignments, confusion, or recurrent questions about instructions or content); and, ultimately, the development of an action plan leading to adjustments and revisions based on the information we gathered (Butler & McMunn, 2014; Suskie, 2018; Walvoord & Banta, 2010). Taking some time to reflect on our experience and analyze student data after each major assignment or maybe only at the end of the term can help us consolidate insights, identify patterns in student performance, and determine the

relationship between what we teach and what students learn. Chapter 6, "Reflect," introduces reflection as one of the critical teaching behaviors along with more suggestions on how you can incorporate reflection into your teaching practice and, potentially, even turn reflective insights into scholarship. Here, we will briefly introduce some practices that help us engage with assessment data specifically.

Depending on course assignments, we will have text-based, qualitative, or numerical, quantitative data or both to provide the basis for our analysis and reflection. Quantitative evidence of student learning can be summarized with tallies, percentages, or averages, among other options; rather than looking at the overall course or assignment grade, it can be helpful to look at student scores on items aligned with specific outcomes, such as comparing evidence for each rubric category or student scores on subgroups of test questions intended to assess discrete learning goals (Suskie, 2018). When we engage with qualitative evidence of student learning, a quick read-through can help us identify any issues we may have to address immediately, while a more extensive thematic analysis allows us to more reliably identify common themes and patterns relevant to our students' learning. In reviewing and analyzing the data, consider: What evidence do you have that students achieved the learning goals? What might have contributed to their success? What evidence of student learning (or the absence of learning) has left you disappointed? What might have contributed to their falling short of goals and expectations? For additional guidance on engaging in these reflections, chapters 24 and 26 in Linda Suskie's *Assessing Student Learning* (2018) provide a wealth of tools and ideas to get you started.

As we make analysis and reflection on assessment data a regular practice, it can be beneficial to create a course portfolio for each course we are teaching to allow us to compare and contrast data across semesters and identify trends over time (Akleh & Wahab, 2020; Sidell, 2003). A course portfolio allows us to document "unfolding of a single course, from conception to results" (Hutchings, 1998, p. 13); it includes course documents (e.g., syllabus, assignment prompts, lecture notes) as well as data on student success combined with our reflection on how things worked out in practice. In keeping a portfolio, we are able to refer to concrete data when identifying how we can improve instruction and student learning rather than relying on perception and our often-overtaxed memory.

What Do We Do?

The CTB framework provides an overview of essential components associated with effective assessment of and for student learning. Importantly, assessment is integrally linked to the critical teaching behavior of "alignment" introduced in chapter 1. Alignment is a driving force in developing an assessment plan for our courses that allows us and our students to gain meaningful insights into the skills and knowledge acquired in a course while increasing transparent communication with our students about our expectations and goals for their learning. Ultimately, whether we are aiming to assess student work or our own instructional practices, assessment, when done well, is an iterative process that integrates goal setting, practice, opportunities to demonstrate knowledge and skills, feedback, and a chance to revise and set new goals. In this context, it is important to remember that assessment cannot happen in isolation; the word *assessment* has its roots in the Latin verb *assidere*, "to sit beside," reminding us that assessment presents us an opportunity to engage in an ongoing dialogue in which students and teachers learn together and from each other. Table 4.1

TABLE 4.1: Assess: Critical Teaching Behaviors in Practice

Behavior	*Step by Step*
AS.1 Schedule regular summative assessments to measure student progress toward learning outcomes	• Ensure assessments align with course outcomes. 　○ Assess skills and knowledge at an appropriate level (e.g., do you want students to remember facts or critically analyze a problem and find a solution). 　○ Make sure all learning outcomes are assessed (or, if an outcome is obsolete, revisit course outcomes listed). • Define and communicate expectations, including criteria that will be used to evaluate assessments (e.g., rubric, checklist, sample work). • When possible, identify authentic assessment tasks and/or opportunities for students to demonstrate their learning through more than one type of assessment to increase fairness and inclusivity. • Appropriately space summative assignments over academic term to allow sufficient time for developing skills and knowledge. • Evaluate grading scheme for your course to make sure grading percentages accurately reflect what is most important. • Consider whether alternative approaches to grading (e.g., ungrading, contract grading, etc.) are appropriate options for driving your approach to assessment.
AS.2 Embed formative assessments and opportunities for self-assessment in instruction	• Plan activities and low-stakes formative assessments that allow students to practice course concepts and skills at the same level as they will be assessed. • Schedule frequent opportunities for low-stakes formative assessments or ungraded self-assessments. 　○ These provide an opportunity for students to identify areas of confusion early on and get a sense of their own strengths and weaknesses in terms of course content. 　○ Regularly testing supports long-term retention of knowledge, according to research on the testing effect.
AS.3 Scaffold assessments	• Provide in-class or guided practice for complex tasks that are essential for students to understand upon completing your course. • If complex tasks are included on an exam, make sure students have an opportunity to practice these and check their understanding through feedback prior to the summative assessment. • Break down complex assignments into smaller tasks that allow students to build up to a more complex product. • Provide opportunities for early feedback on these steps, either by providing feedback yourself, planning peer feedback activities, or engaging students in guided self-assessment.

(Continues)

TABLE 4.1 (*Continued*)

Behavior	Step by Step

AS.4 Communicate purpose, task, and criteria for assessments	• Communicate the purpose, specific instructions for completing the task, and criteria for how the task will be evaluated for each assignment; this supports students' success, especially for minoritized students.
	  ○ *Purpose.* Connect to course learning outcomes or professional skills gained.
	  ○ *Task.* Describe the nuts and bolts of an assignment; be concise or it becomes overwhelming.
	  ○ *Criteria.* Share a rubric, checklist, or sample work to communicate your expectations as clearly as possible.

AS.5 Provide timely, constructive feedback to students	• The best feedback opens a conversation about strengths and areas for growth where students have an opportunity to use the feedback to improve (e.g., revisions or retake, application to a similar future task).
	  ○ Indicate specific areas for improvement rather than leaving vague comments.
	  ○ Offer recognition and encouragement for work well done and be specific about what made the student successful.
	• Investigate whether technology tools can facilitate feedback and streamline your grading process (e.g., audio feedback, rubrics).
	• Consider peer feedback and self-assessment.
	  ○ Peer feedback and self-assessment provide an opportunity for students to familiarize themselves with evaluation criteria.
	  ○ Peer feedback provides students with an opportunity to get insights from multiple perspectives.

AS.6 Review assessment data to make informed decisions about course content, structure, and activities	• Summarize and analyze assessment data after major assessments and/or at the end of a course. • Identify factors that might have contributed to student successes as well as to assessment outcomes that were disappointing. • Keep a record of assessment data over time, for example by creating a course portfolio. • Use assessment data to adjust and revise course details in the future.

presents a summary of "Assess" behaviors discussed in this chapter and suggests step-by-step actions we can take to integrate meaningful assessment practices into our teaching practice.

What Do We Show?

Assessment is an integral part of learning that, if done effectively, helps us and our students understand how well they can navigate and apply the knowledge and skills we want them to take away from our courses. That said, good assessment practices are not as straightforward as asking students to complete a midterm and a final exam; the frequency and type of assessments play a role in supporting learning, the way we frame assignments and communicate expectations supports or hinders students' success, and whether we provide feedback and opportunities to use this feedback to improve can influence student motivation. This provides us with many opportunities—outlined in Table 4.2—to document and discuss how we assess students in our courses and how our practices support student learning.

TABLE 4.2: Documenting Assessment

Teaching Materials	
Provide short annotations for materials to focus attention on the critical teaching behavior(s) you want to showcase.	
Assessments, including instructions, prompts, or questions	Assessments showcase how you evaluate your students' learning. Ideally, you will have a combination of low-stakes formative assessments to provide feedback and summative assessments to evaluate student learning. In annotating assessments, we can emphasize how they help us achieve learning outcomes and allow us to support student learning. *Prompts* can provide a glimpse into your reason behind assigning certain assignments and the outcomes or goals they achieve (Purpose), the task students complete to show their learning (Task), and the way you evaluate their success (Criteria). They also allow you to provide insights into the scaffolding or steps of a longer assignment. Annotations on *test and quiz questions* allow you to discuss your approach to formative and/ or summative assessment and how you leverage them to (a) evaluate student achievement in your course and/or (b) use as a learning tool for students to deepen their understanding of materials. You may also choose to include a test blueprint. Test blueprints are simple tools that help us be more intentional about achieving learning outcomes when creating exams. When creating a test blueprint matrix, you start by listing the learning outcomes you want students to demonstrate through the exam and determine the distribution of questions or performance tasks focused on each of the outcomes.
Lesson plan	Ideally, every learning unit includes some type of assessment to check in with students on what they are learning and where they might still be confused. On a daily basis, we might check in with students in low-key ways such as having an in-class discussion, integrating a few engagement questions using clickers or other audience-response tools, or asking students to complete a quick reflective minute paper on remaining questions at the end of the meeting. Our plans for checking in with students would be noted on the lesson plan.
Representative examples of feedback to students	Feedback on performance is an essential element of the learning process. By including a representative example of feedback you provide to your students, you can address how you support them through the learning process.
Rubrics/grading criteria	Rubrics and grading criteria allow us to communicate our expectations to students from the beginning, supporting students in creating high-quality work. They also promote increased fairness and equity in grading. Maybe we even involve students, to some extent, in the development of grading criteria. In annotations, we may also want to discuss our approach for introducing students to a rubric or grading criteria and any opportunities we provide for them to work with these tools such as peer or self-assessment.
Student data demonstrating achievement of learning outcomes	Summative assignments provide us with a range of data we can present to discuss accomplishments of our students as a whole. Data we discuss may include grade averages on certain tasks or questions linked to specific learning outcomes, or a reflection on student growth over the course of the semester based on pre/post scores on standardized assessments.

(Continues)

TABLE 4.2 (*Continued*)

Syllabus	The course syllabus provides an opportunity to communicate learning outcomes and expectations for students and can provide information on how assessments will allow students to do the following: • demonstrate their learning • self-assess their progress It can also show the relative importance of different assessments throughout the semester (based on point/percentage value). A syllabus might include a course calendar that shows the distribution of assessments over the course of the semester. This allows students to intentionally plan and prioritize their time. Alternatively, a syllabus may also include a course map that visually represents for students the alignment of course learning outcomes with content, assessments, and activities. Creating a course map helps you communicate how you are evaluating course learning outcomes through the assessments you selected.

Materials From Others

Peer feedback and/or observation	Ask your observer to note examples of assessment in your teaching presentation and materials. As an alternative to a classroom observation, you may ask peers to conduct course material reviews. These are similar to a classroom observation as you ask a peer or teaching expert (e.g., your campus teaching center colleagues) to review specific materials or learning units and provide feedback. Here, too, you may ask your colleague to note examples of assessment in your materials. Be sure to share your course syllabus and other relevant materials to ensure your observer is aware of the outcomes you aim to accomplish.
Student feedback	As stated previously, students benefit from assessments that are aligned to learning activities and course materials and are transparently stating purpose, task, and evaluation criteria. Students can provide targeted feedback on their experience in your class through formal and informal feedback. • *CTB midterm feedback.* The CTB midterm feedback survey includes questions that specifically solicit your students' feedback on assessment in your course. • *Select end-of-term surveys.* Questions related to assessment are part of many—but not all—end-of-term student surveys. If no question related to assessment is included on the survey used in your institution, you may be able to add a custom question or facilitate your own survey.

Reflection Questions

1. What is the role and distribution of summative and formative assessments in your course? Do students have regular opportunities to check in on their learning? How do you scaffold learning to ensure students are prepared to succeed on summative assessments?

2. Can you articulate the purpose, task, and criteria for each assignment in your course? If

not, how can you communicate this information more clearly to your students?

3. What opportunities can you create in your courses for providing feedback that opens the door for conversation? How can students apply the feedback you provide to increase their learning gains and improve performance?

4. How might you integrate authentic assessments or alternative approaches to grading in your courses? Do these assessment options align with your course learning outcomes?

References

Adachi, C., Tai, J. H.-M., & Dawson, P. (2018). Academics' perceptions of the benefits and challenges of self and peer assessment in higher education. *Assessment & Evaluation in Higher Education, 43*(2), 294–306. https://doi.org/10.1080/02602938.2017.1339775

Akleh, A., & Wahab, R. A. (2020). Effectiveness of course portfolio in improving course quality at Higher Education. *International Journal of Higher Education, 9*(3), 39–48. https://eric.ed.gov/?id=EJ1248526

Anderson, L. W., Krathwohl, D. R., & Bloom, B. S. (2001). *A taxonomy for learning, teaching, and assessing: A revision of Bloom's taxonomy of educational objectives.* Longman.

Bearman, M., & Ajjawi, R. (2021). Can a rubric do more than be transparent? Invitation as a new metaphor for assessment criteria. *Studies in Higher Education, 46*(2), 359–368. https://doi.org/10.1080/03075079.2019.1637842

Beaumont, C., O'Doherty, M., & Shannon, L. (2011). Reconceptualising assessment feedback: A key to improving student learning? *Studies in Higher Education, 36*(6), 671–687. https://doi.org/10.1080/03075071003731135

Bishop, J., Cofer, J., Domizi, D., McRae, R., & Smitherman, M. (2020, June). *TILTing your online assignments.* University System of Georgia Summer Webinar Series. https://www.usg.edu/facultydevelopment/assets/facultydevelopment/documents/TILT-supplementalmaterials.pdf

Bloom, B. S. (1956). *Taxonomy of educational objectives: The classification of educational goals.* David McKay.

Blum, S. D. (2020a). Just one change (just kidding): Ungrading and its necessary accompaniments. In S. D. Blum (Ed.), *Ungrading* (pp. 53–73). West Virginia University Press.

Blum, S. D. (Ed.). (2020b). *Ungrading.* West Virginia University Press.

Boud, D. (2015). Feedback: Ensuring that it leads to enhanced learning. *The Clinical Teacher, 12*(1), 3–7. https://doi.org/10.1111/tct.12345

Boud, D., & Molloy, E. (2013). Rethinking models of feedback for learning: The challenge of design. *Assessment & Evaluation in Higher Education, 38*(6), 698–712. https://doi.org/10.1080/02602938.2012.691462

Bourke, R. (2018). Self-assessment to incite learning in higher education: Developing ontological awareness. *Assessment & Evaluation in Higher Education, 43*(5), 827–839. https://doi.org/10.1080/02602938.2017.1411881

Boyle, B., Mitchell, R., McDonnell, A., Sharma, N., Biswas, K., & Nicholas, S. (2020). Overcoming the challenge of "fuzzy" assessment and feedback. *Education &*

Training, 62(5), 505–519. http://dx.doi.org/10.1108/ET-08-2019-0183

Bridglall, B. L. (2001). Research and practice on how people learn. *Pedagogical Inquiry and Praxis, 1*, 7. https://files.eric.ed.gov/fulltext/ED452305.pdf

Brookhart, S. M. (2013). *How to create and use rubrics for formative assessment and grading.* Association for Supervision & Curriculum Development.

Brown, G., & Harris, L. (2013). Student self-assessment. In J. H. McMillan (Ed.), *SAGE handbook of research on classroom assessment* (pp. 367–393). SAGE. https://dx.doi.org/10.4135/9781452218649.n21

Brown, P. C., Roediger, H. L., & McDaniel, M. (2014). *Make it stick: The science of successful learning.* The Belknap Press of Harvard University Press.

Brown, S., & Pickford, R. (2006). *Assessing skills and practice* (Vol. 7). Routledge.

Butler, S. M., & McMunn, N. D. (2014). *A teacher's guide to classroom assessment: Understanding and using assessment to improve student learning.* Wiley. http://ebookcentral.proquest.com/lib/erau/detail.action?docID=708115

Cockett, A., & Jackson, C. (2018). The use of assessment rubrics to enhance feedback in higher education: An integrative literature review. *Nurse Education Today, 69*, 8–13. https://doi.org/10.1016/j.nedt.2018.06.022

Cohen, G. L., Steele, C. M., & Ross, L. D. (1999). The mentor's dilemma: Providing critical feedback across the racial divide. *Personality and Social Psychology Bulletin, 25*(10), 1302–1318. https://doi.org/10.1177/0146167299258011

Culver, K. C., Braxton, J., & Pascarella, E. (2019). Does teaching rigorously really enhance undergraduates' intellectual development? The relationship of academic rigor with critical thinking skills and lifelong learning motivations. *Higher Education, 78*(4), 611–627. https://doi.org/10.1007/s10734-019-00361-z

Culver, K. C., Braxton, J. M., & Pascarella, E. T. (2021). What we talk about when we talk about rigor: Examining conceptions of academic rigor. *The Journal of Higher Education, 92*(7), 1140–1163. https://doi.org/10.1080/00221546.2021.1920825

Darley, J. M., & Gross, P. H. (1983). A hypothesis-confirming bias in labeling effects. *Journal of Personality and Social Psychology, 44*(1), 20–33. https://doi.org/10.1037/0022-3514.44.1.20

Darling-Hammond, L., & Snyder, J. (2000). Authentic assessment of teaching in context. *Teaching and Teacher Education, 16*(5), 523–545. https://doi.org/10.1016/S0742-051X(00)00015-9

Deeley, S. J., Fischbacher-Smith, M., Karadzhov, D., & Koristashevskaya, E. (2019). Exploring the "wicked" problem of student dissatisfaction with assessment and feedback in higher education. *Higher Education Pedagogies*, *4*(1), 385–405. http://dx.doi.org/10.1080/237526 96.2019.1644659

DePaul University Teaching Commons. (n.d.). *Types of rubrics*. https://resources.depaul.edu/teaching-commons/teaching-guides/feedback-grading/rubrics/Pages/types-of-rubrics.aspx

Dobson, J. L., & Linderholm, T. (2015). Self-testing promotes superior retention of anatomy and physiology information. *Advances in Health Sciences Education*, *20*(1), 149–161. https://doi.org/10.1007/s10459-014-9514-8

Dovidio, J. F., Gaertner, S. L., & Pearson, A. R. (2016). Aversive racism and contemporary bias. In C. G. Sibley & F. K. Barlow (Eds.), *The Cambridge handbook of the psychology of prejudice* (pp. 267–294). Cambridge University Press. https://doi.org/10.1017/9781316161579.012

Driscoll, A., & Wood, S. (2007). *Developing outcomes-based assessment for learner-centered education: A faculty introduction*. Stylus.

Eyler, J. (2022, March 7). Grades are at the center of the student mental health crisis. *Inside Higher Ed*. https://www.insidehighered.com/blogs/just-visiting/grades-are-center-student-mental-health-crisis

Fletcher, A. K. (2016). Exceeding expectations: Scaffolding agentic engagement through assessment as learning. *Educational Research*, *58*(4), 400–419. https://doi.org/10.1080/00131881.2016.1235909

Frost, R., Matta, V., & Kenyo, L. (2021). A system to automate scaffolding and formative assessment while preventing plagiarism: Enhancing learning in IS and analytics courses that use Excel. *Journal of Information Systems Education*, *32*(4), 228–243. https://aisel.aisnet.org/jise/vol32/iss4/1

Gibbs, L. (2020). Let's talk about grading. In S. D. Blum (Ed.), *Ungrading* (pp. 91–104). West Virginia University Press.

Gower, K. (2021). Let them eat cake: Why the inherent bias in professor grading should change to individual performance assessments. *Journal of Organizational Psychology*, *21*(5), 149–154. https://doi.org/10.33423/jop.v21i5.4724

Hortigüela Alcalá, D., Palacios Picos, A., & López Pastor, V. (2019). The impact of formative and shared or co-assessment on the acquisition of transversal competences in higher education. *Assessment & Evaluation in Higher Education*, *44*(6), 933–945. https://doi.org/10.1080/02602938.2018.1530341

Huisman, B., Saab, N., van den Broek, P., & van Driel, J. (2019). The impact of formative peer feedback on higher education students' academic writing: A meta-analysis. *Assessment & Evaluation in Higher Education*, *44*(6), 863–880. https://doi.org/10.1080/02602938.2018.1545896

Hutchings, P. (1998). *The course portfolio: How faculty can examine their teaching to advance practice and improve student learning. The teaching initiatives*. American Association for Higher Education. https://eric.ed.gov/?id=ED441393

Inoue, A. B. (2019). *Labor-based grading contracts: Building equity and inclusion in the compassionate writing classroom*. The WAC Clearinghouse; University Press of Colorado. https://doi.org/10.37514/PER-B.2019.0216.0

Jack, J., & Sathy, V. (2021, September 24). It's time to cancel the word "rigor." *The Chronicle of Higher Education*. https://www.chronicle.com/article/its-time-to-cancel-the-word-rigor

Karpicke, J. D. (2012). Retrieval-based learning: Active retrieval promotes meaningful learning. *Current Directions in Psychological Science*, *21*(3), 157–163. https://doi.org/10.1177/0963721412443552

Katopodis, C., & Davidson, C. N. (2020). Contract grading and peer review. In S. D. Blum (Ed.), *Ungrading* (pp. 105–122). West Virginia University Press.

Kickert, R., Meeuwisse, M., Stegers-Jager, K. M., Koppenol-Gonzalez, V. G., Arends, R. L., & Prinzie, P. (2019). Assessment policies and academic performance within a single course: The role of motivation and self-regulation. *Assessment & Evaluation in Higher Education*, *44*(8), 1177–1190. https://doi.org/10.1080/02602938.2019.1580674

López-Pastor, V. M. (2011). Best practices in academic assessment in higher education: A case in formative and shared assessment. *Journal of Technology and Science Education*, *1*(2), 25–39.

Masland, L. [@LindsayMasland]. (2022, January 19). *I've got a workshop tomorrow on how student-centered teaching can lead to instructor burnout. (Inclusive Teaching Includes You Too) Does anyone have examples of how you made a choice to be student-centered and then possibly regretted it because it was unsustainable for you?* [Tweet]. Twitter. https://twitter.com/LindsayMasland/status/148385275 8964965382

Meer, N. M., & Chapman, A. (2014). Assessment for confidence: Exploring the impact that low-stakes assessment design has on student retention. *The International Journal of Management Education*, *12*(2), 186–192. https://doi.org/10.1016/j.ijme.2014.01.003

Nilson, L. B. (2014). *Specifications grading: Restoring rigor, motivating students, and saving faculty time*. Stylus.

Oleson, K. C. (2020). *Promoting inclusive classroom dynamics in higher education: A research-based pedagogical guide for faculty*. Stylus.

Panadero, E., Brown, G. T. L., & Strijbos, J.-W. (2016). The future of student self-assessment: A review of known unknowns and potential directions. *Educational Psychology Review*, *28*(4), 803–830. https://doi.org/10.1007/s10648-015-9350-2

Panadero, E., Jonsson, A., & Botella, J. (2017). Effects of self-assessment on self-regulated learning and self-efficacy: Four meta-analyses. *Educational Research Review, 22,* 74–98. https://doi.org/10.1016/j.edurev.2017.08.004

Persellin, D. C., & Daniels, M. B. (2015). *A concise guide to improving student learning: Six evidence-based principles and how to apply them.* Stylus.

Pittman, C., & Tobin, T. (2022, February 7). Academe has a lot to learn about how inclusive teaching affects instructors. *The Chronicle of Higher Education.* https://www.chronicle.com/article/academe-has-a-lot-to-learn-about-how-inclusive-teaching-affects-instructors

Reid, M. A., & Barrington, H. (1994). *Training interventions: Managing employee development.* Institute of Personnel Development.

Roediger, H. L., & Karpicke, J. D. (2006). Test-enhanced learning. *Psychological Science, 17*(3), 249–255. https://doi.org/10.1111/j.1467-9280.2006.01693.x

Sadler, D. R. (1998). Formative assessment: Revisiting the territory. *Assessment in Education, 5*(1), 77–84. http://dx.doi.org/10.1080/0969595980050104

Shepard, L. A. (2000). The role of assessment in a learning culture. *Educational Researcher, 29*(7), 4–14. https://doi.org/10.3102/0013189X029007004

Sidell, N. L. (2003). The course portfolio. *Journal of Teaching in Social Work, 23*(3–4), 91–106. https://doi.org/10.1300/J067v23n03_08

Stommel, J. (2020). How to ungrade. In S. D. Blum (Ed.), *Ungrading* (pp. 25–41). West Virginia University Press.

Supiano, B. (2022, April 29). The unintended consequences of "ungrading." *The Chronicle of Higher Education.* https://www.chronicle.com/article/the-unintended-consequences-of-ungrading

Suskie, L. (2018). *Assessing student learning: A common sense guide.* Wiley. http://ebookcentral.proquest.com/lib/erau/detail.action?docID=5215462

TiLT Higher Ed. (n.d.). *Transparency in teaching and learning.* https://tilthighered.com/

Vye, N. J., Schwartz, D. L., Bransford, J. D., Barron, B. J., Zech, L., & Cognition and Technology Group at Vanderbilt. (1998). SMART environments that support monitoring, reflection, and revision. In D. J. Hacker, J. Dunlosky, & A. C. Graesser (Eds.), *Metacognition in educational theory and practice* (pp. 319–360). Routledge. https://doi.org/10.4324/9781410602350

Walvoord, B. E., & Banta, T. W. (2010). *Assessment clear and simple: A practical guide for institutions, departments, and general education.* Wiley.

Wanner, T., & Palmer, E. (2018). Formative self- and peer assessment for improved student learning: The crucial factors of design, teacher participation and feedback. *Assessment & Evaluation in Higher Education, 43*(7), 1032–1047. https://doi.org/10.1080/02602938.2018.1427698

Wiewiora, A., & Kowalkiewicz, A. (2019). The role of authentic assessment in developing authentic leadership identity and competencies. *Assessment & Evaluation in Higher Education, 44*(3), 415–430. https://doi.org/10.1080/02602938.2018.1516730

Winkelmes, M.-A., Bernacki, M., Butler, J., Zochowski, M., Golanics, J., & Weavil, K. H. (2016). A teaching intervention that increases underserved college students' success. *Peer Review, 18*(1/2), 31–36.

CHAPTER 5

Integrate Technology

DEFINITION

Instructors who integrate technology responsibly use tools to design accessible, high-quality instructional materials and engaging learning opportunities beyond traditional barriers of place and time.

E VERY DAY IN ONLINE and face-to-face (F2F) instruction, we have options to use technology in many ways for many different purposes: We post a course syllabus to the LMS; we use presentation tools to offer information during lectures; we use apps to engage students in physical and virtual learning spaces; we share multimedia resources to enrich the student experience and sometimes we even create these media ourselves. Whether we like it or not, the fact is that we likely use at least some technology for teaching in all our courses. The importance of technology as an essential instructional tool has increased exponentially as a result of the COVID-19 pandemic that required emergency pivots to virtual learning spaces for courses that were previously taught on campus. In response to this complex global problem, many if not all instructors increasingly leveraged technology to facilitate a high-quality learning experience for students while accommodating individual needs. Many students and instructors benefited from the increased awareness of the available options for integrating technology and from the attention paid to implementing technology in a way that supports students' learning. However, if we focused only on recent developments and the emergency adoption of technology tools and online learning in response to the pandemic, we would fail to fully understand the essential nature of technology for instructional purposes. Research from 2017—prior to the emergency pivot of 2020—found that most, if not all, teaching and learning in higher education involves, and even depends on, technology and that using technology effectively is critical when it comes to preparing students for success in and beyond academia (OECD, 2015; Office of Educational Technology, 2017). Additionally, as previewed in chapter 3 ("Engage"), productive engagement with technology is one of the four types of interactions most relevant to student engagement and learning (Anderson, 2003; Nilson & Goodson, 2018). While skepticism regarding the role of instructional technology persists, it is practically impossible to teach a course without it, and therefore we must consider how we can use it well so that it can enhance teaching and learning rather than distract from it.

The CTB framework includes a specific category dedicated to the integration of technology in response to this reality. Technology plays an important role in higher education in on-campus, hybrid, and fully online classes, and instructors have critical roles to play in shaping learning experiences for our students that intentionally and effectively leverage available tools. It is not enough to keep up with the latest trends in educational technology and integrate tools that seem "fun"; instead, integrating technology should be an intentional practice built on evidence and intended to foster course learning outcomes.

What Do We Know?

Effective integration of technology is associated with a range of benefits. Technology can support students' engagement with course materials and ideas and promote higher order thinking. Specifically, access to course materials outside of predetermined class meetings and participation in multimodal communication through visuals, print, and virtual experiences provide learners with opportunities and time to think critically and reflectively (Duderstadt et al., 2002; Robinson & Hullinger, 2008). At the same time, integrating technology plays an important role in preparing students for success in and beyond academia; according to *Students, Computers, and Learning* (OECD, 2015), "students unable to navigate through a complex digital landscape will no longer be able to participate fully in the economic, social and cultural life around them" (p. 3). Using technology for learning and professional purposes is one of the skills we can help students develop through effective and intentional integration of technology into our courses.

Before moving on to some of the specific strategies we can employ to effectively leverage technology tools in our classrooms, we want to provide some context on students' and instructors' preferences and experiences regarding the use of technology in higher education in the United States. Since 2004, the EDUCAUSE Center for Analysis and Research (ECAR) has conducted student and instructor surveys at a range of institutions to capture insights into their perspectives on the increasingly important role of technology in higher education. In 2017, 2018, and 2019, between 43,000–64,000 students responded to the ECAR student survey each year. Their responses indicate an increasing preference for instructional modalities that include some form of blended learning. The 2019 and

2020 surveys expanded on student preferences by providing insights into students' preferred learning environment; the data showed that over half of the respondents preferred a blended learning experience (56% in 2019; 57% in 2020), although most students leaned in the direction of more F2F components than online ones (Gierdowski, 2019; Gierdowski et al., 2020). The Students and Technology Report: Rebalancing the Student Experience, 2022, indicates that following the pandemic overall student preferences are shifting further toward blended courses with more online learning components and fully or mostly online courses; only 41% of respondents indicated a preference for fully or mostly F2F courses in 2022 as compared to 65% in 2020 (Robert, 2022). Regardless of student preference, it is also noteworthy that various research studies indicate that, on average, students in online courses and blended learning environments (courses that combine online and F2F components) perform better than those receiving F2F instruction (Balakrishnan et al., 2021; Means et al., 2013); the advantage of blended learning over F2F classes was especially pronounced (Means et al., 2013). Knowing that blending online and F2F learning, if done well, can positively impact student performance, engagement, and perceptions about learning might be a motivator for some of us teaching primarily F2F to explore how we might effectively integrate some online components into our courses to enrich the learning experience for students. Of course, shifting learning to an online environment is not the only way to integrate technology; technology tools can also help us make an F2F classroom more engaging and focused and help us better achieve some of our learning goals and outcomes.

In fact, regardless of modality, students expect instructors to use technology to share information and materials (Brooks & Pomerantz, 2017) and to integrate tech tools in the classroom for the purpose of facilitating engagement and connections with faculty, materials, and classmates (Gierdowski, 2019). Technology continues to be a growing component of teaching and learning, a fact that good teachers cannot ignore. To be effective in this environment as instructors, we must be intentional about how we integrate and leverage technology in our courses. In the following paragraphs we introduce some of the important considerations that underlie decisions about the role of technology in our courses. Specifically, this chapter will discuss research and implementation ideas related to the following strategies:

- selecting limited and relevant technologies
- leveraging technology to increase access, facilitate ease of use, and optimize the student learning experience
- using technology effectively and efficiently
- training students to use instructional technology and provide basic support
- considering pedagogical needs relevant to instructional modality
- ensuring materials and tools meet legal requirements

Select Limited and Relevant Technologies

Technology integration can have a significant impact on students' engagement (or disengagement) and success. To effectively leverage technology, "careful planning, sound pedagogy, and appropriate tools are vital" (Bond et al., 2020, p. 2), as there is no guarantee technology will promote student engagement and learning unless it is carefully and purposefully integrated into the course. In fact, poorly integrated

educational technology can "promote disengagement and impede rather than help learning" (Bond et al., 2020, p. 4). Technology adoption must be driven by careful consideration of the contextual factors including didactic needs we aim to meet by integrating technology as well as course content and the technologies that are especially well suited to supporting learning in our discipline (de Witt & Gloerfeld, 2017; Koehler & Mishra, 2009). As we learn about technologies and evaluate their usefulness, it is beneficial to keep in mind the dynamic relationship between technology, content, and pedagogical strategies instead of adopting a tech tool or app because it is new or trendy in order to avoid using technology excessively or uncritically.

Technology can be used to achieve a range of different purposes, but as its use becomes more and more common and the tools available to us are ever more abundant, we may be tempted to adopt technology tools just because we see colleagues using them with success or because we are excited about the fun opportunities we associate with a tool; however, our selection of technology should be driven by the pedagogical goals we aim to accomplish through its use. Some of the goals technology can help us achieve are listed in Table 5.1.

TABLE 5.1: Pedagogical Goals Supported by Technology

Goal	Potential Implementation Ideas
Delivery of course content	• Use open educational resources (OER) to provide affordable access to course textbook and other resources. • Create hyperlinked and other interactive materials to encourage students to explore beyond required information. • Show or share instructional videos to illustrate concepts or demonstrate application of skills. • Leverage presentation tools, such as PowerPoint or Prezi, to keep in-class lecture focused and to emphasize key points. • Share course materials on the LMS to allow students to review content on their own time. • Organize course content shared on the LMS to facilitate ease of access—the more time students spend on finding the material or activity, the less time they have to engage with the task.
Student engagement	• Use student response systems for an easy way to incorporate formative assessment and engage students during interactive lectures. • Design online discussion boards to encourage exchange of ideas and collaboration in writing or through voice recordings or videos. • Assign virtual presentations or student-created videos to encourage students to present their ideas. • Create short online quizzes to check in with students on materials they prepare at home or provide an opportunity for self-assessment.

Goal	Potential Implementation Ideas
Teamwork and collaborations	• Foster asynchronous group or teamwork through collaborative document creation using web-based apps such as Google Drive or Office 365. • Promote exchange of ideas while students prepare new materials through collaborative annotation tools such as Perusall or Hypothesis.
Communication	• Post important course announcements, updates, and reminders via LMS or email. • Provide personalized feedback through instructor response videos or voice feedback recordings. • Promote student-to-student support through course back channels using social networking apps.

Once we have determined our purpose for integrating technology, technology implementation models such as SAMR and PICRAT can provide us with a guiding framework and the language to determine what we would like technology integration to look like in our class. Are we looking for small changes driven mostly by the instructor, or are we hoping technology will transform the learning experience for us and the students? The SAMR model, introduced by Ruben Puentedura, guides instructors in their implementation of technology (France, 2018; Puentedura, 2015). SAMR provides a framework to reflect on the level of transformation we want technology to promote in our courses. Technology may be used to *substitute* another tool (e.g., students' use of presentation software to create a report rather than pen and paper); *augment* the learning experience (e.g., students include multimedia materials in their report in addition to text); *modify* the task (e.g., students create a podcast to discuss what they learned preparing the report); or *redefine* what is possible (e.g., student teams collaborate to create a video showcasing their report findings; the video is shared with others using the course website). Especially as we are starting out, technology may be a tool we use to substitute for another activity or mode of delivery, but as we become more comfortable with the technology and fully understand the possibilities available to us, we may move along the continuum to completely rethink activities in our course, making technology a more central part of the learning experience and outcomes. The SAMR model focuses primarily on the teacher's intention behind a shift to increased technology use. The PICRAT model, on one hand, considers the students' relationship

to the technology as well as the instructor intention (Kimmons et al., 2020). Students' engagement with technology may be *passive* (reception of information), *interactive* (engagement with content or other learners), or *creative* (construction of knowledge via construction of artifacts). On the other hand, like the categories introduced in the SAMR model, the instructor's intention for technology use may be to *replace* a more traditional practice, *amplify* learning, or *transform* learning. These models for technology integration give us the language to talk about the changes we desire for ourselves and our students and provide us with an implementation continuum that tells us it is okay to start small, although we have the option to entirely transform our classroom.

Making intentional decisions about our use of technology that take into consideration our learning outcomes, the level of change we are comfortable with, desired level of student interaction with technology, and disciplinary context allows us to select the most appropriate technology tools and integrations for our course. Whereas instructors teaching in an F2F context might choose to use technology to reach only select goals since they have opportunities to reach other goals in the classroom without the use of technology, instructors teaching an online only or a hybrid course with mostly online components will want to identify technology to accomplish all or most of these pedagogical goals in an effort to design and deliver a well-rounded and engaging educational experience for students. That said, we want to be cautious of selecting too many technology tools for use in our courses as it can be overwhelming for faculty and students to efficiently manage tasks on multiple platforms. When designing learning materials, we must minimize the extraneous cognitive load required to complete a task—or the demand to use cognitive resources on tasks not directly related to the desired learning outcomes—so that learning can occur (Jenkins et al., 2013; Paas & Sweller, 2021). Finding materials across multiple platforms and navigating the different demands of various tech tools add to students' workload without directly contributing to their learning of course information and skills. An LMS, with its various tools and functionalities, often allows us to accomplish a range of pedagogical goals without adding additional tech tools into the mix. Frequently, we also have the option to integrate additional technologies and apps into the LMS so students can easily access all tasks in one place, making it easier to locate activities and reducing time on tasks not directly related to course goals. That said, we may have good reasons to look for and use tools outside of the LMS to meet our needs. In these cases, we encourage you to reach out to campus resources such as your teaching center or IT department for guidance. Our colleagues in these departments might have suggestions for tools already supported by the university that can help us and our students accomplish specific goals, or they may be able to help us understand the process of adding additional technologies to the campus toolbox.

Defining and aligning pedagogical purposes and designs with technology remain a significant challenge exacerbated by the ongoing rapid pace of technological innovations and change: as Schneckenberg (2009) observed: "technology development tends to outpace strategic thinking and pedagogical design in universities" (2009, p. 419). As a result, selecting appropriate technologies can be time-consuming, but it is the first important step we must take to ensure that technology promotes the type of engagement and learning we want to see in our class, followed by a critical consideration of how to best integrate the apps and tech tools we chose.

Leverage Technology to Increase Access, Facilitate Ease of Use, and Optimize the Student Learning Experience

In addition to informing the selection of appropriate tools, pedagogical goals must also drive decisions about how we implement technology in our courses to ensure students' use of technology optimizes and enriches their learning experience instead of distracting from it. Learning improves when

pedagogical considerations drive technology integration (Simonson & Schlosser, 2004; Waterhouse, 2005) because what matters most for student learning is good teaching, although, more and more often, good teaching is supported by technology. Many effective behaviors easily translate to a teaching with technology context and help us map our technology implementation plan in general. When it comes to specific questions related to the technology we want to use, we have access to an abundance of research that focuses specifically on best practices for using particular technology tools in the higher education classroom; often a quick search and skim of the available literature on a particular tool can provide us with a great place to start our own implementation journey. It is impossible and unfeasible to share a comprehensive overview of research on each of the educational technology options available to instructors in the quick overview we intend to provide in this chapter, and with the constant emergence of new technology options, information we might provide on specific tools can be quickly outdated. To provide a place to start, however, we share some pedagogical considerations to guide the use of some of the most common technology integrations and questions—the LMS; multimedia resources, especially instructional videos; and the use of personal devices in the traditional F2F classroom.

Leverage the LMS as a Multifunctional Tool and Organizational Framework

In 2019 over 80% of students reported that all or most of their courses used the institution's LMS for at least some aspect of the class, regardless of whether the course was delivered in an F2F, hybrid, or fully online modality (Gierdowski, 2019). Faculty also report using their institutions' LMS at high rates, but the primary use of this multifunctional tool is "mostly only for operational, course management functions like circulating information" (Pomerantz & Brooks, 2017, p. 7). While the LMS is an essential tool to support these logistical functions, it offers a wide range of options beyond these basics, including the following:

- interactive features such as discussion boards, quizzes, and so on that can encourage students to engage with course materials, each other, and the instructor

- communication tools that allow us to send course-related alerts and nudges, which most students find "very" or "extremely" useful (Gierdowski et al., 2020)
- space to share course information and resources so students can review important materials outside of the physical classroom space as often as they need
- space to provide just-in-time resources for students to review information on basic skills and knowledge they may not remember from prerequisite classes

As this list indicates, the LMS can play a significant role in encouraging student engagement with course content and promoting self-regulated learning (both topics we introduced and elaborated on in chapter 3). Interestingly, research on the interrelation between technology and engagement shows that certain tools are more significantly associated with affective, behavioral, and cognitive engagement; the types of tools associated with the highest levels of engagement include text-based tools such as discussion forums and note-taking apps, knowledge organization and sharing tools such as social bookmarking and file sharing, and multimodal production tools such as presentations and digital pinboards (Bond et al., 2020). Many of these tools are available to us as part of the LMS.

The more we increase our use of the LMS, the more important it is to clearly organize shared course materials. Data from the *Study of the Technology Needs of Students With Disabilities, 2020,* shows that students responding to the survey considered the LMS "key to providing access for students with disabilities to online course content, and they would like faculty to use it more" (Gierdowski & Galanek, 2020, p. 5). Gierdowski and Galanek further report that "students want an LMS layout that is intuitively structured, organized, clearly labeled, and updated so that they can find the materials they need with ease" (p. 5). Clear organization of online contents and ease of navigation is also an essential standard of high-quality online courses according to the Quality Matters Higher Education Rubric, used to evaluate and certify online courses. To achieve this standard, the rubric annotations clarify, a course must employ consistent layout and design throughout and the course design must enable learners "to easily locate where they are within the course" (Quality Matters, 2018, p. 39).

To optimally facilitate learning, we need to present online materials in an organized and transparent way; this makes it easy for students to find assigned materials and activities and understand the learning pathway(s) we laid out for them when we designed the course and aligned its elements. We present an overview of organizational principles and how they may be implemented in Table 5.2. We hope that if you are not already a power user of the LMS, these data and ideas encourage you to consider including it as a part of your teaching tool kit.

Multimedia Learning Resources
In addition to providing tools for increasing student engagement, the online environment opens opportunities to present instructional content in different formats, including text, video, and audio sources, and to add interactive elements to engage students. Incorporating multimedia materials allows us to promote engagement and increase access by providing alternative ways for students to interact with course materials (CAST, 2018). Images and sounds can provide learners with information that might not be accessible to them if only presented in text form (Daiute & Morse, 1994). In addition, research shows that students' understanding of material increases if it is presented in both words and pictures (Mayer & Fiorella, 2021). Finally, when we share information in multiple modalities (text/video/audio) more students are able to access the information we provide at a time, a place, and in a format that allows them to work within their context and leverage their strengths to cognitively engage with the course content and ideas (although it is important to ensure that all materials meet accessibility requirements as discussed in chapter 2).

Instructional videos are one of the most common multimedia sources used to deliver instruction (Fiorella, 2021). They are useful for delivering content, demonstrating a procedure, or showing applications of abstract concepts in practice. Sharing a video or screencast of a procedure can help students visualize the process in a way that cannot be conveyed by words alone. Videos recorded by the instructor can also help us humanize the learning experience in the online environment and demonstrate investment in student learning. For example, we may record short videos to further explain a course concept or unpack a misconception in response to student input such as performance on formative assessments or direct

TABLE 5.2: Practical Suggestions for Organizing Asynchronous Online Learning Components

Organizational Principle	*Implementation Examples*
Create a shared mental model of organization with students to facilitate navigation and ease of use.	• A mental model is a representation of how something works. Mental models vary from person to person, so when it comes to organizing course materials, we must take some time to first define a clear organization structure and then communicate it to our students. Especially at the beginning of the semester, take time to explore the organization and navigation of online content during class or with a guided activity such as a start-up quiz. • Make effective use of a course homepage in your LMS (the first page students see once they access your course) to provide easy access to important information and to orient students to the course. You may have to create this page for your course; if your institution provides a home page used by all courses, familiarize yourself with the information shared there and the pathways it provides for accessing information. • Create a course information module that combines and provides easy access to important course documents such as the syllabus and course schedule, contact information, communication guidelines, information about support available to students and how they can access it, and so on. • Within the LMS, modules are useful for clearly creating an organizing structure for our course and make it easy to quickly find and access all materials related to a certain unit. Modules can be organized by week, by textbook chapters, or by thematic units. If you choose not to use modules for your class, clear naming conventions will be even more important. You may also have to spend additional time in class to discuss how your materials are organized online. • For each unit, provide an overview of tasks that students need to complete in this module and describe the order in which to complete them. This is helpful for all classes but especially important in classes with more asynchronous online components as students work independently on completing tasks.
Use consistent and clear naming conventions.	• If using modules, number them in chronological order and assign a descriptive title to each module that allows students to easily identify the topic addressed (e.g., Module 1: Course Introduction, Module 2: Scientific Notations and Vectors, etc.). • As you add pages and tasks, use a descriptive title to allow students and yourself to find a resource more easily for reference purposes (e.g., M1_READ: Learning Physics, M1_DISCUSS: Physics in Our Daily Life, M1_QUIZ: Learning Strategies, etc.). Consider adding an abbreviated module indicator (M1, M2, etc.) for each page or task. • Keep titles simple and brief.
Provide contextual information and scaffolds for materials and tasks.	• For each page/activity provide a short introduction stating, for example, how the reading relates to big questions asked in the course, how the video helps students understand important concepts, why you are excited about the material, etc. As you may remember from chapter 3 ("Engage"), a short introduction can be a great way to capture students' attention and increase motivation. Offering contextual information and communicating expectations also provide students a scaffold to complete the task. • Ask a few guiding questions students should keep in mind as they engage with content; guiding questions can provide students with an anchor to focus their attention. • Create a glossary with the essential terms students need to know and be able to define to fully understand the content of this learning unit. You may decide to ask students to fill in the definitions and/or examples instead of providing them.

questions. This can be a general explanation shared with the whole class or a personalized video in direct response to a specific student's concern. Similarly, when it comes to student questions regarding the use of technology tools or navigation of online content, recording a quick screencast video of the instructor performing a task can provide important clarification more easily than prolonged email exchanges.

Of course, when we share video content with our students, we want them to watch all of it because we consider it important to their understanding and learning. Therefore, we must aim to present these materials in a way that makes it more likely students will stay engaged for the whole duration. When selecting or creating instructional videos for our course, research insights provide guidance on how we can maximize their benefits and avoid student disengagement; Table 5.3 summarizes three important guidelines that apply to both videos we create as well as videos from others we might curate for our course.

As we produce or curate concise videos that pique students' interests and ask students to engage with the information they communicate, it is often essential to provide contextual information that orients students to important takeaways. In doing so, we have an opportunity "to more deeply consider the core elements of the lesson" (Costa, 2020, p. 35): If students remember only one thing from this lesson—what will that be? This focus on what is essential can lead to insights that can benefit us as well as the students. We may find that not all materials are equally important, and some might not make the final cut (pun intended) because we decide to prioritize a deep engagement with one topic over a surface level engagement with many.

Capturing students' attention by orienting them to the main takeaway and relevance of a resource shared and creating opportunities for interaction are also useful strategies for promoting student engagement with other multimedia resources, such as images, podcasts, and others.

TABLE 5.3: Guidelines for Effective Instructional Videos

Keep it short and simple.	**How?** • Keep it short when creating or curating instructional videos; a video should be no longer than 10–15 minutes. • Chunk your content by identifying subtopics, if necessary. If you are recording your own video, you can create multiple shorter videos; if you are curating others' materials, explicitly divide longer videos into distinct sections. **Why?** A 2018 study with 924 participants found that 52% of viewers prefer instructional and informational videos between three to six minutes in length and less than 10% preferred videos longer than 20 minutes (TechSmith, 2021). In a separate study over 50% of undergraduate students reported a preference for videos 10 minutes or less and fewer than 30% of students watched longer lecture recordings; those students who pushed play on the lecture recordings, on average, kept watching for only 22 of the 80 minutes (Patterson et al., 2019).
Create opportunities for interaction and engagement.	**How?** • Embed interactive elements such as low-stakes discussion prompts or quizzes; some LMSs and apps provide the option to embed questions directly in the video. • Provide a worksheet students complete based on information from the video. • Invite students to connect the topic to their own experiences. **Why?** Geri et al. (2017) discovered that adding interactivity (in the form of embedded quizzes) increased the average completion percentage of video lecture viewing by over 20%. Strategically selecting questions related to key ideas for quizzes or discussions also provides us with the opportunity to highlight important concepts and allows us to gather information on whether students are understanding the new content and where they may struggle.

(Continues)

TABLE 5.3 (*Continued*)

Capture students' attention.	**How?** • Begin with a challenging question you are going to answer. • Share an interesting fact about the subject matter. • Present an authentic problem from your discipline the video will help them solve. • Contextualize the content by telling a story or sharing an experience. • Include illustrations and diagrams to limit text on slides and maximize visual learning. • Include an advance organizer that tells students what the video will address; this can be either a slide included in a screencast or a short verbal overview at the beginning of the video. • Bring your personality into the video to humanize the online learning experience. Do not try to be perfect. **Why?** Learning requires attention and students must use limited cognitive resources to select the most relevant information, organize it into a coherent structure, and integrate it with their existing knowledge (Fiorella, 2021). Alpert and Hodkinson (2019) find that, in terms of incorporating video into a class, students disliked a video being played without introduction; "they felt that, if a video was to be shown in class, it should be part of scaffolded learning in that they should be told why and what they should watch for" (p. 6). This demonstrates that we must provide a context for the video and guidance on important takeaways if we want to keep students' attention.

In-Class Use of Technology

While instructors may be reluctant to promote the use of technology during class meetings, many students expect technology to be integrated in the classroom, especially for the purpose of facilitating engagement and connections with faculty, materials, and classmates (Gierdowski, 2019). In the past, the use of personal devices for in-class learning activities has often been discouraged due to concerns that not all students may have access to such a device. Recent data indicate that concerns regarding student access to devices must no longer present a barrier to their use during class; students have near universal access to a desktop computer, a laptop, a tablet, a smartphone, or a combination (Gierdowski, 2019; Gierdowski et al., 2020). Another concern is that access to personal devices may distract students from focused attention and engaged learning (Al-Furaih & Al-Awidi, 2021; Mueller & Oppenheimer, 2014; Ravizza et al., 2017). While concerns that technology may distract students are merited, placing limitations on the use of technology in the classroom may do more harm than good. Restricting or banning technology use in the classroom can unfairly disadvantage certain student groups; in particular,

policies that ban and discourage student device use in the classroom may very well undermine the efforts of women, students of color, lower-income students, and students with disabilities to leverage their devices in ways that help them succeed in college. (Galanek et al., 2018, p. 11)

In the classroom, technology can help us enhance access for students in ways that range from allowing students to use preferred personal devices to access course materials and engage in class activities to creatively using technology to, for example, live caption in-class presentations. Allowing and encouraging students to leverage their preferred device for learning in- and outside the classroom is especially relevant in light of an increasing move toward "digital-first" textbooks and OER that lower cost and barriers associated with course materials. Students who want to access OER course materials during lectures or class discussions must be able to use their personal devices to do so.

Research indicates additional benefits of using personal devices in the classroom. Technology in the classroom can open channels of communication, collaboration, and support, ranging from discussion and engagement with other students to access to additional information on a specific topic (Anshari et al., 2017; Fernandez, 2018; Twum, 2017). These interactions with content and peers can help to clarify content and allow students to explore topics in more depth. Instructors who integrate laptops and smartphones for class activities can also minimize distractions from these devices as students who are using them in a focused and intentional way are less likely to go online shopping or check the latest posts on social media (Anshari et al., 2017). Despite an overall positive attitude toward the use of personal devices, several scholars suggest developing and implementing rules for their acceptable use during class time, ideally with input from students to increase buy-in (Gierdowski et al., 2020; Langmia & Glass, 2014; Twum, 2017). Overall, using personal technology devices in the classroom offers more advantages than disadvantages provided we set clear expectations for their use and utilize them to engage students by asking them to complete, for example, short quizzes, collaborative activities, or a self-driven exploration of information related to the course topic.

Regardless of the technology you use in your course we recommend you ensure that the tools and tasks are clearly linked to course outcomes and that you transparently communicate your reasons for integrating the selected technology to your students. Openly communicating about goals and expectations allows you to establish trust and minimize perceptions of activities as busywork.

Use Technology Effectively and Efficiently

Have you ever stood in front of a class ready to present your best lecture supported by a snazzy, well-thought-out PowerPoint complete with illustrations, embedded videos, instructions for activities and all that jazz just to find that the projector bulb was burned out or the class computer would not start after a recent software update? Or maybe you were excited to use this new tool with your students only to find that you could not get it to work? (No, we would not be speaking from experience, of course!) In all seriousness, however, technology fails are a part of teaching—a very frustrating part, for us and for the students. In this section, we explore a few strategies that can help us minimize the disruption associated with technology fails.

First, as we prepare for a class session, we should consider how we might adapt a lesson if technology fails. Unless there is a quick fix, time that is dedicated to problem-solving technology issues in the classroom takes away from our students' learning experience. Having a low-tech or no-tech backup plan in case technology fails during a course meeting can help us keep our students engaged. For example, if you cannot project a visual, maybe students can pull it up on their phones or laptop instead. If the classroom response system (aka clickers) does not work, ask students to write down their responses and then discuss them in small groups before reporting out to the class. We may even find our new favorite activity by making these emergency adaptations to our original plan.

Second, we must familiarize ourselves with any technologies used for teaching to ensure we can confidently navigate the tool and complete basic troubleshooting. The 2017 ECAR faculty survey found that a considerable number of faculty believe that "they could be more effective instructors if they were better skilled at integrating various technologies into their courses" (Pomerantz & Brooks, 2017, p. 7). As we plan our courses, we know that each technology used presents a learning curve for us and our students. If we choose to integrate technology into our classrooms, not only do we need to be able to operate it efficiently and effectively but we also need to be sufficiently fluent in its use to provide basic training and troubleshooting for our students. Even when external tutorials and support are available, we must invest the time to get to know the tool. Depending on our personal context, this can be a significant barrier to overcome and may prompt us to stick with familiar tools rather than trying new options. That is okay. If we consistently fumble through the integration of a technology we did not have time to explore fully, we create a frustrating experience for ourselves and our students. It is okay to postpone exploring interesting technology options until we can commit time to learning how to use them well. That said, for many of us, there are a few technologies, such as the LMS or presentation software, we need to familiarize ourselves with sooner rather than later, as we may be required by institutional policies to use them for certain aspects of our instructional practice.

Train Students to Use Instructional Technology and Provide Support

While it is important for us to be comfortable with the functionalities and navigation of technology tools used in our courses, it is also important for students to be able to efficiently navigate technology they need to access course content or complete assignments (Cochrane, 2010; Quality Matters, 2018). Research shows that students with higher computer self-efficacy (remember that self-efficacy describes an individual's belief in his or her ability to successfully complete a task) "consistently demonstrate greater self-regulation and achievement in computer-mediated learning environments" (Maymon et al., 2018, p. 2). These findings underline the importance of providing explicit instructions and support for helping students develop confidence in their ability to complete tasks that ask them to use technology. If we want students to use a tool for the purpose of learning and assessment in our course, we need to provide the necessary guidance, training, and support that allows them to do so with as little frustration as possible, especially knowing that all of us, including our students, have limited time and any time spent on figuring out how to operate the technology in our course is time that is no longer available to actually complete the task.

While we need to be able to navigate the technology and support students in basic troubleshooting ourselves, not all training or guidance has to come from us. The Quality Matters (QM) *Course Design Rubric Standards* (2018) requires that all courses earning the QM certification provide students with instructions that "articulate or link to a clear description of the technical support offered and how to obtain it" (p. 36). This requirement confirms the importance of making technical support available, but our primary responsibility is to clearly describe how students can access this support, whether through campus or vendor resources. In addition to pointing students toward available tech support, we may want to plan a basic introduction to a new technology to be presented in the classroom or in a quick video—this can be especially important if the way we use a tool differs from the ordinary use or we only want students to complete a very specific task. It can be helpful to first use a tool for a low-stakes assignment; this allows us to identify any challenges with the tool and allows students to ask questions they might have early on.

Consider Pedagogical Needs Relevant to Instructional Modality

Even though technology has a place in all classrooms across instructional modalities, how and why we integrate it will vary slightly whether we incorporate it to enrich F2F teaching or rely on it exclusively for fully online courses. The more we shift from synchronous and F2F modalities to asynchronous online modalities of instruction, the more up-front guidance we must provide to support students' learning and success. As you know by now, in all instructional modalities we should intentionally align materials and tools to intended outcomes, make efforts to create a community that is inclusive of all learners, provide opportunities for learners to actively engage in the learning experience, and include regular check-ins to assess students' progress and provide feedback. Technology provides us with tools we can use to optimize the learning experience in all these behavioral categories, but to do so effectively we must let pedagogical considerations drive our implementation of these tools. Before exploring differing pedagogical needs of the diverse modalities, we want to take a moment to provide a brief overview of some of the most common instructional formats.

- Traditional F2F instruction generally refers to instruction that happens in a physical classroom where students and teachers are synchronously present in the same space at the same time. Traditionally, F2F instruction has focused on lecture presentations, although more and more instructors incorporate active learning elements such as polling, group work, and so on (Center for Excellence in Learning and Teaching, n.d.).
- In flipped instruction, students engage with content prior to the class meeting (e.g., watching a prerecorded lecture, reading a textbook, etc.). In the classroom or group space, students then apply this information to complete higher order learning activities (e.g., case studies, simulations, problem sets, or activities that would traditionally be assigned as homework, etc.). Online activities generally do not replace F2F time but prepare students to fully engage in application and expansion tasks during class meetings (O'Flaherty & Phillips, 2015; Talbert, 2017; Vidic & Clark, 2016). Flipped is one specific form of blended instruction, or instruction combining F2F and online components.
- Hybrid instruction also combines F2F and online components. In this modality,

students complete a significant amount of learning activities online in their own time (asynchronously), and time spent in a classroom is reduced (Garnham & Kaleta, 2002). Asynchronous online and synchronous classroom teaching and learning activities "are fused in a way that capitalizes on the strengths of each" (Garrison & Vaughan, 2013, p. 24). Ideally, that means that students in a hybrid course are experiencing active and engaged learning in the classroom and online and that activities and information from each modality are well connected (Linder, 2016; Tucker, 2018).

- Fully online instruction uses the internet for all components of learning including delivering content, engaging students, and assessing learning. All content and activities are intentionally designed in advance to be delivered fully online in a way that promotes effective interactions between learners, instructors, and content (Bates, 2016, 2019; Mathes, 2020; Nilson & Goodson, 2018).

While the critical teaching behaviors we have explored so far—Align, Include, Engage, Assess—are relevant to all modalities, each modality also has unique needs and provides us with distinct opportunities to leverage technology for good teaching. Table 5.4 presents considerations for leveraging technology across modalities to effectively enact other critical teaching behavior.

The table focuses on ideas for effective integration of technology across modalities in the context of the critical teaching behaviors; more comprehensive models such as the OLC *OSCQR Course Design Review Scorecard* (Online Learning Consortium, n.d.)—a scorecard based on the Suny Online Course Quality Rubric (OSCQR), OLC *Quality Scorecard for Blended Learning Programs* (Online Learning Consortium, 2015), and Quality Matters *Course Design Rubric Standards* (Quality Matters, 2018) are available to help us assess the quality of our online or hybrid course design. These tools can be a wonderful resource to ensure that a course that integrates technology meets widely accepted, research-based standards and while these tools are targeted for use with online or hybrid courses, many instructors who significantly integrate technology into a F2F course have also found them to be a useful resource in identifying good practices for setting up an effective course.

Ensure Materials and Tools Meet Legal Requirements

Beyond careful and intentional planning to maximize technology's potential to engage students, ensuring technology tools and digital materials are integrated keeping all applicable legal requirements in mind is an essential step to avoid potential repercussions for ourselves, our students, and our institutions. Some of the legal requirements to consider include regulations guiding the accessibility of content and laws protecting the privacy of students' educational records, as well as copyright rules; we briefly address each of these areas in the following.

Accessibility

Technology has the potential to increase accessibility in multiple ways. For instance, technology can be leveraged to reduce limitations of time and space that otherwise might prevent a number of students from participating fully in the learning experience or enrolling in higher education at all. However, this is only possible if we ensure all materials are accessible to all students. As we presented in more detail in chapter 2, "Include," creating accessible course materials and learning opportunities is required by law. The Americans with Disabilities Act and the Rehabilitation Act require institutions that receive federal funding to ensure that "no otherwise qualified individual with a disability in the United States [shall] be excluded from the participation in, be denied the benefits of, or be subjected to discrimination" (Section 504 of the Rehabilitation Act, 1973, para. 1) and that diverse learners have equivalent access to digital course materials including text, media, and learning activities (Section 508 of the Rehabilitation Act, 1973). We encourage you to refer to this section in chapter 2 for specific information on ensuring accessibility of online materials. Here it is important to note, however, that these requirements are in effect for all technologies we use. For example, whether we ask students to watch a video on YouTube, our LMS, or embedded in an interactive presentation tool, we must ensure that the video is captioned or includes a transcript. As you investigate the technologies you plan to use in your course, make sure to inquire about accessibility features to guide your decisions about whether to adopt a tool for your course.

TABLE 5.4: Leveraging Technology for Good Teaching Across Modalities

Behavior	F2F	Flipped	Hybrid	Online
Align	• Select technology aligned with learning outcomes to support and optimize the learning experience.			
		• Determine what content and activities are better suited to online versus F2F modality; generally it is preferable to use the online space for students' first engagement with new materials so that meeting time can be used to guide students through answering higher order questions and application tasks. • Plan classroom activities so that they connect to and build on the online materials and activities rather than review materials students prepared outside of class (Asarta & Schmidt, 2015).		
Include	• Provide access to technical support; this is important any time students complete asynchronous activity using technology tools, but especially in courses with more significant online components.			
			• Pay extra attention to clear and frequent communication as students rely heavily on the static instructions we provide and responses to student questions posted through electronic media may be delayed. • Plan low-stakes assignments that allow students to get to know each other and foster community through collaboration.	
				• Get to know your students personally and allow them to get to know you through video introduction, personal phone call, and so on.
Engage	• Share information (e.g., videos, readings, etc.) with students; for material students prepare outside the classroom, ensure expectations are reasonable in terms of complexity and workload. • Share information in multimedia formats.			
		• Engage students in class, with online quizzes, polls, collaborative assignments such as cocreation of documents, and so on. • Dedicate time to answering student questions and concerns about asynchronous preparation of materials but do not reteach the entire content.		
			• Develop interactivity in the online environment through integration of active learning tasks and collaborative assignments such as self-assessment quizzes, discussion boards, collaborative creation of materials, and so on.	

Behavior	F2F	Flipped	Hybrid	Online
Assess	• Collect, grade, and provide feedback on assignments using the LMS tools. • Plan low-stakes assignments that allow students to become familiar with technology tools used for summative assessments. • Create autograded self-assessment quizzes students can use at any time to test their understanding.			
		• Assign formative assessment tasks (e.g., online quiz, learning journal, etc.) to check in on students' understanding of new content prior to class meetings.		

Note. Informed by Asarta & Schmidt, 2015; Linder, 2016; Nilson & Goodson, 2018; Stavredes, 2011; Talbert, 2017.

Family Educational Rights and Privacy Act

The Family Educational Rights and Privacy Act (FERPA) is a federal law that protects the privacy of student education records. Generally, schools and school officials (in this case instructors) must have written permission from a student (or their parent/guardian in case the student is not yet 18 years old) in order to release any information from a student's education record (U.S. Department of Education, 2021); this also applies to sharing information with parents of students who are older than 18. In the context of day-to-day teaching, we need to consider FERPA particularly when it comes to computerized record-keeping and sharing student grades electronically; in either case, we must ensure that we do so in a way that protects the confidentiality of those records. Some technology tools offer autograding options and therefore store student grade data. Using your campus-approved technologies ensures that any such tool meets FERPA regulations by adequately protecting access to student grades in the event of a data breach. Because many tools also ask for personal information that could result in identity theft if leaked, like birthday, email, phone number, and address, we should always ensure that the technology we want to use protects all user data in compliance with campus policies, not just FERPA-related data.

Copyright

When sharing materials with our students we must ensure we observe copyright restrictions and requirements. In the traditional classroom, or F2F instruction, all performances and displays of a legally acquired work are allowed. Even when we share materials outside of the traditional classroom, the Technology, Education and Copyright Harmonization (TEACH) act and fair use exceptions to copyright still allow us to limited use of many copyrighted materials without obtaining permission as long as the use can be considered fair. The Purdue University Copyright Office (n.d.) provides an excellent and easy to use fair use analysis tool (www.lib.purdue.edu/uco/fair-use) that can serve as a starting point to evaluate whether you are legally allowed to share copyrighted materials with your students. However, we also recommend checking with local campus resources such as the library for additional guidance.

The benefits and challenges associated with instructional technology seem best summarized in the observation that "technology can amplify great teaching, but great technology cannot replace poor teaching" (OECD, 2015, p. 4). In other words, educational technology offers many opportunities, including "the potential to make teaching and learning processes more intensive, improve student self-regulation and self-efficacy, increase participation and involvement in courses as well as the wider university community, and predict increased student engagement" (Bond et al., 2020, p. 2). Integrating technology challenges us to advance our pedagogical skills so we are able to use selected tools to their full potential.

While the rapidly changing landscape of instructional technology can make it difficult to keep up with new tools and research findings on their best use for teaching, we recommend identifying and using resources on your campus that can help with this. Instructional technologists and other teaching and learning experts are doing this work on a daily basis and are a fantastic resource for information on best practices as well as training and support for using the tools available to you. Your investment into building skills and knowledge supports what you do in the classroom and serves as an important scaffold for effectively integrating technology in the design and delivery of a course. The benefits associated with responsible and intentional integration of technology justify investing time into building a repertoire of educational strategies that leverage technology tools to enhance student learning and promote engagement.

What Do We Do?

The best ways to integrate technology and the most appropriate tools to use will differ depending on course type, format, and size as well as instructors' teaching preferences. However, research tells us that there are some cross-disciplinary best practices related to implementing technology. In this chapter, we aggregated extensive research on these best practices into critical teaching behaviors that indicate specific actions you

can take to design and deliver learning experiences that effectively integrate technology in the classroom (F2F, hybrid, online, etc.) to support student learning. During the design phase you make important decisions regarding the learning outcomes and structure of your course; you determine tools and assessments that will support your students in developing knowledge and skills and help them demonstrate their learning through specific, measurable actions. The delivery of a course includes any interactions with students through presentations, activities, feedback, and so on. Critical teaching behaviors that support the effective integration of technology span both components of teaching practice.

In both the design and delivery of instruction that integrates and leverages technology, the critical teaching behaviors outlined in this chapter provide us with guidelines for making decisions that are driven by an interest in maximizing student learning and supporting our students in the achievement of the course learning outcomes; Table 5.5 presents a concise summary of behaviors and outlines step by step strategies to guide implementation of technology tools for instructional purposes.

TABLE 5.5: Integrate Technology: Critical Teaching Behaviors in Practice

Behavior	Step by Step
Select limited technologies from available options to enhance student learning and meet outcomes	• Keep learning outcomes in mind when deciding how to best integrate technology into courses. Does the technology support (rather than drive) learning? • Consider disciplinary context to select appropriate and relevant technologies (e.g., What tech tools will students use as professionals in their field to complete tasks?). • Determine the level of technology integration you are comfortable with and the depth of engagement you desire for your students (SAMR, PICRAT models can help). These can vary from activity to activity. • Ensure technology used for activities and assignments is well integrated into course and clearly linked to course outcomes to avoid student disengagement as activities can be perceived as busywork.
Leverage technology to increase access, facilitate ease of use, and optimize the student learning experience	• Apply pedagogical knowledge to designing content delivery and learning activities when teaching with technology in F2F course and online. • Take advantage of pedagogical research and SoTL to learn more about benefits and challenges of different instructional technologies as well as implementation examples. • Be attentive to consistency and transparency in the organization of online learning components (in the LMS) to facilitate access and ease of use for all students. • Create modules or learning units to present information in a consistent and transparent manner from week to week. Files and materials that are poorly organized can make it difficult and frustrating for students to find the resources they need, presenting a barrier to their learning.

Behavior	Step by Step
	• Use multimodal course media, including written text, audio, video, and visuals, to provide multiple means of engagement. • During class meetings, leverage technology, including students' personal devices, to foster engagement with content and peers. • Involve students in the creation of acceptable use expectations for personal devices that are inclusive but minimize distraction.
Use technology effectively and efficiently	• Familiarize yourself with any technologies used for teaching to ensure confident navigation and ability to support students in using the technology tools for learning. • Have a backup plan for instruction in case technology fails. Time that is dedicated to problem-solving in the classroom takes away from our students' learning experience. • Present materials in a clear and well-organized manner. Consider providing an outline of what to expect, incorporating guiding questions that emphasize the main concepts, and so on.
Train students to use instructional technology and provide basic support	• Provide support (e.g., in-class training, self-paced tutorials, etc.) to help students use technology confidently and efficiently. Just like us, students face a learning curve when using technology tools. When we ask students to use technology, it is important that we provide the resources and support necessary to turn technology into a tool for advancing learning rather than a barrier to completing the task. • Check with students on whether they can access all course materials; this can include verifying that information presented on a screen or whiteboard is visible and legible for all students. • Limit the number of different technologies used in a course and leverage institutional tools, such as the LMS, that students will use in multiple courses to support the development of students' self-efficacy and efficient use of technology for learning.
Consider pedagogical needs relevant to instructional modality	• Investigate the expectations associated with different instructional modalities at your institution and identify the advantages and limitations of the instructional modality. • Evaluate which materials and activities are best completed by students on their own time (e.g., self-paced online activities) and which should take place during synchronous or on-campus class meetings. Be strategic about using online and on-campus spaces to maximize engagement. • Consider leveraging technology to help students prepare introductory materials before class meetings to free up time for application and practice tasks, which often require higher order thinking and benefit from instructor guidance. • Implement good teaching practices most appropriate to instructional modality.
Ensure materials and tools meet legal requirements	• Guidelines for creating accessible materials are widely available, including, for example, in a Penn State resource (Accessibility and Usability at Penn State: Website Accessibility). • Verify that web pages are following responsive design principles, which facilitate the viewing of pages and documents on a range of devices with different screen sizes. • Make sure to meet all FERPA, cybersecurity, and copyright requirements. • Understand why institutionally approved technology matters. • See chapter 2 for additional ideas on creating inclusive and accessible course materials and activities.

What Do We Show?

There are many ways to document our efforts to effectively integrate technology into our teaching. In addition to feedback from students (e.g., midterm feedback, end-of-course evaluations, unsolicited comments) related to technology, we can solicit feedback from our peers through course review and teaching observations that could be conducted by departmental colleagues, centers for teaching and learning, or—more

formally—by external entities such as Quality Matters. When we intentionally approach the task of integrating technology, we will produce a range of artifacts that document our efforts, which can be combined with strategic annotations and data collected in our courses to showcase our effectiveness. In addition, materials we create for our courses can also serve as evidence of our effectiveness. Table 5.6 provides an overview of the materials we may gather and how they can showcase effective integration of technology.

TABLE 5.6: Documenting Integration of Technology	
Teaching Materials *Provide short annotations for materials to focus attention on the critical teaching behavior(s) you want to showcase.*	
Activity or task instructions or prompt	When technology is used to complete course assignments, prompts should include guidance on how to use the technology (especially if students are using it for the first time). Guidance can be a short video, a step-by-step overview, or even a link to an existing tutorial. When sharing this type of material, consider explicitly stating how and why technology is used to support learning outcomes for the assignment and course.
Examples or screenshots of activities conducted through technology	Specific examples or screenshots of technology facilitated activities you integrate into your classroom are another option to showcase implementation. Annotate these examples to explicitly state learning outcomes you wanted to achieve and how the example demonstrates student learning achievements.
Instructional units focused on the development of technology and/or digital literacy skills	In addition to serving as an instructional tool, development of technology skills and/or digital literacy can be the intended outcome of a course or lesson. You may create custom tutorial videos or written instructions to support your students. These can be especially useful if you are using the technology in a unique way.
Instructor-created media (text, video, audio, etc.) or online learning units	Creating learning materials takes time. If we record instructional videos, create interactive course pages, or develop other forms of multimedia materials for our course, it may be worth showcasing and reflecting on the result of this work.
Lesson plans	Instructors use technology during class meetings for a range of purposes; lesson plans can allow us to showcase integration of technology and explain the goals we are pursuing through the technology tools used.
Syllabus	The course syllabus is a great place to introduce students to the technologies used for learning in your course. Consider including a technology statement that describes the integration of technology and its relevance for the course. An accessibility statement can inform students about technology tools used and accessibility measures put into place to support their learning.

Materials From Others	
Provide short annotations for any materials you include to emphasize how the feedback and training has impacted your instructional practices.	
Peer feedback and/or observation	Ask your observer to note examples of integrating technology in your teaching presentation and materials. Be sure to give your observer access to any technology you are using to ensure they have the option to explore and experience the tools you use for themselves. Especially in fully online courses, a peer observation may take the form of course material review, although this type of feedback can be helpful for any instructor. Material reviews are similar to a classroom observation as you ask a peer or teaching expert (e.g., your campus teaching center colleagues) to review specific materials or learning units and provide feedback.
Student feedback	As stated previously, students benefit from the integration of technology as it can increase access and self-directed learning. Students can provide targeted feedback on their experience in your class through formal and informal feedback. • *CTB midterm feedback.* The CTB midterm feedback survey includes questions that specifically solicit your students' feedback on integration of technology in your course. • *Select end-of-term surveys.* Questions related to technology use are sometimes part of end-of term student surveys. If no question related to assessment is included on the survey used in your institution, you may be able to add a custom question or facilitate your own survey.

Reflection Questions

1. What pedagogical goals (see Table 5.1) are you most interested to accomplish by integrating technology tools in your instruction? Which technology options are most appropriate for accomplishing these goals?

2. How will you facilitate navigation and ease of use of the tools you select? What instructions and other resources will you provide to guide students' use of these tools?

3. What specific needs related to the instructional modality of your course do you need to consider? How will you use technology to include, engage, and assess students in your course?

4. What resources are available to you at your institution to make technology decisions (including but not limited to legal considerations) and get support with its implementation?

References

Al-Furaih, S. A. A., & Al-Awidi, H. M. (2021). Fear of missing out (FoMO) among undergraduate students in relation to attention distraction and learning disengagement in lectures. *Education and Information Technologies*, *26*(2), 2355–2373. https://doi.org/10.1007/s10639-020-10361-7

Alpert, F., & Hodkinson, C. S. (2019). Video use in lecture classes: Current practices, student perceptions and preferences. *Education & Training*, *61*(1), 31–45. https://doi.org/10.1108/ET-12-2017-0185

Anderson, T. (2003). Getting the mix right again: An updated and theoretical rationale for interaction. *International Review of Research in Open and Distance Learning*, *4*(2). https://www.proquest.com/docview/1634543750/abstract/890BBF41FD044109PQ/1

Anshari, M., Almunawar, M. N., Shahrill, M., Wicaksono, D. K., & Huda, M. (2017). Smartphones usage in the classrooms: Learning aid or interference? *Education and*

Information Technologies, 22(6), 3063–3079. https://doi-org.ezproxy.libproxy.db.erau.edu/10.1007/s10639-017-9572-7

Asarta, C. J., & Schmidt, J. R. (2015). The choice of reduced seat time in a blended course. *The Internet and Higher Education, 27*, 24–31. https://doi.org/10.1016/j.iheduc.2015.04.006

Balakrishnan, A., Puthean, S., Satheesh, G., Unnikrishnan, M. K., Rashid, M., Nair, S., & Thunga, G. (2021). Effectiveness of blended learning in pharmacy education: A systematic review and meta-analysis. *PLoS ONE, 16*(6), Article e0252461. https://doi.org/10.1371/journal.pone.0252461

Bates, A. W. (2016, July 16). *Online learning for beginners: 1. What is online learning?* https://www.tonybates.ca/2016/07/15/online-learning-for-beginners-1-what-is-online-learning/

Bates, A. W. (2019). *Teaching in a digital age* (2nd ed.). Tony Bates Associates. https://pressbooks.bccampus.ca/teachinginadigitalagev2/

Bond, M., Buntins, K., Bedenlier, S., Zawacki-Richter, O., & Kerres, M. (2020). Mapping research in student engagement and educational technology in higher education: A systematic evidence map. *International Journal of Educational Technology in Higher Education, 17*(1), 1–30. https://doi.org/10.1186/s41239-019-0176-8

Brooks, D. C., & Pomerantz, J. (2017). *ECAR study of undergraduate students and information technology, 2017* [Research report]. ECAR. https://library.educause.edu/resources/2017/10/ecar-study-of-undergraduate-students-and-information-technology-2017

CAST. (2018). *Universal design for learning guidelines version 2.2.* http://udlguidelines.cast.org

Center for Excellence in Learning and Teaching. (n.d.). *Traditional face-to-face.* Iowa State University. https://www.celt.iastate.edu/instructional-strategies/teaching-format/traditional-face-to-face/

Cochrane, T. D. (2010). Exploring mobile learning success factors. *ALT-J: Research in Learning Technology, 18*(2), 133–148. https://doi.org/10.1080/09687769.2010.494718

Costa, K. (2020). *99 tips for creating simple and sustainable educational videos: A guide for online teachers and flipped classes.* Stylus.

Daiute, C., & Morse, F. (1994). Access to knowledge and expression: Multimedia writing tools for students with diverse needs and strengths. *Journal of Special Education Technology, 12*(3), 221–256. https://doi.org/10.1177/016264349401200305

de Witt, C., & Gloerfeld, C. (2017). Mobile learning and higher education. In D. Kergel, B. Heidkamp, P. Kjaersdam Telléus, T. Rachwal, & S. Nowakowski (Eds.), *The digital turn in higher education* (pp. 61–79). Springer Fachmedien Wiesbaden. https://doi.org/10.1007/978-3-658-19925-8_6

Duderstadt, J., Atkins, D., & Houweling, D. (2002). *Higher education in the digital age: Technology issues and strategies for American colleges and universities.* Praeger.

Fernandez, S. (2018). University student's perspectives on using cell phones in classrooms—Are they dialing up disaster? *Turkish Online Journal of Educational Technology—TOJET, 17*(1), 246–258.

Fiorella, L. (2021). Multimedia learning with instructional video. In R. E. Mayer & L. Fiorella (Eds.), *The Cambridge handbook of multimedia learning* (pp. 487–497). Cambridge University Press. https://doi.org/10.1017/9781108894333.050

France, P. E. (2018, October 18). *What the SAMR model may be missing.* EdSurge. https://www.edsurge.com/news/2018-10-18-what-the-samr-model-may-be-missing

Galanek, J. D., Gierdowski, D. C., & Brooks, D. C. (2018). *ECAR study of undergraduate students and information technology, 2018* [Research report]. ECAR. https://library.educause.edu/-/media/files/library/2018/10/studentitstudy2018.pdf?la=en

Garnham, C., & Kaleta, R. (2002). Lessons learned from the Hybrid Course Project. *Teaching With Technology Today, 6*(33). https://hcclearning.files.wordpress.com/2010/09/lessons-learned-from-the-hybrid-course-project.pdf

Garrison, D. R., & Vaughan, N. D. (2013). Institutional change and leadership associated with blended learning innovation: Two case studies. *The Internet and Higher Education, 18*, 24–28. https://doi.org/10.1016/j.iheduc.2012.09.001

Geri, N., Winer, A., & Zaks, B. (2017). A learning analytics approach for evaluating the impact of interactivity in online video lectures on the attention span of students. *Interdisciplinary Journal of E-Skills and Lifelong Learning, 13*, 215–228. https://doi.org/10.28945/3875

Gierdowski, D. C. (2019). *ECAR study of undergraduate students and information technology, 2019* [Research report]. ECAR. https://library.educause.edu/resources/2019/10/2019-study-of-undergraduate-students-and-information-technology

Gierdowski, D. C., Brooks, D. C., & Galanek, J. D. (2020). *EDUCAUSE 2020 student technology report: Supporting the whole student.* EDUCAUSE Research. https://www.educause.edu/ecar/research-publications/student-technology-report-supporting-the-whole-student/2020/introduction

Gierdowski, D. C., & Galanek, J. D. (2020). *ECAR study of the technology needs of students with disabilities, 2020.* ECAR. https://er.educause.edu/blogs/2020/6/ecar-study-of-the-technology-needs-of-students-with-disabilities-2020

Jenkins, J. L., Durcikova, A., & Burns, M. B. (2013). Simplicity is bliss: Controlling extraneous cognitive load in online security training to promote secure behavior. *Journal of Organizational and End User Computing, 25*(3), 52–67. https://doi.org/10.4018/joeuc.2013070104

Kimmons, R., Graham, C. R., & West, R. E. (2020). The PICRAT model for technology integration in teacher preparation. *Contemporary Issues in Technology and Teacher Education* (CITE Journal), *20*(1).

Koehler, M., & Mishra, P. (2009). What is technological pedagogical content knowledge (TPACK)? *Contemporary Issues in Technology and Teacher Education, 9*(1), 60–70.

Langmia, K., & Glass, A. (2014). Coping with smart phone "distractions" in a college classroom. *Teaching Journalism & Mass Communication, 4*(1), 13–23.

Linder, K. E. (2016). *The blended course design workbook: A practical guide.* Stylus.

Mathes, J. (2020, April 13). *A defining moment for online learning.* OLC. https://onlinelearningconsortium.org/a-defining-moment-for-online-learning/

Mayer, R. E., & Fiorella, L. (2021). Introduction to multimedia learning. In L. Fiorella & R. E. Mayer (Eds.), *The Cambridge handbook of multimedia learning* (3rd ed., pp. 3–16). Cambridge University Press. https://doi.org/10.1017/9781108894333.003

Maymon, R., Hall, N. C., & Goetz, T. D. (2018, November 7). When academic technology fails: Effects of students' attributions for computing difficulties on emotions and achievement. *The Social Sciences.* Advance online publication. https://api.semanticscholar.org/CorpusID:150042997

Means, B., Toyama, Y., Murphy, R., & Baki, M. (2013). The effectiveness of online and blended learning: A meta-analysis of the empirical literature. *Teachers College Record, 115*(3), 1–47. https://doi.org/10.1177/016146811311500307

Mueller, P. A., & Oppenheimer, D. M. (2014). The pen is mightier than the keyboard: Advantages of longhand over laptop note taking. *Psychological Science, 25*(6), 1159–1168. https://doi.org/10.1177/0956797614524581

Nilson, L. B., & Goodson, L. A. (2018). *Online teaching at its best: Merging instructional design with teaching and learning research.* Jossey-Bass.

Office of Educational Technology. (2017). *Reimagining the role of technology in higher education. A supplement to the National Education Technology Plan.* U.S. Department of Education.

O'Flaherty, J., & Phillips, C. (2015). The use of flipped classrooms in higher education: A scoping review. *The Internet and Higher Education, 25,* 85–95. https://doi.org/10.1016/j.iheduc.2015.02.002

Online Learning Consortium. (n.d.). *OSCQR course design review scorecard.* https://onlinelearningconsortium.org/consult/oscqr-course-design-review/

Online Learning Consortium. (2015). *Quality scorecard for blended learning programs.* https://onlinelearningconsortium.org/consult/olc-quality-scorecard-blended-learning-programs/

Organization for Economic Co-operation and Development. (2015). *Students, computers and learning: Making the connection.* https://doi.org/10.1787/9789264239555-en

Paas, F., & Sweller, J. (2021). Implications of cognitive load theory for multimedia learning. In L. Fiorella & R. E. Mayer (Eds.), *The Cambridge handbook of multimedia learning* (3rd ed., pp. 73–81). Cambridge University Press. https://doi.org/10.1017/9781108894333.009

Patterson, N., Rasua, R. T., Hobbs, M., Wood-Bradley, G., Currey, J., & Lanham, E. (2019, August 15–16). *Chunked lectures: A new model for conducting online lectures within information technology higher education* [Paper presentation]. EAISR International Academic Conferences Proceedings, Berlin, Germany. https://arxiv.org/pdf/1909.03041.pdf

Pomerantz, J., & Brooks, D. C. (2017). *ECAR study of faculty and information technology, 2017* [Research report]. ECAR. https://library.educause.edu/-/media/files/library/2017/10/facultyitstudy2017.pdf

Puentedura, R. R. (2015). SAMR: A brief introduction. *Hippasus.* http://hippasus.com/blog/archives/227

Purdue University Copyright Office. (n.d.). *Fair use.* https://www.lib.purdue.edu/uco/fair-use

Quality Matters. (2018). *Course design rubric standards.* https://www.qualitymatters.org/qa-resources/rubric-standards/higher-ed-rubric

Ravizza, S. M., Uitvlugt, M. G., & Fenn, K. M. (2017). Logged in and zoned out: How laptop internet use relates to classroom learning. *Psychological Science, 28*(2), 171–180. https://doi.org/10.1177/0956797616677314

Robert, J. (2022, October 3). *Modality preferences. 2022 students and technology report: Rebalancing the student experience.* EDUCAUSE. https://www.educause.edu/ecar/research-publications/2022/students-and-technology-report-rebalancing-the-student-experience/modality-preferences

Robinson, C. C., & Hullinger, H. (2008). New benchmarks in higher education: Student engagement in online learning. *Journal of Education for Business, 84*(2), 101–109. https://doi.org/10.3200/JOEB.84.2.101-109

Schneckenberg, D. (2009). Understanding the real barriers to technology-enhanced innovation in higher education. *Educational Research, 51*(4), 411–424. https://doi.org/10.1080/00131880903354741

Section 504, Rehabilitation Act of 1973. (1973). U.S. Department of Labor. https://www.dol.gov/agencies/oasam/centers-offices/civil-rights-center/statutes/section-504-rehabilitation-act-of-1973

Section 508 of the Rehabilitation Act. (1973). Federal Communications Commission. https://www.fcc.gov/general/section-508-rehabilitation-act

Simonson, M., & Schlosser, C. (2004). We need a plan: An instructional design approach for distance education courses. *Distance Learning, 1*(4), 29–38.

Stavredes, T. (2011). *Effective online teaching: Foundations and strategies for student success.* Jossey-Bass.

Talbert, R. (2017). *Flipped learning: A guide for higher education faculty.* Stylus.

TechSmith. (2021, November 11). Video statistics, habits, and trends you need to know. *The TechSmith Blog.* https://www.techsmith.com/blog/video-statistics/

Tucker, C. (Host). (2018, October 8). *Catlin Tucker on blended learning on Apple podcasts* (Audio podcast no. 20). Vrain Waves. https://vrainwaves.simplecast.com/episodes/catlin-tucker-on-blended-learning-039ce6b8

Twum, R. (2017). Utilization of smartphones in science teaching and learning in selected universities in Ghana. *Journal of Education and Practice, 8*(7), 216–228.

U.S. Department of Education. (2021, August 25). Family Educational Rights and Privacy Act (FERPA) [Guide]. https://www2.ed.gov/policy/gen/guid/fpco/ferpa/index.html

Vidic, N. S., & Clark, R. M. (2016, June 26). *Comparison of a partially flipped vs. fully-flipped introductory probability and statistics course for engineers: Lessons learned* [Paper presentation]. 2016 ASEE Annual Conference & Exposition, New Orleans, LA, United States. https://216.185.13.174/comparison-of-a-partially-flipped-vs-fully-flipped-introductory-probability-and-statistics-course-for-engineers-lessons-learned

Waterhouse, S. (2005). *The power of eLearning: The essential guide for teaching in the digital age.* Pearson.

CHAPTER 6

Reflect

DEFINITION

Instructors who reflect gather feedback on their teaching from self-assessment, peers, and students to regularly identify opportunities for growth. They pursue improvements to their instruction through engagement with professional development and scholarship.

AT THE BEGINNING OF this book, we introduced the CTB diagram (Figure I.1) to help you understand how the individual CTB categories relate to each other. As we close our overview of the framework, we ask you to turn your attention to this diagram once again. Notice that "Reflect" encompasses all of the other categories. We made this choice because good teaching is a feedback loop powered by reflection on the impact of our behaviors on student learning. "Reflection," explains Jennifer Porter (2017), an executive coach, "gives the brain an opportunity to pause amidst the chaos, untangle and sort through observations and experiences, consider multiple possible interpretations, and create meaning. This meaning becomes learning, which can then inform future mindsets and actions" (p. 3). Effective reflection distills our teaching experiences into learning and focuses our efforts by allowing us to identify existing strengths as well as areas for growth. The process requires us to take stock of where we currently are (present), how we got there (past), and where we want to go (future); done correctly, reflection will also be informed by external data and perspectives, not simply our own ruminations. This kind of reflection helps us make informed decisions about changes we need to make to our teaching, professional development we would like to pursue, scholarship we want to read, innovations we will implement, or findings we want to share, thereby enabling us to hone our skills over the course of our careers to become better instructors.

Not all reflection is created equal, however, when it comes to better teaching. In their study of university instructors' reflection practices, McAlpine and Weston (2000) ask, "Does better teaching knowledge lead to better teaching?" "Not necessarily," they conclude (p. 375). A basic experience of teaching and knowledge of pedagogy provide an essential foundation for instructor growth, but McAlpine and Weston found that neither reflecting on experience nor increasing pedagogical knowledge alone leads to better teaching. For you as the reader of this book, this finding means that you could study each of the critical teaching behaviors without necessarily improving your teaching or seeing any gains in student learning. Productive reflection supplies the missing piece of the "good" teaching puzzle. To ensure that your time is well spent when engaging in this critical teaching behavior, we devote this chapter to the benefits of reflective teaching and best practices for effective reflection.

What Do We Know?

Reflection is how we transform experience into learning, which makes it an essential component of a good teacher's tool kit (Boud et al., 1985; Sternberg & Horvath, 1995). McAlpine and Weston (2000) explain that this kind of "reflection requires linking existing knowledge to an analysis of the relationship between current experience and future actions or applications. . . . The outcome of the process of reflection is the building of or expansion of knowledge" (p. 374). In other words, effective reflection makes a connection between what you already know about teaching, either from experience or other learning, to an understanding of your current experience of teaching as well as future actions. By connecting past learning and experience with present and future, we learn and grow our knowledge of teaching. This process is also the most likely means of ensuring the permanency of any changes we make to our teaching as a result of learning. "Reflection as a way of learning," says Haras (2018), "works especially well for faculty who want to change their practice. . . . If the goal is to transform practice, then ongoing reflection is seminal to faculty professional development" (p. 4). We hope this gives insight into the purpose behind the reflection questions embedded at the end of each chapter (and the importance of completing them). The purpose of this book is to help you document your critical teaching behaviors, but we also want to help you "transform practice" by engaging in even more of these evidence-based behaviors. Reflection increases the likelihood that your learning will stick and that you will subsequently make meaningful changes to your teaching. For an overview of only some of the research-based benefits of reflection, see Table 6.1. In the sections that follow, we explore the characteristics of effective reflection practices.

Assess Personal Growth

Whether we intentionally collect and record them or not, we all experience spontaneous thoughts both during and outside of class about what is going well, what is not going well, why, and how these insights will impact our teaching in the future. Often our decisions about what to do in the learning environment spring from instinct, and instinct, when left unexplored, can be riddled with unstated assumptions and biases, both good and bad. When we encounter a bias or an assumption, we cannot responsibly set it aside and continue as we were. Instead, reflective practitioners make time to examine their biases, as we discuss at more length in the "Assess Personal Biases and Mitigate Their Potential Impact on Student Learning and Success" portion of chapter 2. We assess personal growth by regularly asking ourselves probing questions about our teaching and being honest in our answers to ferret out our biases. Asking superficial questions or failing to probe the veracity of our conclusions can lead us to dangerous and unproductive assumptions. Reflection that leads to growth does not simply stop at asking, "How do I teach, and how do my actions impact student learning?" The kind of reflection that qualifies as a critical teaching behavior asks the important why questions: "Why do I teach this way? Why does that behavior impact student learning in that way? Why do I respond this way to that type of student behavior?" It also asks forward-looking questions: "Now that I know, how will this affect my teaching? What changes will I make?"

Exploring all these questions at once can be overwhelming. In her book *Inspired College Teaching*, Weimer (2010) breaks reflective questioning into two steps. First, she advocates instructors focus on "what" questions by objectively observing what happens in their classrooms like scientists recording experimental data. Resist making judgments about why things happen and instead focus on collecting as much data as possible about what you do, how you do it, and what students do. We encourage you to use the critical teaching behaviors to help you identify and list your behaviors—we created them, in part, to simplify the reflection process for you. As we will discuss further in chapter 8 ("Peer Observation"), a CTB-aligned peer observation provides you an excellent opportunity to identify your own behaviors and discuss your reflections with a colleague who has also made notes on your teaching behaviors.

Once you have data to answer the "what" questions, you may move into the second stage of the process by asking "why" questions. "Why" questions require deeper investigation of your underlying assumptions,

TABLE 6.1: Benefits of Reflection

Reflection helps us make meaning out of our experiences, a process necessary for significant learning to occur in adult learners (Mezirow & Associates, 1990).

Critical reflection is a vital part of learning for adults. To learn and grow from experience, adults must first recognize their actions and unpack the values that underlie them. Adult learners can then examine, challenge, and change these values on the path to transforming their actions.

Reflection questions that prompt specific, internal explanations of events encourage people to develop a sense of personal responsibility for behavior, which can make them more likely to change their behaviors (Ellis et al., 2006).

If we want to develop a deeper sense of personal responsibility for our actions or coach others to do so, we should carefully select the questions we use to prompt reflection. Questions like "How did [insert instructor's specific action here] contribute to student behaviors, classroom climate, and so on?" or "How effective were your behaviors in this context?" encourage people to see themselves as the source of their successes and failures. When people see their actions as the cause leading to specific effects, whether positive or negative, they are more likely to feel a sense of control that leads them to make behavioral changes.

Reflection on failed experiences is more beneficial than reflection on successful experiences (Ellis et al., 2014).

Participants in this study learned most from reflecting both on what they did well and what they did poorly in moments of failure. Reflecting on what they did well after a success yielded little growth. Reflecting on what they did poorly after a success yielded some benefits. By far, however, reflecting on what they did well and poorly after a failure most improved learning outcomes in future tests. Encouraging participants first to think about what they did well in moments of failure seemed to foster a sense of psychological safety necessary to allow participants to think productively about behaviors that led to the failure.

Regular reflection helps turn thoughts and ideas into behavioral changes (Haras, 2018).

A study of reflective statements generated by participants in an Association of College and University Educators training indicated that regular reflections written throughout ongoing professional development experiences offer several benefits over reflections conducted only at the end of a long-term training experience. Specifically, spaced reflection allowed faculty to do the following:

- utilize classroom experience to contextualize new learning
- structure their growing teaching knowledge
- find personal meaning in the process of learning about teaching
- remain focused and intentional in their teaching development
- turn experience into knowledge
- make decisions about future action based on knowledge

Researchers noted that these benefits were more pronounced for individuals who engaged in repetitive training, feedback, and reflection cycles.

motivations, and goals as a teacher, which can make this an emotionally exhausting task. Thankfully, many institutions have instructional support units that often host faculty learning communities, book discussion groups, and other opportunities to engage in this kind of reflection with the support of other instructors undergoing the same process. If you do not have access to this type of support at your institution, consider looking for online instructor support groups that often spring up spontaneously through conferences or social media.

To help you capture your personal reflections as well as interrogate your previously undiscovered assumptions, consider keeping a course journal. This does not need to be a time-consuming activity to yield impactful results. Set aside 10–15 minutes after a class session or module to record your thoughts on what went well, what did not go well, why you think that might be the case, and changes you plan to make before you teach the lesson again. You might also limit the time you spend journaling by choosing to focus on one course per semester—a new prep, format, or modality; a course that has traditionally been difficult to teach; a course that has become boring to teach; a course to which you have made significant changes, and so on—rather than journaling about all courses you teach. Alternatively, you can journal thematically by selecting one of the CTB framework categories as your lens through which to filter your experience in the classroom. Journals can be written, typed, or recorded; the format of your journal should be convenient for your needs. Insights and extracts from these journals can be used for documentation purposes if you so choose. If you journal across your career, these artifacts can help you identify themes in and assess your growth over time.

External Perspectives on Teaching

Our thoughts about our own teaching form an important foundation for effective reflection. However, ours is not the only perspective, nor is it always the most useful perspective, from which we can reflect on our teaching. In fact, if we never consider perspectives beyond our own impressions of our teaching, we may begin to believe that we are the sole cause of everything that happens in our classrooms, both good and bad. Britzman (1991) found that beginning teachers, in particular, struggle because they assume what happens in the learning environment depends solely on them; when anything goes wrong, new teachers tend to blame themselves. Brookfield (1995) noted that instructors at all stages of their careers are susceptible to this kind of self-blame, but we must acknowledge the converse to be true as well: When we remain trapped in our personal perspectives about our teaching, we may more likely assume that students are to blame for struggles we face in the learning environment. Regardless of where we place the blame (or the credit), reflection conducted in a vacuum does not lead to better teaching because it "can never avoid the risks of denial and distortion" that follow from solitary rumination (Brookfield, 1995, p. 33). Beyond our own perceptions of our teaching, we should also intentionally seek external perspectives by soliciting peer and student feedback as well as scholarship encountered in professional development or research activities. We explore each of these perspectives briefly in the following.

Invite Feedback From Colleagues

Peer feedback usually requires preplanning, including a formal request for someone to observe a class/module(s). As a result, we might be less likely to collect peer feedback on a regular basis, yet our peers offer unique and important perspectives on our teaching. Peers can be instructors in your discipline, at your institution, or even at a different institution; they can also be pedagogy specialists in a center on campus. Although they are outsiders to our courses, peers bring their disciplinary and/or pedagogical expertise to bear on what they see happening in the learning environment. This external perspective can help us answer questions and make decisions about what to do in our courses when our self-assessments conflict with input we receive from students. Aside from offering solutions for and alternate understandings of what is happening in your learning environment, peers can affirm good practices and provide emotional support based on common experiences. In chapter 8, we talk about the CTB protocol for promoting productive peer observation experiences.

Solicit Student Feedback

Much like our personal insights, we continuously collect informal student feedback in the learning environment. Enthusiastic chatter, blank stares, assessment performance, and so on tell us much about how our teaching methods are impacting students, and we use this feedback to inform our self-assessment, perhaps deciding we need to do more of this and less of that. However, we may not always collect formal feedback about our teaching from students in their own words, or if we do, we wait to read students' comments in their end-of-semester evaluations when it is too late for us to address their feedback with them. Collecting midterm student feedback allows us to hear about our teaching from the student perspective and to be more responsive with our teaching techniques. Chapter 9 covers student feedback sessions and the aligned CTB instrument for gathering feedback in greater depth.

Engage With Scholarship and Professional Development Related to Teaching

When we encounter a question or problem in our chosen fields of study, we turn to the literature and experts. The same should be true when we encounter a question or problem in our teaching, yet because most of us in higher education are not trained in the field of pedagogy, we sometimes forget that we can consult external expertise on teaching as well. Reading the literature related to a teaching topic of interest can help us realize we are not alone in our classroom struggles; it can also yield insights and strategies we might never have considered. As the research on teaching and learning continues to expand, consulting the literature can inform our classroom practices and keep us on the cutting edge of effective teaching techniques. We might also investigate development opportunities offered by professional organizations and campus experts. Such trainings are usually led by pedagogy specialists who have condensed extensive reviews of literature on a topic into seminars of manageable length and content. If, like most faculty, you find yourself pressed for time, professional development sessions related to teaching can be a time-effective means of learning more about a pedagogical topic while gaining a new perspective on your teaching practices.

Each of these four perspectives enriches our reflection on teaching by providing missing pieces of the teaching and learning puzzle. While each perspective is essential to improving our teaching, reflection begins and ends with self-exploration. Once we gather and analyze the external data on our teaching, we return to the initial questioning introduced previously. Reflection is an iterative process; this means that questioning should lead to data collection, which should inevitably lead to more questioning and data collection. In the process of answering questions about our teaching, we frequently find that we uncover just as many new questions as we do answers. This cycle of reflection can help keep teaching fresh and interesting as an object of inquiry while also helping us to continuously improve (and document our improvement) as instructors.

Plan for Personal Growth by Identifying Categories for Development and Setting Goals

Reflection is a messy process. To illustrate how reflecting on self-assessment and external perspectives can help us set goals and grow, consider the following scenario: You observe that students often do not respond to your questions in class. This observation in itself means nothing beyond a statement of fact based on behavior. Reflecting on the "why" that drives this type of interaction between you and your students helps you make meaning out of the pattern, but reflecting on the "why" without enough data could lead you to inaccurate conclusions based on unfounded assumptions. For instance, if you question your rapport with

students or lack confidence in yourself as a likable instructor, you might easily conclude that students do not answer your questions because they dislike you. At this juncture, you either accept this assumption as truth or you probe further into what led you to this conclusion, lacking any other concrete evidence of student dislike. Without challenging your assumptions, this type of conclusion might lead you to pander to students in the hopes that they will like you more or to be stricter and less tolerant in your interactions with students as a result of a growing bitterness toward them. Neither of these outcomes will lead to better teaching or learning.

If we engage in the reflection cycle introduced previously—self-assessment informed by external perspectives—we might reach a vastly different conclusion to our classroom silence scenario. When you identify this trend in student behavior, you step back to observe your own behaviors in these moments and make a plan to gather additional data. You invite a colleague to observe your class and provide feedback on this specific issue to help you gain a more objective perspective. Next you decide to collect input from students by asking a colleague to perform a student feedback session or by gathering anonymous feedback through an electronic form. Finally, you seek out research on what prevents students from responding to questions in class. Having gathered your data, you now proceed to consider the question of why students do not respond to your questions. Notice that the process outlined here incorporates each of the four perspectives introduced previously: self, peers, students, and scholarship. In collecting these data points, you become equipped with the multiple perspectives necessary to answer the "why" question effectively. You may discover that you tend to answer your own questions or to ask questions that students need more time to think about. As you consider why you answer your own questions instead of giving students enough time to think, you realize you feel uncomfortable with silence in the classroom (as most of us do). You use your review of research to help you identify strategies you can implement to become more comfortable with silence and allow students time to think and develop confidence in their answers. Since you are in the middle of the semester and need something quick and easy to implement, you decide to incorporate think-pair-share activities before asking students to answer a question in class. Through this process of reflection, you discover insights about yourself and your students as well as pedagogical strategies you can implement to help you overcome student silence and your own fears as a teacher. As you dive deeper into your initial question, you might develop follow-up questions based on the changes you make to your teaching (e.g., Does this think-pair-share activity really improve students' willingness and/or ability to answer my questions?). This reflection cycle can lead you to hone specific aspects of your teaching over time.

While we must learn to take an objective stance on our teaching if we are to develop effective reflection practices, nagging doubts and subjective responses to the "why" questions often crop up on their own, and they should not be ignored. In fact, identifying and probing these underlying assumptions is an essential part of reflective teaching. Following Weimer's advice, you may choose in the previous scenario to suspend your belief that students do not respond to you because they dislike you and instead focus on recording behaviors. By doing so, you escape the downward spiral precipitated by this assumption, but if you choose never to address this assumption, it will affect the way you teach and the way you interact with students because it shapes your subconscious perceptions of situations.

When you discover these underlying assumptions, make time to sit with them and examine them more closely. In this scenario, you might ask yourself why your first explanation of a common classroom scenario was to assume students dislike you. Can you identify personal insecurities that might lead you here? Have you had previous experiences that are coloring your current situation? Did instructors in your experience model an antagonistic relationship with students that you feel doomed to repeat? Identifying what led you to this assumption is an essential part of growing as an instructor. When you pair this assumption hunting with data gathering, you are able to ask yourself what other, more reasonable explanations exist for student behavior and set goals for personal growth. What behavior of yours might be prompting students to withhold a response? Are you asking the right questions, waiting long enough for an answer, answering your own questions, and so on? At the end of this journey, you will not only have identified behaviors you can implement to elicit the desired behavior from students but you will also have begun to unravel a destructive assumption that could be hindering your development as a teacher. Table 6.2 provides an

---

TABLE 6.2: Example: Using Multiple Perspectives on Teaching to Ask Questions, Probe Assumptions, and Make Changes

As a student, Lauren hated group work because she felt the burden of ensuring a successful outcome always fell on her. She consequently resisted using group work early in her teaching career because she assumed all students must experience the same frustrations with it. Lauren did, however, enjoy and learn best through classroom discussions. Her early experiences discussing literature in high school inspired her to pursue degrees in English, and she assumed that all students felt just as eager to engage in discussion as she did. During a classroom observation debrief, an educational developer noted that the same students tended to dominate discussion throughout the class period while others engaged infrequently, if at all. The consultant also collected feedback from students, which included requests for more small-group activities. Feedback from the consultant and students led Lauren to question her initial assumptions based exclusively on personal experience as she began to understand that not all students process information in the same way. She continued her inquiry by reading research indicating the learning gains that can be achieved through well-designed group work and concluded that all her students could benefit from more variety of engagement. To ensure that she implemented group work strategies effectively, she once again reached out to an educational developer on campus to discuss her ideas. As a result of this reflective journey, Lauren's classes look quite different now. She incorporates more low-stakes individual as well as group activities to prepare students to engage more fully in discussion. While she still values whole-class discussions, she also acknowledges the importance of allowing students time to prepare to engage through small-group conversations. Consequently, she has seen improvements in the quality of student discussions as well as the variety of students who regularly choose to participate. She no longer talks with the same three students all semester, and she is much closer to reaching her goal of meaningful discussions that engage *all* students in some way rather than a select few.

example from Lauren's own experience engaging in this process.

Conduct Research on Teaching and Learning

Just as we involve others in the process of reflecting on teaching, we may want to share the findings of our endeavors with interested colleagues. We have all engaged in conversations with colleagues where we share our classroom struggles as well as solutions. These informal exchanges can be invaluable sources of information and inspiration when reflecting on our own teaching, but they can also offer us an opportunity to share our experiences in a way that changes how our colleagues teach and broadens the impact of our personal reflections. After engaging in productive reflections, we may find that we want to share our insights more extensively with other instructors. Doing so usually requires that we study our insights more rigorously by reformulating our reflection questions into research questions that we can systematically investigate through structured studies and thorough data analysis. When we do this, we move beyond reflective practice and toward the scholarship of teaching and learning (SoTL). According to Bishop-Clark and Dietz-Uhler (2012), SoTL "is the study of teaching and learning and the communication of findings so that a body of knowledge can be established" (p. 1). An entry-level interest in SoTL often stems from systematic reflection on teaching and learning that leads us to ask questions about what is happening and why. For instance, Poole (2018) tells us that SoTL questions may arise when our beliefs, which he identifies as springing from intuitions, conversational anecdotes, and observations about teaching, become curiosities we can study. In other words, we probe our intuitions, conversational assumptions, and observations rather than taking for granted that they are, in fact, true; we push past the easy questions and answers to identify something of deep importance to both teachers and learners.

Although reflection provides the starting place,

> SoTL differs from scholarly and reflective teaching in that it not only involves questioning one's teaching or a teaching strategy, but also formally gathering and exploring evidence, researching the literature, refining and testing practices, and finally going public. The purpose of SoTL is not just to make an impact on

student learning, but through formal, peer-reviewed communication, to contribute to the larger knowledge base on teaching and learning. (Bishop-Clark & Dietz-Uhler, 2012, p. 19)

Conducting a study of your interesting question or problem and finding an appropriate place to share your findings may initially feel daunting as you step outside your home discipline, but the "big tent" of SoTL encompasses and welcomes a wide variety of disciplinary backgrounds, teaching and learning questions, study methodologies, and purposes (Huber & Hutchings, 2005). For a study to be considered SoTL, it must be shared publicly through peer-reviewed channels such as conferences and journals with the intention of improving teaching and learning as a field. If you are interested in beginning or sharing a SoTL project but are struggling to know what to do next, consider reaching out to an educational developer or colleague who can guide you. You might also consult Bishop-Clark and Dietz-Uhler's *Engaging in the Scholarship of Teaching and Learning* (2012), which provides excellent step-by-step directions for designing, conducting, analyzing, and sharing a SoTL study.

What Do We Do?

The CTB framework provides a useful starting place for reflecting on your teaching because it encourages you to focus on behaviors. Sometimes the most difficult part of reflection is simply getting an accurate picture of what you do as a teacher rather than what you think you do. We cannot make useful changes to our teaching if we do not know how we teach. By starting with behaviors, you can get outside your head and take a more objective approach to reflection. As you begin to take conscious notice of your behaviors, you can invite peers and students to provide additional feedback so you can balance your perceptions and identify behavioral trends. You can then consult the literature to compare your behaviors to evidence-based practices to gain further insights. While you probably undertake some level of regular if informal reflection on your teaching, Table 6.3 offers concrete, step-by-step actions you can take to engage in this critical teaching behavior more formally and systematically.

TABLE 6.3: Reflect: Critical Teaching Behaviors in Practice

Behaviors	Step by Step
RE.1 Assess personal growth	• *Keep a course journal.* Jotting down your thoughts after class or as you have them can help you identify patterns, remember key insights, plan for future improvement, and track your growth over time. • *Track behaviors.* If you notice a particular student response, pay attention to your behaviors before and after to begin to understand how your actions affect student behaviors. This strategy can help you identify a particularly effective or ineffective teaching behavior. • *Review previous course journals, reflections, observation reports, and teaching philosophy statements to identify how you have grown as an instructor.* Seeing concrete changes to your perspective on and approach to teaching can provide encouragement and inspiration. You might review your materials through the lens of a particular CTB category to see where you have grown and where you might still need to grow.
RE.2 Invite feedback on teaching from colleagues	• *Invite a colleague to observe your class/module and provide feedback.* Consider seeking an observation at least every other year if this practice is not already required for your position. • *Ask a colleague to review teaching materials.* Chapter 8 provides more guidance to assist in the peer observation process.
RE.3 Solicit student feedback	• *Gather midsemester student feedback.* If your institution has a center for teaching and learning, you can ask a trained educational developer to conduct an anonymous feedback and discussion session with your students. Colleagues may also conduct these sessions (see chapter 9 for instruments and instructions). • *Review end-of-semester student evaluations of instruction.* Look for themes in the feedback across responses, courses, and semesters. Identifying broader trends in student feedback can keep you from fruitlessly focusing on a few negative comments and can help you make the most of the data you receive. Consider reaching out to an educational developer to help you process student feedback.
RE.4 Engage with scholarship and professional development related to teaching	• *Read about your teaching topic of interest.* Scholarly teachers turn to the literature for insights they can apply to improve their learning environments. You can find articles and blog posts online or, for a deeper dive, read books related to your growth area. Ask a colleague or educational developer for recommendations, conduct a literature review, or start with the references in this book. • *Seek professional development opportunities* that will help you move toward those goals. Units on campus may offer a one-off workshop, intensive institute, or other opportunity related to your goal. You may also find conference sessions or entire conferences relevant to your growth area.
RE.5 Plan for personal growth by identifying categories for development and setting goals	• *Use the CTB categories* to help you make sense of themes across the feedback you collect and reflections you generate. Do you notice an alignment of themes across sources, or do student and/or peer feedback seem to diverge from your own reflections on your teaching? • *Identify categories of strength* based on the different insights into your teaching that you gather. • *Establish goals for growth* by selecting a category in which you need or want to develop. You might read more about that category, identify a few behaviors you can implement, and then reflect on their implementation.
RE.6 Conduct research on teaching and learning	• *Formalize your questions about teaching and learning into SoTL/discipline-based education research (DBER) projects.* Engaging in research on your teaching can re-energize you when teaching starts to grow dull and help you stay committed to continuous improvement as an instructor. • *Present or publish your study results.* Sharing your findings with a broader community of instructors can change the way others teach and lead to improvements not just in your own discipline or at your own institution but across disciplines and institutions.

What Do We Show?

If you want to show your dedication to growing as an instructor, documenting your reflection efforts is essential. Like alignment, reflection often falls into the category of invisible yet foundational labor that goes into good teaching. Therefore, we must actively plan to capture the work we do in this area. Table 6.4 lists possible materials you can use as evidence of reflective practice. Since most of these artifacts do not in and of themselves illustrate reflection, the table also includes suggestions for how to capture the reflective aspects of these materials for an external audience to whom they might not be as readily apparent.

TABLE 6.4: Documenting Reflection

Personal Materials
Provide short annotations for materials to focus attention on the critical teaching behavior(s) you want to showcase.

Course journal	Excerpts from course journals can serve as evidence of ongoing reflective practice; they can also be excellent sources of questions about your teaching that can lead to SoTL/DBER projects.
Written reflection on peer feedback and/or observation	To maximize the value of the observation and to demonstrate reflective practice, we recommend that you do the following: • write a reflection on the class period or module(s) observed • generate a professional development plan based on the feedback you receive These reflection documents can be included in a teaching portfolio along with the observation report. The CTB peer observation protocol includes prompts to promote meaningful reflection on observations.
Written reflection on student feedback (midterm and/or end of term)	We strongly encourage you to frame student feedback with your own reflection on that feedback. Not only can that reflection help clarify points of concern raised by students but it can also help you process feedback productively and make concrete plans for growth.
Teaching statement	A teaching statement can be the cornerstone of reflective teaching. While it may be a required component of a job application, tenure, promotion, or annual review package, the act of writing such a statement prompts you to reflect on what you value as a teacher, why you value it, and what you do as a result. Taking time to review and revise your statement periodically, regardless of whether you need to submit it to someone else, can spark meaningful reflections on how your teaching values continue to evolve over the course of your career. In the next chapter, we will set the foundation for your teaching philosophy by exploring how you can use the CTB framework to identify a core teaching value. The final chapter of this book guides you through the process of pulling the disparate component pieces of evidence into a coherent, compelling narrative that documents your teaching effectively.
Presentations led on teaching topics	If a teaching strategy you implement works particularly well, you may be invited to share it in a presentation with your colleagues or you may choose to submit it to a conference focused on teaching and learning. Preparing this presentation will require reflecting on what you did, how students responded, why you think it worked, what you would do differently, and how others can implement a similar practice in their contexts. Be sure to include a description of your workshop if you choose to list it as evidence of reflection.

(Continues)

TABLE 6.4 (*Continued*)

SoTL/DBER presentations and/or publications	Both SoTL as well as DBER prompt you to ask questions about what works and why when it comes to student learning. Formalizing your reflective questions into a research study allows you to share your findings with interested colleagues to help improve teaching within your discipline and beyond. Tracking the impact of your findings on how others teach, either in your own department or in the broader discipline, can provide compelling evidence of the impact of your reflective teaching practices.
Materials From Others	
Participation in teaching-related professional development	Often, units and organizations that offer professional development opportunities related to teaching provide you with some sort of recognition for or documentation of your participation. These materials might include the following: • workshop transcripts • microcredentials • certificates • letters of participation • professional development stipends When you receive these items, be sure to save in a digital or physical file for possible use as evidence of reflective teaching. Like the listed materials, these items do not speak for themselves but are most persuasive as evidence of effective teaching practice when accompanied by reflective statements. In this case, your reflective statement might include the following: • the description of the event you attended • a summary of what you did during the event • thoughts about what you learned • how your learning will impact your teaching
SoTL/DBER recognition	As SoTL and DBER gain more acceptance as valid and important research fields, the recognition for those engaging in this type of research also grows. Your institution may already offer awards, fellowships, or minigrants for this kind of research. Many state, regional, national, and even international organizations host annual SoTL/DBER awards for which you can apply.

Reflection Questions

Unless we take the time to critically examine why we do what we do, we usually default to teaching the way we were taught or to the way that was most effective for our learning. While we may have the best of intentions, it is entirely a matter of chance as to whether our practices align with research-based pedagogies. As we close this chapter on reflection, the last of the CTB categories, we once again invite you to pause to reflect on the following questions. If you have not taken time to answer the reflection questions before now, we hope you are more convinced of the importance of doing so.

1. Who are you as an instructor currently? What evidence do you have (behaviors, feedback from peers and/or students, etc.) to confirm your self-perceptions?
a. If you have student or peer feedback, what patterns do you see across that feedback?
b. Do those patterns align with your perceptions of who you believe you are as an instructor? Why or why not?

2. Who do you want to become as an instructor and why? How do you want students to perceive you?

   a. How can you use insights gained from your answers to Question 1 to grow toward the instructor you want to become?

   b. What do you plan to do to help you become that instructor?

3. Reflect on a teaching strength. Why do you consider it a strength? Was it always a strength? How did you develop this strength?

4. Think about a particular struggle you have faced during your teaching career. What have you done to overcome that struggle? How have you grown? Where might you still need to grow?

References

Bishop-Clark, C., & Dietz-Uhler, B. (2012). _Engaging in the scholarship of teaching and learning: A guide to the process, and how to develop a project from start to finish._ Stylus.

Boud, D., Keogh, R., & Walker, D. (Eds.). (1985). _Reflection: Turning experience into learning._ Kogan Page.

Britzman, D. P. (1991). _Practice makes practice: A critical study of learning to teach._ State University of New York Press.

Brookfield, S. D. (1995). _Becoming a critically reflective teacher._ Jossey-Bass.

Ellis, S., Mendel, R., & Nir, M. (2006). Learning from successful and failed experience: The moderating role of kind of after-event review. _Journal of Applied Psychology, 91,_ 669–680.

Ellis, S., Carette, B., Anseel, F., & Lievens, F. (2014). Systematic reflections: Implications for learning from failures and successes. _Association for Psychological Science, 23_(1), 67–72.

Haras, C. (2018). _Improving teaching through reflection._ Association of College and University Educators. https://acue.org/wp-content/uploads/2018/11/Improving TeachingThroughReflection-Cat-Haras-1.pdf

Huber, M. T., & Hutchings, P. (2005). _The advancement of learning: Building the teaching commons._ Jossey-Bass.

McAlpine, L., & Weston, C. (2000). Reflection: Issues related to improving professors' teaching and students' learning. _Instructional Science, 28_(5), 363–385.

Mezirow, J., & Associates. (1990). _Fostering critical reflection in adulthood: A guide to transformative and emancipatory learning._ Jossey-Bass.

Poole, G. (2018). Using intuition, anecdote, and observation: Rich sources of SoTL projects. In N. Chick (Ed.), _SoTL in action: Illuminating critical moments of practice_ (pp. 7–14). Stylus.

Porter, J. (2017, March 21). Why you should make time for self-reflection (even if you hate doing it). _Harvard Business Review._ https://hbr.org/2017/03/why-you-should-make-time-for-self-reflection-even-if-you-hate-doing-it

Sternberg, R. J., & Horvath, J. A. (1995). A prototype view of expert teaching. _Educational Researcher, 24_(6), 9–17.

Weimer, M. (2010). _Inspired college teaching._ Jossey-Bass.

PART TWO

APPLICATIONS OF THE CRITICAL TEACHING BEHAVIORS FRAMEWORK

CHAPTER 7

Identifying Your Core Value

NOW THAT YOU ARE familiar with the research underlying the development of the CTB framework, you are ready to explore its practical applications and accompanying tools. If you recall from the previous chapter, we introduced four inputs for reflection: self-assessment, peer feedback, student feedback, and professional development and scholarship. In this second half of the book, we will explore instruments aligned with the CTB framework that help you gather teaching insights and documentation from each of these sources (by reading this book, you are already engaging in professional development). The following chapters will guide you through several processes:

- conducting peer observations
- gathering student feedback
- crafting a reflective narrative of teaching effectiveness using CTB materials

While many frameworks, protocols, instruments, and guides exist to assist you with each of these tasks, few of them offer comprehensive alignment across instruments. We designed each instrument to complement the other components of the CTB tool kit and to work together to help you generate a complete picture of your teaching. Instrument alignment with the CTB framework helps create coherence across your materials, making it easier for you to craft a persuasive narrative of teaching effectiveness.

As we transition, we invite you first to engage in a self-assessment activity to identify your core teaching value. Articulating a core teaching value helps you personalize the content as you read and ensures that you get the most out of the chapters that follow. The reflection activities in this brief interlude between sections prepare you to frame your teaching narrative using the CTB instruments to:

- define your core teaching value
- align your core teaching value with a broader CTB category

Be sure not to skip this important step as we will refer to your core teaching value throughout the remaining chapters.

What Is My Core Teaching Value?

We use the term *core teaching value* to refer to a clear, concise statement of your underlying motivation for teaching the way that you do. A well-written core value statement might be the sentence that drives your teaching philosophy statement and provides coherence to your teaching portfolio. The process of discovering your core teaching value requires reflection, an openness to exploration, and time. To generate one well-crafted, specific sentence expressing a core teaching value, most of us need to do a lot of reflecting first. If you have been answering the reflection questions at the end of each of the previous chapters, you have already engaged in some of the self-exploration necessary to articulate a core value. You might begin this process by reviewing your responses to those prompts before answering one or more of the following guiding questions:

- What motivates your approach to teaching?
- What is the one thing you believe an effective instructor *must* do or believe to promote student learning?
- What are your immediate and future (10+ years) goals for students when teaching your subject?
- What do you believe is the foundation of good teaching?
- Which CTB category definition and/or behavior resonates most with your approach to teaching? Why?

You need not answer all of these questions (unless you want to); instead, choose the prompt(s) that most appeal to you. The goal of this activity is to discover what beliefs or approaches define you as an instructor so you can convey that clearly to an external audience. If you find it difficult to get started with your reflections, try one of the brainstorming methods in the following.

Write

Set a timer for two to five minutes and keep writing until the timer goes off. Ignore word choice, grammar, or complete sentences. Write in bullet points if you prefer. If nothing comes to mind, start by narrating your thoughts on paper, even if that means writing, "I'm struggling to answer any of these prompts. Why?" The idea behind this kind of freewriting is to write yourself out of a block by keeping your pen moving. In reviewing the preceding prompts, you may find that you have more questions than answers, and if that is the case, start by writing all of the related questions that come to mind. Doing so can help you delve deeper into the reflection process by asking or reframing questions to be relevant to you. Often, answers will start to flow if you allow yourself to write without self-judgment for any length of time. When time is up, stop writing and read your

thoughts. Rarely does one round of freewriting like this reach the intended goal, so do not be afraid to identify a theme, ask a new question, and start a new round. This kind of iterative reflection can help you produce a well-articulated core value.

Draw

If you prefer a more visual approach, consider concept mapping, creating a word cloud, or drawing a picture of what your value looks like in action. A concept map helps you visualize connections between ideas and sort out complex relationships between thoughts. Along similar lines, a word cloud allows you to visually gather descriptions of good teaching so you can identify themes and patterns in your words. Finally, you might try visualizing and drawing your typical (or perhaps your ideal) class period. Consider what you are doing, what students are doing, where everyone is located, what technology you have in the room, and so on. Once you have sketched your drawing, begin explaining why you chose to represent your classroom this way. What does your drawing reveal about your approach to or beliefs about teaching? Regardless of the drawing method you choose, review the final product and look for themes to help you identify implicit beliefs you hold about teaching and learning. Reflect on the connections between these themes and the CTB categories.

Talk

Verbal processors may desire to record themselves talking through their answers so they can distill key thoughts through playback. You might even try this as a partner exercise. Use the prompts to begin talking out your answers with a trusted colleague who can write down your responses. Set a timer and swap roles to allow your partner to discuss their responses while you write them down. Ask probing questions if necessary to encourage your partner to delve more deeply into a thought. Such an activity may lead to a fruitful conversation that can give you the insights you need to identify your core teaching value; it can also provide an excellent opportunity to learn more about how your colleagues approach teaching.

Review

However you arrive at your answers, review your notes for recurring themes. Are there any particular words, phrases, concepts, or ideas that appear repeatedly?

Make note of them. Draft one statement about your teaching that you feel accurately communicates your value. While you will likely find that there are many considerations that shape your thoughts about teaching, we encourage you to distill your thoughts down to one central idea that you can use to create a coherent narrative about your teaching. Your statement need not be perfect or permanent. You may end up revising your statement several times before using it to frame your narrative of teaching effectiveness. We encourage you to try multiple brainstorming methods as you dig deeper into your core value reflection. Remember, the goal is to give you a direction to pursue, a lens through which to view and present your teaching as we explore options for documenting your effectiveness in the chapters to come.

What Is My Core Value Category?

Once you have generated a statement that you feel accurately reflects your core value, review the CTB framework (Appendix A). Carefully read the definitions of each of the categories and answer the following questions:

- Into which category does your value statement best fit?
- Why do you think your statement fits into this category?
- Does it surprise you that your core value fits best in this category? Why or why not?
- Is there another category into which your core value might fit? If so, which of the two (or more) categories would you choose to represent your core teaching value and why?
- Do you have a secondary value that falls into a different category?
- What connection do you see between your primary and secondary values if you had more than one?

To help you approach the process from a fresh perspective, consider trying a different brainstorming method for this set of questions than the method you chose previously. For a blank reflection worksheet and an example of a completed reflection, see the "Core Value Reflection Worksheet and Example" in Appendix B.

As you complete these steps, you may find it difficult to fit your statement into a single category or to narrow yourself to one value; if so, do not be concerned. Most faculty who engage in this process find that different aspects of their value span more than one category or that they have two deeply held values. Even faculty who can easily fit their value into a single category typically find that they have a primary and secondary category. For the purposes of crafting a coherent, directed narrative, we recommend that you select a dominant category to frame your narrative. While engaging in behaviors from all categories is necessary to be a well-rounded instructor, be wary of trying to frame your narrative from too many categorical angles as this may create a fragmented, ineffective story for your readers. Selecting a category that fits your core value does not limit you solely to providing evidence of your teaching effectiveness in that category. Instead, you will use your core value category to frame how you present evidence of behaviors from other categories. We will discuss strategies for crafting your teaching narrative in depth in chapter 10, "Creating a Narrative of Teaching Effectiveness."

The outlined process will help you not only define a core value statement but also identify a broader core value category that will allow you to collect materials and frame your narrative. Remember, the CTB is merely a framing device, not a reductive tool designed to box you permanently into a single category. As you grow and change, you may find that your core value category also changes. For this reason, consider revisiting this activity periodically to reflect on ways that you have developed or circumstances that have changed your teaching motivations. Repeating this activity over time will help you develop a long-term narrative of growth and provide depth and nuance to your materials. Keep your core value category and statement handy as we move forward with our exploration of the CTB instruments, as we will reference how you can use your category in relation to each instrument.

CHAPTER 8

Peer Observation

A S WE DISCUSSED IN chapter 6, "Reflect," the perspective of peers plays a vital role in our efforts to reflect on teaching. When we invite peers to observe our teaching, they can also generate reports that help us document our strengths and make plans to grow as professionals. Engaging with a trusted peer in this way can moreover foster a greater sense of community related to teaching. The benefits of peer observation make it worth pursuing even if your unit does not have a formalized process for doing so. If you are seeking guidance to perform a peer observation or begin a peer observation program, this chapter provides an overview of research-based individual and collective benefits before offering a protocol for conducting effective, efficient observations. The protocol's grounding in the CTB framework not only provides clarity, structure, and increased objectivity to the process; it also makes it easier for teams to start the observation with a shared understanding of the characteristics of effective teaching, all with the intention of fostering collegial conversations around teaching. Your reflections and voice as an instructor are at the heart of the CTB approach; consequently, as you review the peer observation instrument in this chapter, you may find that it requests more active engagement from you, the observed faculty, than what you may expect based on your experience with other observations. That said, we recognize the heavy demands on faculty time and have designed the protocol to streamline the observation process as much as possible for both observers and observed without losing the important element of faculty voice and agency in documenting effective

teaching. As we dive deeper into CTB peer observations, we will explore the following questions:

- What can effective peer observation accomplish?
- How does the CTB observation protocol promote effective peer observation?
- What is the CTB process for conducting observations?
- How can you adapt the CTB observation protocol to your needs?

Readers seeking to build a peer observation program may find it particularly valuable to review the next section on benefits, as it provides a concise overview of what research tells us about peer observations. Readers who desire to learn only about the CTB peer observation process may choose to skip directly to the "What Is the CTB Process for Conducting Peer Observations?" section.

What Are the Benefits of Effective Peer Observations?

If requesting peer observations has not been a regular part of your instructional practice, let the research convince you to start now. While peer observations are becoming a more standard practice and sometimes even a requirement for faculty, there can be a great deal of variability in terms of the guidance provided for requesting and conducting peer observations. Research studies make the case that well-designed peer observation programs can offer substantial collective benefits, indicating that the effort required to establish such a program can pay dividends in "kick-start[ing] transformational [teaching] reforms within an institution" (Thomas et al., 2014, p. 153). Regardless of whether your goals are more personally focused on making meaningful changes to your teaching or more institutionally focused on inspiring a culture of reflective and innovative teaching among your colleagues, peer observation deserves your time and attention. Let's take a closer look at the benefits of well-conducted peer observations. Refer to Table 8.1 for a condensed overview of the benefits of peer review.

Reflection and Growth

You may initially feel vulnerable making the request, but inviting a peer to observe a class opens the door for fresh perspectives that can guide your self-reflection on teaching and lead to transformative learning and teaching innovation (Bell & Mladenovic, 2008; Wubbels & Korthagen, 1990). Peers can help us identify strengths as well as weaknesses in our teaching, provide specific feedback on a new instructional technique or learning activity, or offer suggestions for alternate strategies we might try in the future (Kell & Annetts, 2009). If we seek professional development opportunities or resources, peers may be able to help us explore available options. They can also give us insight into student reception of our teaching that students themselves might not know how to voice. Such insights include feedback on student progress toward learning goals (Gleason & Sanger, 2017). As novices, students may not recognize that they do not understand a concept, but a perceptive observer may notice signs of confusion or lack of comprehension. Aside from providing observable facts about our teaching for us to consider, peers can also ask probing questions that make us reflect more deeply on why we teach the way we teach. If you have peer observations performed with some regularity over a few years, you will develop a treasure trove of reflective materials that allow you to consider your growth over time and make more focused plans for future growth.

Confidence and Community

We can be our own harshest critics, especially when we care deeply about doing something well, like teaching in a way that promotes student success. An objective outsider may more readily identify our strengths than we do. Receiving confirmation of strengths supported with observable evidence not only boosts our confidence in our teaching abilities but also provides us with documentation to use as support in a teaching effectiveness narrative (Hanson, 1993). Conversely, questions raised during debrief conversations can lead us to ponder our teaching decisions. While that may lead us to make productive changes, reflecting on why we teach the way we teach may also lead us to deeper conviction for and confidence in the merit of our approach. As we become more self-aware in our teaching, we grow in self-regulation, allowing us to share our expertise in some areas while identifying and pursuing relevant professional development opportunities in others (Al Qahtani et al., 2011).

Effective peer observations benefit observers as well and can be just as much of a learning experience for the observer as for the observed. Rather than a feedback monologue delivered by the observer, a well-conducted observation debrief looks more like a dialogue between observer and observed. These discussions between peers can develop collegiality, promote respect for diverse teaching practices, encourage cross-cultural or cross-disciplinary exchanges, and foster productive, professional debates on pedagogy (Quinlan & Akerlind, 2000). The community created by peer observation conversations cultivates a sense of professional responsibility and peer accountability related to teaching (Al Qahtani et al., 2011). If your goal is to open collegial conversations about teaching, a well-designed peer observation program is a good place to start.

Equity and Fairness

Recently, in light of a growing body of research on bias in student evaluations of teaching (SETs), many departments and institutions have begun exploring peer observations as a less biased means of assessing teaching effectiveness (Boring, 2017; MacNell et al., 2015; Wagner et al., 2016). The reports generated by faculty peers can provide an alternate perspective on our teaching effectiveness, helping to offset the prejudices that may skew data collected in SETs (Gleason & Sanger, 2017). An objective report that captures evidence of teaching behaviors functions as strong proof of effectiveness when included in a portfolio (Hurst et al., 1998; Knapper & Wright, 2001). As fellow instructors, observers also notice and provide feedback on aspects of teaching that go unnoticed by students, including our subject matter expertise, pedagogical innovations, and course design and delivery (Bernstein, 2008). In this regard, peer observations can push beyond the tip of the teaching iceberg to document some of the invisible labor involved.

As noted, semiregular peer observation offers the additional benefit of allowing you to document your teaching journey over time. While this is useful for personal reflection, it can also strengthen your growth narrative. A single snapshot of teaching may or may not accurately reflect your teaching effectiveness, but multiple snapshots over the course of your career allow you to create a narrative arc that demonstrates your commitment to growth with specific evidence of improvement. There is no such thing as a perfect teacher; no matter how good a teacher we are, we will always have room for improvement. Constructing a narrative that includes identified weaknesses and your ongoing efforts to improve throughout your career humanizes and strengthens your narrative, creating a more fair and accurate reflection of who you are as a teacher. Refer to chapter 10 to further explore how you can build a narrative of teaching effectiveness with evidence collected over time.

Problems and Pitfalls

Realistically, peer observation frequently falls short of this idealistic potential. Instead, discussions about peer observation can become a source of controversy at the departmental, college, or even institutional level. Policies requiring regular peer observations may be well intentioned, but such requirements, especially when created with limited faculty input, more often inspire faculty opposition than enthusiasm as instructors resist what they perceive as the loss of academic autonomy (Keig & Waggoner, 1994). Peer observation programs are most effective when faculty feel a sense of ownership over the process; however, getting faculty to agree on what constitutes effective teaching practice poses its own challenge (Cavanagh, 1996; Kell & Annetts, 2009). Moreover, even if a consensus can be reached, instructors report distrust in their peers' ability to provide objective, pedagogy-focused feedback and may experience fear and anxiety related to receiving judgmental feedback from insufficiently trained peers (Atwood et al., 2000; Hanson, 1993). High-stakes outcomes based on observation reports, like evaluation for promotion, tenure, and other forms of recognition, validate these concerns. Vague expectations, unclear processes, and biased feedback can leave the observed feeling confused, frustrated, or unfairly treated, to say nothing of the complications generated by the power disparities frequently involved in the

---

TABLE 8.1: At a Glance—Potential of Peer Observation

Reflection and Growth

- guide self-reflection, which can encourage a change in perspective on teaching, prompt transformatory learning, and foster innovation
- gain insight into progress toward student learning goals
- identify and correct weaknesses; identify and build on strengths

Confidence and Community

- promote autonomy and self-regulation related to teaching by confirming teaching strengths with observable evidence
- develop collegiality, respect for diverse teaching practices, cross-cultural or multidisciplinary exchanges, and professional debates about instruction
- create a sense of professional responsibility and peer accountability

Equity and Fairness

- assess aspects of teaching that cannot be captured in SETs
- offset data collected in SETs, which is often influenced by students' implicit biases
- provide objective evidence of teaching effectiveness to be included in a teaching portfolio

> **TABLE 8.2: At a Glance—Problems With Peer Observation**
>
> **Autonomy and Power**
>
> - anxiety over the perceived threat to academic autonomy
> - tensions due to faculty pulling rank and power disparities between observer and observed
> - lack of departmental and/or institutional culture that recognizes and values the benefits of peer observation
>
> **Judgment and Fairness**
>
> - fear of judgment by peers
> - concerns about fairness and/or bias in the process or report
> - misgivings about peers' ability to conduct effective peer observations (e.g., understand approach to teaching, provide objective feedback, focus on pedagogy rather than content)
>
> **Confusion and Lack of Guidance**
>
> - lack of agreement on what characterizes good teaching practice
> - concerns about how much time the process will take
> - uncertainty about what should be reviewed

observer–observed relationship.[1] Observers may experience their own frustrations from a lack of instruction on how to perform effective observations, the need to juggle yet another demand on their limited time, or restrictive instruments that do not fit their contextual needs. Lacking more specific guidance, observers may unintentionally privilege their own teaching preferences when giving feedback or focus on more familiar lesson content rather than less familiar pedagogical insights. Interdepartmentally, the myriad of protocols and instruments used complicates requests for observations from peers in different disciplines. Rather than opening dialogues about good teaching, poorly conceived and implemented peer observations run the risk of becoming another box to check for already-overtaxed faculty, or worse, they become a point of contention that drives a divide between faculty and administration, tenured and nontenured, full-time and part-time instructors. Ill-conceived peer observations can shut down conversations about teaching and perpetuate biases against minoritized instructors or innovative pedagogies. Table 8.2 summarizes key issues with peer observation.

Potential problems aside, research on peer observation overwhelmingly indicates its value in fostering collegiality, personal reflection, and improvement of teaching effectiveness (Fletcher, 2018; Goldberg et al., 2010; Lowder et al., 2017). Its ability to function as either a formative or evaluative assessment of teaching effectiveness and its long-standing recognition as a means of measuring teaching effectiveness make

peer observation a powerful tool in your documentation tool kit (Alabi & Weare, 2014; Chism, 2007). To promote positive experience, Thomas et al. (2014) recommend that successful peer observations meet the following criteria:

1. Utilize a process that can be adapted to meet faculty needs and promote a sense of ownership rather than a sense of obligation or requirement.
2. Clarify the process for both observer and observed by providing clear instructions on what both parties should do and expect at each stage of the observation process.
3. Provide flexible instruments that accommodate a variety of teaching styles.
4. Guide reflection to encourage debate and conversation about teaching among colleagues.

With these criteria in mind, we now turn our attention to the design of the CTB peer observation protocol.

How Does the CTB Observation Protocol Promote Effective Peer Observation?

We designed the CTB observation process and instruments with these benefits, pain points, and best practices in mind. In this section, we will look more closely at the peer observation instruments as we discuss how their design promotes peer observations that maximize the benefits of the experience. Before proceeding, take a moment to review the Teaching Observation Instructor Worksheet (Appendix C) and the Observation Report (Appendix D). Familiarity with these instruments will enhance your understanding of potential benefits offered by their unique design. You may also wish to refer to the peer teaching observation instructions in Appendix E ("CTB Observation Process Introduction and Overview").

Reflection and Growth

By actively prompting instructor reflection throughout the observation process, the CTB protocol encourages faculty to strengthen their reflective muscles. We may sometimes think of a peer observation as a passive experience for the instructor observed—just teach as usual and wait for feedback—but many of the key benefits of peer observation are associated with guided reflection upon the experience. The Teaching Observation Instructor Worksheet (Appendix C), meant to be completed by the instructor before an observation, prompts you to provide necessary information about your course to the observer, but more importantly, it frames the CTB peer observation as a reflective process by asking you specifically to consider how you teach your course, what professional development you have pursued to improve the course, and any feedback requests you have for your observer.

Notice that the Observation Report form includes an "Instructor Reflection" column and a final "Reflect" section. The postobservation reflection column invites you to record specific thoughts about the class or module(s) observed while the final "Reflect" box bookends the observation experience by asking you to take a more holistic approach to reflection that summarizes your strengths, identifies areas for growth, and plans for professional development. These features take a past, present, future approach to reflection, providing you a record of your accomplishments as well as goals to which you can refer when developing your teaching narrative. If you have multiple observations conducted over the course of years, the reflection components allow you to hear about your teaching from yourself and yield insights about how your approach to teaching has changed. They also let you check in on your progress toward your teaching goals.

Confidence and Community

The CTB protocol overall offers needed transparency and structure that can ease some of the apprehensions associated with vague peer observation procedures. When observers and observed are clear on what is expected from them at each stage of the process, they can focus on having insightful conversations about teaching rather than sorting out what to do, when, and how. The CTB's focus on observable behaviors pushes observers to take notes on what they can see happening in the learning environment and align their feedback with research-based practices instead of commenting on content. Knowing that your observer has guidance on effective pedagogies going into the observation can instill confidence in the feedback you receive and promote a more trusting relationship between observer and observed. By guiding both you and your observer to look for evidence-based practices in each of the CTB categories, the observation report form also offers a common language for conversations about teaching, thus helping to build community around good teaching.

Although the protocol brings needed structure to peer observation, our intentional inclusion of space for your voice in the process enables you to explain and take ownership of your pedagogical choices, which can build your confidence in your teaching. Research defines certain effective, evidence-based practices conducive to student learning, but the expression and implementation of these practices looks different across disciplines, modalities, instructors, and even courses taught by the same instructor. There is no "one-size-fits-all" model of good teaching. Although we list example evidence observers might look for in each category, these examples are not intended to be used as a checklist but as a guide to simplify the feedback process and foster a mutual understanding of effective teaching practices. Using the step-by-step behavior breakdown provided in the first section of this book, individuals, departments, or institutions can adapt the example evidence column to reflect what good teaching looks like more specifically in their context. The reflection components allow you further freedom and flexibility to define good teaching by making space for you to explain your pedagogical choices. Do your part to foster meaningful conversations about your teaching by providing these reflections to your observer before the debrief session. Your reflections can clarify confusion or misunderstandings in advance of your debrief, allowing you to use your scheduled debrief time for deeper conversations. You may also use this protocol flexibly by choosing to identify categories in which to receive targeted feedback from your observer, perhaps your core value category as well as a growth category. Peer feedback that confirms areas of strength offers persuasive evidence of teaching effectiveness, especially when that feedback bolsters your core value narrative.

Equity and Fairness

Many faculty express valid concerns about bias in observation reports. We mention this not because we believe observers intentionally provide biased feedback; rather, we address this concern in recognition that, regardless of our intentions, we all bring implicit biases with us when we observe someone else's class.[2] These biases may be professional, based on our disciplinary background or preferred teaching style; these factors sometimes cause observers to bring a bias for or against certain pedagogies to the learning environment. However, as we are becoming increasingly aware, biases may also be personal, based on race, age, sex, gender, culture, and so on. By guiding observers to look for objective behaviors as evidence of effective teaching practices, the critical teaching behaviors encourage a focus on pedagogy rather than content or evaluation of the instructor on the basis of non-teaching-related qualities. The list of evidence-based behaviors encourages observers to record what they see that aligns or does not align with listed examples rather than privileging their own preferred pedagogies.

Concerns about equity and bias in observations can be reduced further by having observers review teaching competencies through multiple artifacts, including syllabi, assignment prompts, lesson plans, course welcome modules, and so on (Hanson, 1993). For this reason, the protocol asks you to provide your syllabus at the very least and invites you to supply additional relevant materials as part of the observation. One of our goals with the CTB project, as you know by now, is to help faculty document teaching beyond the tip of the iceberg—what we can see in the learning environment. You may think that the purpose of an observation is to record what happens in the learning environment, but these additional materials provide evidence of the time-intensive labor that goes into designing and delivering a great class session. Providing them can help the observer document your teaching efforts beyond a single lesson or module.

Finally, we assert that incorporating instructors' thoughts in the observation process does more than foster reflective habits; it also has the potential to make peer observation a more equitable process by acknowledging instructors as authorities on their own teaching. Rather than privileging the authoritative voice of the observer, the "Instructor Reflection" column gives faculty an opportunity to redefine what characterizes good teaching in their contexts and to offer additional pieces of evidence that observers might not have noticed. This peer observation process no longer silences the faculty observed; instead, our reflection components treat the voices of the observer and the observed as equally important perspectives. The equal value given to the voice of the observed becomes especially important when reports are used for evaluative purposes as the observed is no longer rendered mute in the evaluation process.

Purpose, Modality, and Discipline

The CTB instrument can be used flexibly for both formative and evaluative purposes as well as across teaching modalities and disciplines. While our background as educational developers leads us to privilege the reflection and formative feedback aspects of observations, we balance our own bias with a recognition that observations can play an integral role in the evaluative assessment of an instructor's teaching effectiveness. We felt remiss in dismissing this (justified) instructor concern, and consequently, in developing this protocol, we prioritized a balance between the formative and evaluative purposes of peer observation, taking a both/and approach to assessment rather than an either/or stance. When using the CTB observation form for evaluative purposes, you will want to focus more attention on your summary of instructor strengths and areas for improvement in the "Reflect" box. Approach this box as the "executive summary" of your notes and use it in place of the traditional observation memo you might write. In the other categories, make brief notes about specific behaviors and to provide evidence. For formative observations, you might give more detailed feedback in each of the categories, reserving a brief, big picture summary of strength and improvement categories for the "Reflect" box. You can use the behavior numbers as a shorthand for referencing specific items in the observation list.

With the proliferation of course modalities beyond traditional F2F environments, finding an observation protocol flexible enough to accommodate the differences in teaching behaviors required by online, blended, hybrid, hyflex, flipped, synchronous, and asynchronous spaces poses a significant challenge. The expansion of these environments has stimulated a multiplication of instruments designed to help faculty conduct observations in particular course modalities. Even in traditional F2F environments, discipline-specific tools abound as well as instruments designed to track certain kinds of teaching behaviors or instructor–student interactions. While each of these tools offers advantages to users, the sheer number of them means that institutions, colleges, departments, and even colleagues within the same discipline are often speaking very different languages when it comes to teaching. We designed the CTB framework as well as the associated observation protocol to work across modalities and disciplines, offering a unifying alternative intended to create a common campus language around good teaching rather than furthering the modality and disciplinary divisions created by niche instruments. Nevertheless, the Creative Commons licensing on the observation materials allows you to customize the instruments to meet specific needs using the step-by-step breakdowns listed in Part One while maintaining a common foundation that makes it more efficient and meaningful to talk about good teaching across modalities and disciplines.

What Is the CTB Process for Conducting Peer Observations?

Now that you have a sense of how the design of the CTB protocol promotes effective peer observations, we will dive into the steps of the CTB observation process and how to use the report form. While the pre- and during observation procedures may not differ substantially from processes with which you are already familiar, the postobservation process involved in completing and debriefing the report form requires more instruction as it departs from established observation conventions. We approach the process from the observer perspective and subdivide this section into "pre, during, post, report form, and debrief" to make it easier for you to reference the section you need as you complete the CTB peer observation process. For a printable overview of the peer observation process for both observers and instructors, please visit https://criticalteachingbehaviors.com to download the peer teaching Observation Report (Appendix D).

Preobservation

Upon receiving an observation request, an observer should respond by asking the instructor to do the following:[3]

1. Familiarize themselves with the CTB Observation Process Introduction and Overview (Appendix E) and follow up with any questions about the process.
2. Complete and return the Teaching Observation Instructor Worksheet (Appendix C).
3. Review the CTB observation report form—for formative observations, you might also invite the instructor to identify one or two categories in which to receive specific feedback if they so choose.

In the CTB protocol, the Teaching Observation Instructor Worksheet takes the place of the preobservation consultation that typically forms part of the peer observation process. Traditionally, these discussions allow the observer to gather information about the class or module to be observed and build rapport with the instructor. The instructor may also share any relevant context not covered in the observer's information-gathering questions. As should be clear by now, we value conversation as a part of the observation process, but we find that supplying instructors with the instructor worksheet yields the same information as a consultation while reducing the amount of time spent on a single observation. Faculty, administrators, and educational developers who perform a large number of observations will find that eliminating this meeting allows them to allocate more time to valuable debrief conversations. The worksheet also ensures that you collect all the necessary information (date, time, location, module[s] for review) in one place rather than potentially losing that information in a long email thread. Of course, if you prefer to hold preobservation consultations, you may use the instructor worksheet to guide your conversation and prompt your note-taking. If you choose to use the instructor worksheet in place of an initial consultation, consider extending instructors the option to schedule a discussion if it helps them feel more comfortable with the process.

The CTB observation protocol requires instructors to engage in pre- and postreflections to be shared with observers, which may be more effort than instructors are used to expending for an observation. Instead of presenting reflection as yet another task busy instructors must complete, our communications with instructors emphasize the importance of these reflections in giving them a voice in the observation process. Reflections offer an opportunity for instructors to become active agents in the observation process rather than passive receivers of someone else's assessment of their teaching. Interested adopters of the CTB observation protocol regularly express concerns about getting instructors to engage in the reflective components of the process, but this has not proven to be an issue in our experience. We attribute our success primarily to the way we frame the purpose of these components. When instructors see these reflections for what they are—opportunities to offer their own perspectives on their teaching—they readily participate. The pre- and postobservation email templates in Appendix H provide you with step-by-step instructions and framing language you can adapt to suit your needs. We provide these email templates not to prescript your responses but to offer guidance. The templates ensure that requesters know what they will need to do before and after the observation and include direct hyperlinks to relevant forms the instructor will need to complete throughout the process. Furthermore, the templates frame the purpose of the work the instructor will need to invest in completing and submitting requested materials as part of the CTB observation process.

To prepare for the observation, review the instructor's returned worksheet, the syllabus, and any additional relevant materials. Make note of any categories in which the instructor has requested feedback as well as any other requests the instructor included. Observers unfamiliar with the CTB report form should make time to review the categories and example behaviors in each category. Keeping these examples in mind will help direct your attention during the observation. You may wish to print a copy of the CTB report form or keep an electronic version handy to use as a reference while taking notes during the observation.

During Observation

Plan to arrive at least 5 minutes early for synchronous observations to get a sense of how students interact with the instructor and with each other. While you may find it helpful to have a copy of the CTB report form available during the observation, we do not recommend taking notes in the form, particularly in synchronous contexts. Things happen quickly in synchronous environments, and if you try to take notes in the CTB report form, you will likely be distracted as you try to organize notes into the categories. Instead, focus on recording what you see happening in the learning environment. Two of the more common approaches to note-taking include chronologically recording events as they happen, noting down the time, or organizing observations into instructor and student behaviors. You might also take notes in a hybrid format, organizing by instructor/student behaviors and noting the time at which things happen. Whatever method you choose, the goal with a CTB observation should be to record what happens, when, and how students respond rather than your thoughts or impressions.

For asynchronous or hybrid courses, set aside one to two hours during which you can focus on reviewing the relevant online course materials. The instructor worksheet collected before the observation prompts faculty to select at least one module for review, although faculty may choose more than one module depending on your policies. We recommend also including the welcome, orientation, or introduction module in your observation as this will give you a sense of how the instructor sets the tone for the course, creates community in the online environment, and establishes clear policies and communication with students. As an observer in an online environment, you may find it easier to take notes on the structure and design of the course than the delivery, but look for evidence of student engagement (discussion boards, activities, assignments, etc.) and instructor tone (recordings, written content, announcements, etc.) to make notes on course delivery as well. Online observation protocols often prompt observers to look for student–student, student–instructor, and student–content interactions. These forms of engagement are essential regardless of course modality, but in an online course, they require more intentional planning from the instructor. You may find it useful to keep these relationships in mind while reviewing the course. If you struggle to find evidence of student engagement in the module the instructor selected, consider following up with a few delivery-related questions for the instructor or asking the instructor to choose a module that might provide more examples of student engagement.

Regardless of modality, approach the observation as an exercise in raw data collection. Use the following questions to prompt your note-taking if necessary:

- How is the instructor presenting information? How is information organized? What is the instructor's tone in presenting material?
- Are students engaged in learning? Are they attentive and responsive or distracted? Are there opportunities embedded throughout the class period or module for them to engage?
- What do the instructor's and students' behaviors indicate about the learning environment in this course? How does the environment feel?
- How does the instructor use technology? Are students able to navigate selected technologies?
- How do class structure and activities support each other and prepare students to perform desired tasks?
- How does the instructor know students achieved the learning outcomes for the lesson? What opportunities do students have to measure their understanding?
- Jot down any questions you want to ask the instructor—what additional information do you need?

Postobservation

In synchronous environments, plan to stay a few minutes after the observation to remind the instructor what to expect next, specifically an email from you with a request for their completed reflections and meeting options to debrief the report. Regardless of the environment, email the instructor as soon as possible after completing the observation to keep the process moving forward. Observations can be nerve-wracking experiences for instructors; you may want to acknowledge this in your email by providing some encouragement or thanking the instructor for inviting you to observe the class, even if the observation is required. Your email should also ask the instructor to do the following:

1. Complete and return responses to the center reflection column of the peer observation report form (Appendix D) for the class period or module observed.[4]

2. Summarize categories of strength and potential categories for growth along with plans for professional development in the "Reflection" box.
3. Schedule a time to debrief the observation report.

Keep in mind that how you frame the reflection component of the observation process helps determine whether the instructor considers this an opportunity to have their voice heard or an additional chore to complete. The postobservation email template in Appendix H gives you language you can adapt encouraging the instructor to complete the reflection and schedule the debrief in a timely manner.

You might also choose to take a few moments to skim your notes to clarify, fill in gaps, or write down additional information while the observation is still fresh in your mind. While you wait for the instructor to return their reflections, you may begin writing your report. Lauren prefers to wait to start her report until after she can review the reflections so she can more effectively respond to the instructor's thoughts in her report; Claudia prefers to start her report and make any necessary updates after receiving the instructor's reflections. When you start your report is a matter of preference and workflow. As long as you take clear notes and schedule the debrief within a week of the observation, the experience should still be recent enough for you to consolidate your notes into a useful report.

Report Form

If you are accustomed to writing observation reports in another format, you may find it takes some practice to adjust to the CTB report form. You might begin your report by grouping your notes into the broader categories. Alternatively, you might choose to review the example behaviors in a category and look for evidence of them in your notes. Remember also to look for behavioral evidence in the instructor's syllabus, welcome module, and any other course materials supplied. We also encourage you to review the instructor's reflections before compiling your report. Doing so can help clarify aspects of the observation that raised questions for you and allow you to write a more thorough, tailored report. However you approach the process, keep in mind that the CTB categories are artificially neat: In reality, behaviors, and your notes on them, often fall into more than one category. Rather than repeating observations in multiple categories, make decisions about which category best represents the impact of the behavior on student learning. That said, sometimes an instructor does something that demonstrates such a multifaceted strength that it is worth referring back to previous comments to note that the behavior had an impact across categories. For instance, you might see that the instructor incorporated ADA-compliant technology seamlessly, which created an inclusive environment for the student who needed accommodations and served to engage all students effectively in the lesson. In this case, you might make a note under "Integrate Technology" stating the seamless operation and incorporation of ADA-compliant technology. Under "Include," you could mention that the accessible nature of this technology allowed the student with screen reader needs to use it without a barrier. Finally, in the "Engage" section, you might point out that students engaged with the technology enthusiastically and that it helped them to make sense of a complex concept. This is not a direct repetition but rather a documentation of the different impacts of a particularly effective behavior.

Be specific with your evidence in each category by describing the instructor and student behaviors you observed, both positive and negative. Remember, the goal is to provide objective evidence of what happened in the instructional space, whether synchronous or asynchronous. Review the instructor's reflections so you can provide evidence to confirm a point they made, answer a question they asked, or point out an issue or outcome they had not considered, as in the following examples:

- You state that you used a small-group activity to engage students in a deeper discussion of this topic. The level of energy in the classroom as students worked in small groups and the questions and conversations overheard (give examples if you recorded them) confirm the effectiveness of this technique in reaching your pedagogical goal.
- You question whether students understood the purpose of the activity. I overheard students in small-group conversations asking, "What were we supposed to do again?" and "What does this have to do with what we're learning?"

- The size and volume of text on the PowerPoint slide made it difficult for students in the back of the lecture hall to read, as evidenced by several students squinting and asking their neighbors what the slide said.

Finally, use the "Reflect" box to provide holistic feedback on the instructor's teaching. Start by noting one or two categories in which the instructor demonstrates particular strength. Be sure to explain how you identified this category as a strength by summarizing some of the key evidence that indicates their success, including student responses to instructional behaviors. Address any special requests or categories in which the instructor requested feedback. Identify one or two categories for growth, giving special attention to issues the instructor identified or things that did not work well for student learning. Avoid listing problems without also giving feedback for improvement; offer specific solutions, techniques, resources, professional development opportunities, or other support options to give the instructor a way forward. You might also pose probing questions to further the instructor's self-reflection. For evaluative observations, keep in mind that the "Reflect" box may be the only part of your report that a committee or supervisor reads, and strive to strike a balanced, objective tone that neither endorses nor criticizes the instructor observed. In most cases, your job as an observer is not to evaluate the instructor, unless explicitly stated otherwise. Rather, your goal should be to collect the evidence necessary to foster productive reflection on teaching. If you know the observation will be used as part of an evaluation package, your goal might be to document behaviors so reviewers can "see" the instructor in action and make an informed decision. Table 8.3 offers an overview of best observation practices for quick and easy reference.

Debriefing the Observation

When leading a debrief, the observer takes on the role of the consultant. In this role, your goals should be "working with a teacher to enhance the teacher's comfort and skill in the classroom; knowledge of instruction; and ability to identify, solve and assess problems of teaching and learning with the end goal of improving student learning" (Border, 2012, p. 9). Unless it is explicitly your responsibility to evaluate the instructor on their teaching, approach the debrief

TABLE 8.3: At a Glance—CTB Observation Best Practices

- Ideally, schedule the observation to take place during the middle of the term (Weeks 5–10 for a 15-week course).
- Discuss expectations for confidentiality of the observation report. To promote formative, collegial dialogue, reports should be confidential, unless otherwise stipulated.
- Ask the instructor to complete the Teaching Observation Instructor Worksheet and review the Observation Report form.
- Offer the observed the opportunity to select a category or two in which they would particularly like feedback.
- Schedule a follow-up debrief session within one week of the observation.
- Remind the instructor to share their reflections as comments in the "Instructor Reflection" column of the form within a day or two to inform the report you write.
- Use the "Reflect" box in place of the memo or letter you might have written by summarizing the instructor's strengths and your suggestions for growth.
- Offer resources, opportunities, and support relevant to your suggestions for growth.
- Record specific evidence of behaviors in each category to support your "Reflect" summary.
- Provide contextualizing information for behaviors (e.g., The instructor did x, and students responded . . .) to explain what made them successful (or not) for student learning.
- Frame the debrief conversation as an opportunity to discuss the class, share strategies, reflect, and make plans for growth.

Specific to Synchronous Environments

- Arrive early and stay late to observe student interactions with each other and the instructor.
- Refrain from participating in class or interviewing students—conduct a student feedback session at the instructor's request if they desire input from students (see chapter 9).
- Take notes on instructor and student behaviors to get a sense of how instruction is being received.

Specific to Asynchronous Environments

- Review the course introduction, welcome, or overview module as well as the module(s) selected by the instructor.
- Look for evidence of course delivery and student engagement. This may mean looking at embedded activities and assignments.

Evaluative

- Let the instructor know whether they will receive a copy of the report.
- If reports must be shared with a supervisor or committee for review, be clear with the observed about who will see the report.
- If an observation report is required outside the Week 5–10 window, ask the instructor to identify a class session that most accurately reflects the way they teach.

as a conversation in which your role is to elicit further insights and reflections from the instructor. This means that you will likely do more probing and listening than talking. You should, of course, answer the instructor's questions and discuss your feedback, but keep the focus on the instructor and their thoughts rather than your own, especially if you are conducting a formative observation. While a productive debrief session might include sharing some of the strategies that work in your own teaching, be careful not to monopolize the conversation or sound overly didactic in telling the instructor what they should do. Share your experiences when relevant but approach the conversation as both a guide and a learner. Consider the debrief an opportunity to learn from your colleague's strengths while also prompting them to grow. If you are conducting an evaluative observation, you might need to give more verbal feedback as you talk through the report. Keep in mind, however, that the transformative potential of observations lies in their

---

TABLE 8.4: At a Glance—Tips for Leading an Effective Debrief Conversation

Do

- Approach the debrief as a consultant rather than as an evaluator (unless that is your stated role).
- Allow the instructor to take the lead in the conversation.
- Listen actively and take notes as the instructor speaks.
- Facilitate discussion and reflection by asking open-ended, nonjudgmental questions.
- Invite clarification or further explanation to encourage the instructor to delve deeper.
- Identify two to three strengths and support them with behavioral evidence.
- Focus feedback on one or two areas for growth and provide behavioral evidence.
- Encourage the instructor to problem-solve and develop an appropriate action plan.
- Offer strategies, resources, professional development opportunities, and other relevant support options to help the instructor make concrete plans for growth.
- Help the instructor set SMART goals (specific, measurable, attainable, relevant, and time-bound).

Don't

- Dominate discussion, interrupt, or talk over the instructor.
- Explain what you would do differently if it were your class.
- Present alternative teaching strategies as the only right way to do things.
- Focus on problems without balancing them against strengths.
- Offer feedback entirely based on praise without noting growth opportunities.
- Make comparisons to other faculty, including yourself, positively or negatively.
- Point out weaknesses without offering suggestions or helping the instructor develop plans for improvement.

---

ability to prompt self-reflection. Probing questions and dialogue should still factor significantly into the debrief of an evaluative observation if you would like the experience to be useful for the instructor's growth. For more tips on how to make the most of this time with the instructor, see Table 8.4 on leading effective debriefs.

How you begin the debrief conversation depends on your consulting style. Until you feel comfortable leading conversations as a consultant, you may prefer to start by providing the instructor with a copy of your report to review and inviting them to ask questions or identify items they want to talk about more. We typically reserve the report until later in the conversation and open by asking the instructor to share any questions, comments, or insights about the class period or module observed. If the instructor has nothing to say, we might ask more specific probing questions about what they think went well or where they think they struggled. These conversations often provide a segue into discussing themes that emerged in the report. As consultants, we can use the themes we identified to answer the instructor's questions, provide data to clarify or complicate an insight, ask further questions,

confirm a strength, or suggest an area for growth. We use the data in the report to fuel robust, reflective conversations about the class period observed and about the instructor's approach to teaching more generally. If you have reserved the report, at some point in the conversation you will want to give the instructor a copy to review and allow them time to ask clarifying questions or to identify areas of interest not yet covered.

Planning for future growth is an important part of the CTB observation process. Before the end of the consultation, cocreate a few actionable suggestions for growth with the instructor. You may already have identified a few you want to share but be sure to invite the instructor to name a few of the actions they will take as a result of your feedback as well. To ensure the instructor can use this feedback, set SMART goals (see Table 8.4). A growth goal that is too broad or too ambitious can leave an instructor feeling overwhelmed and discouraged rather than motivated to make positive change. Encourage the instructor to generate a professional development plan to be included in the instructor reflection box at the top of the report. This plan should be related to the outcomes of the debrief conversation and might include, for example, trying a new instructional strategy, reviewing a shared resource, or participating in a relevant professional development opportunity. Either ask the instructor to write down these goals and give them to you or take notes so you can add this plan to the "Reflect" box of the report. You will also want to make note of any clarifications or adjustments that need to be made to the report during your conversation. Once you make these updates, send the instructor and/or the relevant parties a final PDF copy of the report.

How Can You Adapt the CTB Observation Protocol to Your Needs?

The CTB peer observation instruments are Creative Commons licensed to allow you the freedom to adapt these materials in ways that best meet your needs. For instance, Janice Dawson, a faculty developer at Mesa Community College, worked with senate leadership, instructional deans, the department chair association leadership, and the senior associate vice president to adapt the CTB protocol to fit the college's needs for an evaluative instrument. Adaptations included removing the instructor reflection column, as instructors are required to submit a reflection as part of their portfolios, of which peer observations are only one component. While we recommend that reflection play a key role in peer observation, in this case, removing the reflection column eliminates a redundancy as instructors will complete a reflection elsewhere as part of the larger review process. We offer this as only one example of how you can adapt the CTB peer observation protocol to suit your context. For more adaptation examples, visit https://criticalteachingbehaviors.com. We also invite you to share your story and adaptations with us at criticalteachingbehaviors@gmail.com so we can create a collaborative repository of options.

Chapter Takeaways

The CTB protocol by no means resolves all of the complications related to peer observations. However, our emphasis on creating a common language in which to discuss the characteristics of good teaching lends a valuable consistency to peer observation conversations, and our instruments, aligned to the CTB framework, provide a clear structure to the process for both observer and observed. As we close this chapter, you should now be able to explain the following:

- the research-based benefits of effective peer observation
- how the design of the CTB peer observation protocol promotes these benefits
- the process for conducting a CTB peer observation

In the next chapter, we will explore the aligned student feedback instrument to consider how you can incorporate the student voice into the documentation of your teaching.

Notes

1. Unsurprisingly, Kell and Annetts (2009) have found that faculty rank impacts perceptions of peer observations. Senior faculty tend to view peer observation as a professional development experience, whereas junior faculty may experience even formative observations as judgments on their teaching.

2. "Implicit bias refers to the attitudes or stereotypes that unconsciously affect our understanding, actions, and decisions. These biases include both favourable and unfavourable assessments, and are activated without one's awareness or intentional control. Individuals therefore do not consciously hide these biases, and they also do not necessarily align with our declared beliefs. Instead, implicit biases are inaccessible to one's conscious mind. Early life experiences and the media are common origins of implicit associations" (Kirwan Institute for the Study of Race and Ethnicity, 2012, p. 1).

3. See Appendix H ("Peer Observation Email Templates") for a template email you can adapt.

4. For asynchronous observations, you may choose to request these observations prior to your review of the course. Obviously, the nature of a synchronous course requires that the instructor complete their reflections on the class period after the observation.

References

Alabi, J., & Weare, W. H. (2014). Peer review of teaching: Best practices for a non-programmatic approach. *Communications in Information Literacy, 8*(2), 180–191.

Al Qahtani, S., Kattan, T., Al Harbi, K., & Seefeldt, M. (2011). Some thoughts on educational peer evaluation.

South-East Asian Journal of Medical Education, *5*(1), 47–49. http://seajme.md.chula.ac.th/articleVol5No1/SP1_Saad%20Al%20Qahtani.pdf

Atwood, C. H., Taylor, J. W., & Hutchings, P. A. (2000). Why are chemists and other scientists afraid of the peer review of teaching? *Journal of Chemical Education, 77*, 239–244. http://pubs.acs.org.ezproxy.lib.monash.edu.au/doi/pdf/10.1021/ed077p239

Bell, A., & Mladenovic, R. (2008). The benefits of peer observation of teaching for tutor development. *Higher Education, 55*, 735–752. https://doi.org/10.1007/s10734-007-9093-1

Bernstein, D. J. (2008). Peer review and evaluation on the intellectual work of teaching. *Change, 40*(2), 48–51. http://www.nus.edu.sg/teachingacademy/docs/Resource%20Review.pdf

Border, L. L. B. (2012). Understanding and implementing effective consultations. In K. T. Brinko (Ed.), *Practically speaking: A sourcebook for instruction consultants in higher education* (pp. 8–15). New Forums.

Boring, A. (2017). Gender biases in student evaluations of teaching. *Journal of Public Economics, 145*, 27–41.

Cavanagh, R. R. (1996). Formative and summative evaluation in the faculty peer review of teaching. *Innovative Higher Education, 20*, 235–240. http://www.metapress.com.ezproxy.lib.monash.edu.au/content/h274g1432208jg30/fulltext.pdf

Chism, N. (2007). *Peer review of teaching, A sourcebook* (2nd ed.). Anker Publishing.

Fletcher, J. A. (2018). Peer observation of teaching: A practical tool in higher education. *Journal of Faculty Development, 32*(1), 1–14.

Gleason, N. W., & Sanger, C. S. (2017). *Guidelines for peer observation of teaching: A sourcebook for international liberal arts learning* [White paper]. Centre for Teaching and Learning, Yale-NUS College, Singapore. https://www.yale-nus.edu.sg/academics/wp-content/uploads/sites/8/2022/01/Peer-Observation-Booklet-web-version.pdf

Goldberg, L. R., Parham, D. F., Coufal, K. L., Maeda, M., Scudder, R. R., & Sechtem, P. P. (2010). Peer review: The importance of education for best practice. *Journal of College Teaching and Learning, 7*(2), 71–84. https://doi.org/10.19030/tlc.v7i2.91

Hanson, J. (1993). Observing classroom teaching in higher education: A case study. *Quality Assurance in Education, 1*, 26–30. https://doi.org/10.1108/09684889310046176

Hurst, B., Wilson, C., & Cramer, G. (1998). Professional teaching portfolios: Tools for reflection, growth, and advancement. *Phi Delta Kappan, 79*, 578–582. Http://www.jstor.org/stable/pdfplus/20439279.pdf

Keig, L., & Waggoner, M. D. (1994). *Collaborative peer review: The role of faculty in improving college teaching* (Technical Report No. 2). (ED378925). George Washington University School of Education and Human Development.

Kell, C., & Annetts, S. (2009). Peer review of teaching embedded practice or policy-holding complacency? *Innovations in Education and Teaching International, 46*, 61–70. https://doi.org/10.1080/14703290802646156

Kirwan Institute for the Study of Race and Ethnicity. (2012). *Understanding implicit bias*. Kirwan Institute for the Study of Race and Ethnicity, Ohio State University. https://kirwaninstitute.osu.edu/article/understanding-implicit-bias

Knapper, C., & Wright, W. A. (2001). Using portfolios to document good teaching: Premises, purposes, practices. In C. Knapper & P. Cranton (Eds.), *Fresh Approaches to the Evaluation of Teaching* (New Directions for Teaching and Learning, no. 88, pp. 19–29). Wiley. http://onlinelibrary.wiley.com.ezproxy.lib.monash.edu.au/doi/10.1002/tl.34/pdf

Lowder, L., Atiqullah, M., Colebeck, D., Das, S., Karim, M. A., Khalid, A., Singh, R., & Utschig, T. (2017). Peer observation: improvement of teaching effectiveness through class participation at a polytechnic university. *Journal of STEM Education, 18*(4), 51–56.

MacNell, L., Driscoll, A., & Hun, A. N. (2015). What's in a name: Exposing gender bias in student ratings of teaching. *Innovative Higher Education, 40*(4), 291–303.

Quinlan, K. M., & Akerlind, G. S. (2000). Factors affecting departmental peer collaboration for faculty development: Two cases in context. *Higher Education, 40*, 23–52. http://www.jstor.org.ezproxy.lib.monash.edu.au/stable/pdfplus/3447950.pdf

Thomas, S., Abraham, M., Raj, S. J., & Beh, L. S. (2014). A qualitative review of literature on peer review of teaching in higher education: An application of the SWOT framework. *Review of Educational Research, 84*(1), 112–159. https://doi.org/10.3102/0034654313499617

Wagner, N., Rieger, M., & Voorvelt, K. (2016). Gender, ethnicity and teaching evaluations: Evidence from mixed teaching teams. *Economics of Education Review, 54*, 79–94.

Wubbels, T., & Korthagen, F. A. J. (1990). The effects of a pre-service teacher education program for the preparation of reflective teachers. *Journal of Education for Teaching, 16*, 29–43. https://doi.org/10.1080/0260747900160102

CHAPTER 9

Midterm Student Feedback

WE KNOW THAT STUDENT perspectives are essential for improving our teaching and showcasing our effectiveness. Most institutions acknowledge the importance of the student voice with the collection of SETs at the end of each semester. While the intention behind SETs may be in part to provide instructors formative feedback on their teaching practices, too often these results become the sole metric by which teaching effectiveness is assessed, prompting more anxiety and aversion than reflection and growth. The student voice becomes the entire narrative rather than an essential component of the larger story of our teaching. While SETs can yield valuable data worthy of reflection and incorporation into a teaching portfolio, this chapter will focus instead on a supplemental means of gathering student feedback that allows us to incorporate student voices into our teaching narratives without losing our own voices or the perspectives of our colleagues in the process.

Typically gathered somewhere between Weeks 5 and 10 of a 15-week semester, midterm student feedback offers a more formative means of gathering student input than SETs. Some instructors collect their own anonymous student feedback through electronic questionnaires or facilitated conversations. In the absence of other options, these practices yield better outcomes for both instructors and students than traditional end-of-term feedback alone. Certainly the feedback an instructor may gather through these means can lead to positive conversations with students and changes in the course. However, as Hurney et al. (2022) note, "if a curious, reflective instructor chooses to gather mid-semester feedback through an anonymous survey or even an instructor-facilitated class discussion, chances are high that the resulting feedback will not be particularly detailed or frank" (p. 85). Students may feel uncomfortable honestly expressing their thoughts through instructor-supplied means, even if the collection method anonymizes the data. Furthermore, instructors may struggle to interpret and respond to contradictory feedback, and if they never follow up with students, students can begin to feel that their feedback is not really valued.

The group instructional feedback technique (GIFT), or the related small-group instructional diagnosis (SGID) method, for collecting midterm student feedback remedies these problems by structuring the process around a series of conversations facilitated by a third-party consultant or colleague (Diamond, 2004). At the request of the instructor, a consultant (a colleague or educational developer) visits the class for as little as 15 but up to 30 minutes to speak confidentially with students after the instructor leaves the room. In the first step of a GIFT, students complete an individual questionnaire. They may then optionally discuss their responses in small groups before the facilitator invites groups to share their responses to the questionnaire and opens the floor for general discussion of feedback. Throughout the conversation, the facilitator takes notes and asks probing questions when necessary to prompt students to provide clarifying information. After the class visit, the consultant compiles a report of student responses and notes from the ensuing discussion to share with the instructor. During the debrief discussion, the consultant and the instructor work together to determine how the instructor can respond to the feedback received. The instructor then returns to the classroom to thank students for their comments and address their input.

While research indicates that collecting and responding to midterm feedback increases SET ratings, engaging in conversation with an external consultant about that feedback further increases SET rating gains over instructors who interpret feedback on their own; conversations about feedback may also help retain these gains over future semesters (Cohen, 1980; Lammers et al., 2017; McGowan, 2009; Piccinin, 1999). For these reasons, the CTB protocol presented in this chapter focuses on midterm student feedback collected through GIFTs, but because we recognize not everyone has access to a colleague who can perform a GIFT on their behalf, we provide notes on how to collect your own feedback using CTB instruments. Following the format established in the previous chapter, we start by providing an overview of what research says about midterm student feedback before taking a closer look at the CTB-aligned instrument and outlining the process for conducting a CTB GIFT. By the end of this chapter, we will have answered the following questions:

- What are the benefits of effective GIFTs?
- What are the instructor benefits of the CTB GIFT protocol?
- What is the CTB process for conducting GIFTs?
- How can you adapt the CTB GIFT to meet your needs?

If you already conduct or receive GIFTs, you will note that neither the CTB protocol nor the instrument differ substantially from what you might already expect based on experience. As you will see, the most significant innovations relate to features we have added to create alignment between the instrument and the CTB framework to help you interpret, use, and explain your report more effectively.

What Are the Benefits of Effective GIFTs?

In our years as educational developers, we have encountered more than a few faculty who feel a great deal of anxiety about reading student feedback at the end of each semester. Sometimes these concerns are related to performance evaluations that may be tied to SET ratings; other times, instructors fear that students will use the opportunity to make unkind, unhelpful, or unfair comments. A growing body of research reveals bias in SETs against instructors belonging to minoritized populations and justifies these fears, especially when significant job outcomes are tied to these reports (Boring, 2016; Kreitzer & Sweet-Cushman, 2021; Mitchell & Martin, 2018). Even instructors who do not experience these apprehensions may feel frustration or disappointment when they read feedback they could have used to improve the course sooner had they known. This kind of feedback can improve the learning experience for next semester's students, but conscientious instructors regret that it is too late to do anything for this semester's students. The GIFT experience, by contrast, often leaves faculty with opposite reactions. We have consulted with faculty who confessed to feeling deeply anxious about what their students would say in a midterm feedback session. Afterward, these same faculty have noted the experience to be much more insightful and encouraging than they expected given their experience with SETs. While GIFTs do not offer a silver bullet alternative to SETs, nor do we advocate that they become the new means by which administrators assess teaching effectiveness, studies have found a host of benefits associated with collecting midterm feedback, particularly through the GIFT method. In the following, we summarize some of these findings for instructors, students, and institutions. Refer to Table 9.1 for a condensed overview of the benefits of midterm student feedback.

Instructor Reflection and Growth

Because they are confidential between the consultant and instructor and designed to gather formative rather than evaluative feedback, GIFTs can lower the instructor anxiety associated with receiving student feedback and help create a constructive atmosphere for reflection and growth as a teacher (Diamond, 2004). During the classroom conversation, questions posed to students and the probing clarifications of the consultant prompt students to provide concrete feedback and actionable suggestions. The GIFT debrief process promotes critical reflection on this feedback in conjunction with guidance and probing from the consultant. Thus, a crucial component of effective GIFTs is allowing adequate time for this conversation to take place (Penny & Coe, 2004). Reflection can and should continue long after that conversation ends; taking time to close the feedback loop by debriefing with students or making improvements to course materials for next semester are just two examples of such ongoing reflection. In a survey of faculty who had participated in the GIFT process, one study found that 90% of respondents indicated they had made changes to their courses as a result of the feedback they received (Finelli et al., 2011). Another study found that only 4% of respondents did not make immediate changes to their courses following GIFT feedback (Diamond, 2004). Multiple studies have found that the benefits of GIFTs are largely predicated upon instructors meaningfully debriefing the experience with students to let them know how it will impact the course both now and in the future (Abbott et al., 1990; Lewis, 2001; McDonnell & Dodd, 2017). When asked about the overall impact of the GIFT, faculty note an improvement in the learning environment as a consequence of improved rapport and communication with students as well as insights into the student learning experience in the course (Clark & Redmond, 1982; Diamond, 2004; Finelli et al., 2011). GIFTs can even improve end-of-semester ratings for the course (Finelli et al., 2008; Wickramasinghe & Timpson, 2006).

Student Motivation and Satisfaction

No doubt as a result of the changes made in response to feedback, instructors who receive GIFT feedback report seeing an increase in student motivation and participation as well as generally improved student attitudes toward the course and instructor (Mauger, 2010; Lewis, 2001; Svinicki, 2001). This ability to gain insight into students' thoughts on our courses while we still have time to make adjustments is one of the chief values of midterm feedback. We can then make informed decisions about what we should do more often, what we might need to clarify before a miscommunication develops into student frustration, and what we can do differently to meet student needs. Rarely can we address all feedback in the immediate moment, but we can let students know how we intend to use their feedback to improve the course in future semesters. Sometimes we receive feedback that we cannot address, either because it does not serve our overall learning goals or because it is beyond our ability to control (e.g., the time and length of the class period). In these cases, we can address student feedback by explaining our rationale for not making changes. This kind of follow-up communicates

a value for student input that can increase instructor–student rapport and trust (Cook-Sather, 2009; Hurney et al., 2014; Richardson, 2005; Wickramasinghe & Timpson, 2006). When surveyed, students themselves indicate an increased sense of camaraderie with each other and ownership over the success of the course (Cook-Sather, 2009). If you have ever conducted a GIFT, you may have seen this finding in action. During the class discussion, one group may offer feedback ("We never know when things are going to be due") only for another student to offer a clarifying correction ("The course calendar is posted in the LMS with all of our due dates"). GIFT conversations make possible this kind of valuable peer learning. In courses where a GIFT was conducted, student responsibility for learning increased as demonstrated through behaviors like studying for and participating in class (Hurney et al., 2014).

As we can see, GIFTs offer demonstrable benefits to students, but can we trust student feedback? Do students know enough about their own learning to offer productive feedback? Findings reveal that students almost ubiquitously agree that GIFTs are more valuable than SETs (Mauger, 2010). Moreover, students tend to engage more thoroughly in GIFTs than in SETs, giving deeper feedback than usual (Sherry et al., 1998; Veeck et al., 2016). Finally, several studies show that, while they may not know everything about what constitutes good teaching, students do have a decent sense of what helps them learn and regularly identify course aspects that align with what we know about best practices in teaching and learning (Blue et al., 2014; Newby et al., 1991; Sozer et al., 2019). We can rely on our students to give honest, useful feedback for the most part, and where discrepancies arise, we can turn to our consultant for further discussion.

Institutional Community and Belonging

As instructors, collecting midterm student feedback is a simple yet high-impact means of improving our teaching as well as student experience in our courses, but we would be remiss if we did not mention the far-reaching impact this kind of feedback can have on programs, departments, colleges, institutions, and potentially all of higher education as well. We do not advocate that administrators require GIFTs from faculty as part of their evaluation as this defeats the formative purpose of the exercise; however, administrators who encourage their faculty to engage

> **TABLE 9.1: At a Glance—Benefits of Midterm Student Feedback**
>
> **Instructor Reflection and Growth**
>
> - provide formative, actionable feedback for growth
> - promote collaborative and individual reflection
> - improve instructor–student rapport and communication, including SET ratings
>
> **Student Motivation and Satisfaction**
>
> - increase student motivation and participation
> - communicate value for student perspectives
> - encourage student camaraderie and peer learning
>
> **Institutional Community and Belonging**
>
> - cultivate a culture that values teaching
> - reduce the sense of isolation in teaching by creating community among faculty
> - foster a sense of both student and faculty belonging to the institution

in GIFTs, or at the very least to collect their own midterm feedback, promote "a culture with greater emphasis on the act of teaching and learning about teaching" (Hurney et al., 2022, p. 108). Departments may benefit from GIFT insights when designing new programs, implementing new curricula, or revamping general education courses. Institutions can ultimately benefit because GIFTs foster both student and faculty sense of belonging to a community (Clark & Redmond, 1982; Hunt, 2003; Wulff et al., 1985). The more instructors collect and respond to student feedback voluntarily, the more students feel the institution values what they have to say. Because GIFTs require collaboration with a colleague who serves as a feedback facilitator and consultant, they can help instructors connect over their teaching, reducing the sense of isolation commonly associated with teaching and replacing it with a feeling of community (Snooks et al., 2004). The power of GIFTs lies in their potential to create conversations about teaching that include all of the relevant players for effective reflection: the instructor, peers, and students.

What Are the Instructor Benefits of the CTB GIFT Protocol?

As we move into this discussion of the CTB GIFT protocol, you will want to first review the Midterm Student Feedback Survey (Appendix F) and the accompanying Midsemester Student Feedback Report (Appendix G) to help you better understand the design features we will highlight. While we have not significantly altered either the process or the report form, a basic knowledge of standard GIFT protocol will help you better understand the adaptations we have made as we move forward. There are a variety of quantitative and qualitative instruments to choose from when designing a student survey form, but the most common GIFT survey includes three standard qualitative questions: What about this course is helping your learning? What about this course is hindering your learning? What suggestions do you have for the instructor? The survey may also include quantitative Likert-scale questions. Occasionally it may include metacognitive questions that ask students to reflect on their responsibilities and contributions to the learning process (e.g, What do *you* do that facilitates your learning?). The GIFT process asks students to complete these surveys individually.[1] Depending on the length of the session and preferences of the instructor and consultant, the consultant may then ask students to discuss their responses to the survey in small groups of three to five or skip to convening a whole-class discussion by inviting students to share their individual responses. As students report on their feedback, the facilitator captures statements on the board or screen. Students "vote" on their agreement with statements by show of hands, which the facilitator also notes. Before leaving, the consultant collects the anonymous questionnaires to use in the final report (we recommend using digital surveys to skip this step). The facilitator's report usually contains raw data, including how many students responded to the surveys, themes that emerged in the whole-group conversation, the number of students who agreed with a given statement, and all or most of the individual responses. Feedback may be organized in the report by perceived priority (number of students who agreed with a statement), by theme (instructor, course delivery, assignments, etc.), or both or neither. There is no standard report form used for GIFTs. Now that we have established a baseline for GIFTs, we turn our attention to the design benefits of the CTB protocol.

Streamlining and Focus

GIFT reports can be overwhelming to read because they consist almost exclusively of qualitative data—a lot of it. Although the consultant's role is to help draw the instructor's focus to salient feedback, we have noticed that it is common for instructors to get sidetracked by a few minor comments that only a handful of students agreed with and that may not have come up in conversation at all rather than turning their attention to the most important feedback that emerged. When designing the CTB GIFT report form, we considered approaches for sharing feedback in a digestible manner that promotes focus. Rather than giving the instructor all the raw data, the report form instead shares only the feedback that students found to be most important based on the whole-class conversation or responses frequently repeated across individual questionnaires. As you can see in the form, we accomplish this by subdividing each of the three GIFT questions into themes that emerged from the whole-class debrief and small-group responses that confirmed or expanded on these themes. This approach limits instructor distraction by red herring comments and allows them to dedicate their limited time and resources to the feedback that students most wanted them to know.

Qualitative and Quantitative Data

Depending on disciplinary background, we tend to prefer working with either qualitative or quantitative data, but we can all benefit from seeing our teaching from the multiple angles each kind of data can provide. The classic GIFT privileges a qualitative approach to student feedback, and for good reason. SETs often consist almost exclusively of quantitative questions, so by collecting only qualitative responses, GIFTs provide a different type of data and move away from the SET model. Quantitative questions are also often associated with evaluation and evaluative feedback rather than the formative feedback GIFTs are designed to promote. Much like our students, we can get in the habit of looking for our "score" rather than reading and reflecting on the written feedback so we can appropriately recognize strengths and growth opportunities. Recognizing the potential benefits of quantitative data and taking these drawbacks into consideration, we made the decision to develop 10 short Likert-scale questions aligned to CTB categories that we have also included in the student survey. The purpose of these questions is not to reintroduce a sense of evaluation to the student feedback process but rather to offer supplemental data to help instructors reflect more effectively on their teaching across the CTB categories that are visible to students. The quantitative and qualitative portions of the survey complement each other, providing data on both big picture behaviors across categories and deeper dive insights into specific behaviors, or lack of behaviors, and their impact on student learning. If instructors receive multiple CTB GIFT reports for different classes or across their careers, the quantitative data can offer quick comparisons about what might be affecting student performance in one course as opposed to another or help the instructor easily see the areas in which they have improved or remained constant over the years. Having reviewed the literature on issues with SETs, we carefully designed the quantitative questions to focus student attention on the prevalence of instructor behaviors to help mitigate some of the biases that tend to emerge in quantitative student ratings. While more research needs to be done on this aspect of the form, our initial data suggest that the questions achieve that goal.[2]

Instructor Reflection and Voice

The "Reflect" box on the last page of the form encourages instructors to continue the reflection process on their own. For instructors who may need more guidance on how to get started, we provide the following prompts: "Based on feedback from students and the debrief conversation, how will you follow up with students about the insights provided? What steps do you plan to take to enhance teaching strengths and address areas for improvement?" These prompts invite instructors to consider feedback from both students and the consultant, list ideas they want to cover when debriefing with students, and make plans for future professional development opportunities or course improvements they would like to pursue. Of course, we always encourage instructors to take notes during the debrief conversation, but the addition of the "Reflect" box to the form allows the instructor's thoughts to become a recorded part of the final report, which serves multiple purposes. First and most importantly, the inclusion of the "Reflect" box ensures that the instructor's perspective continues to be an ever-present part of the documentation of their teaching, a core value for us in designing the CTB tool kit. The thoughts recorded in this section can become part of the larger narrative instructors construct about their teaching and can even serve as narrative guides for external reviewers with whom the report might eventually be shared if included in a portfolio. For instructors who seek student feedback over multiple semesters using this form, their reflections can act as checkpoints to which they can refer in future years, helping them to see what goals they set for themselves, how they have grown to meet those goals, and how they would like to continue to grow.

Purpose, Modality, and Discipline

As this is a midsemester student feedback instrument, we feel strongly that the GIFT survey and protocol should be used for formative rather than evaluative purposes. If this protocol were to be used for evaluative purposes, many of the reflective, conversational components would be rendered ineffective. However, the survey and report could be adapted for this type of use if desired as the survey provides a balanced alternative to SETs that prioritize quantitative data. Because GIFTs require synchronous conversations with students, we designed this protocol to function primarily in an F2F or online synchronous environment. Instructors teaching in an asynchronous online environment may still find the survey

useful for collecting midterm student feedback but will miss out on the small-group conversation portion of the GIFT experience unless they are able to schedule synchronous student feedback conversations. In the adaptations section near the end of the chapter we provide more information on how to use the CTB student feedback survey in an online environment. The mixed-methods data collected by the CTB student feedback form lends itself to use across disciplines.

What Is the CTB Process for Conducting GIFTs?

GIFTs, as Hurney et al. (2022) argue, revolve around leading effective conversations. The CTB process for conducting GIFTs does not differ significantly from existing guidance, so in this section, we summarize best practices from existing literature and our own experiences for facilitating effective GIFT discussions. Keep in mind that there are many variations in the execution of this process, some of which we will discuss in the adaptations section. Our process differs most significantly from existing protocols in terms of the quantitative questions and how we prepare and report the data. With these caveats in mind, readers who are familiar with the process for conducting GIFTs may wish to skim ahead to the "Report Form" subsection.

Presession

Depending on your position and context, you may receive student feedback requests through casual conversations, emails, or a designated request system such as an online form or calendar app. Regardless of how you receive the request, your first step should be to reach out to the instructor by email to clarify the process and confirm necessary details. We recommend that you collect the following information at a minimum:

- course title and number
- preferred date(s) for the session
- course start and end time
- preferred timing for the visit (beginning or end of class)
- meeting location

- number of students
- preferred dates/times for a debrief conversation

You may also want to provide the instructor an overview of the process if they are unfamiliar with what happens during and after a GIFT. The Pre-GIFT email template in Appendix I includes the information you might want to collect from the instructor and provides an overview of the process that you can adapt and share with instructors. To save time and make this process easier for the instructor and the consultant, we recommend gathering and sharing information electronically rather than holding presession consultations, as is customary. As you can see in the email template, we invite the instructor to request a consultation should they have any additional questions they would like to discuss before the GIFT.

To prepare for the classroom visit, think about how you will administer the survey. We prefer to collect student responses through an online form as it saves the step of having to type written data into our reports and easily ensures the anonymity of student responses. If you choose this option, you will want to create a shortened URL or QR code in advance that you can share with students. Consider setting the form to send or show students their responses after submitting the survey so they can refer to their written notes during the debrief conversation. Most students carry technology with them but bring a few printed copies of the survey just in case a student forgets their technology, experiences technical difficulties, or does not have regular access to such technology.

Leading a Student Feedback Session

When you arrive to lead the session, the instructor should introduce you to the students and briefly state that you are there to talk with them about their experience in the class. The instructor and any teaching assistants should then leave the room. Before administering the survey, take a moment to positively frame the experience. Let students know that their responses to the survey are completely anonymous and remind them that the instructor has requested this feedback voluntarily because they care about what students have to say. Lauren prompts students to think about the value the instructor places on their feedback by asking students when they usually give feedback on their courses (end of semester) and what the instructor does with that feedback (they never find out). By contrast, midterm feedback allows them to work with their instructor to create a better learning environment while there is still time to make positive changes. This is also a good opportunity to read or summarize a bias statement. The sample bias statement we provide in Appendix I shifts student focus away from static instructor attributes and toward dynamic teaching behaviors. As a final step before administering the survey, outline for students what will happen in the remaining time. Students will spend 5 to 7 minutes completing the survey individually. At the end of that time, you will invite volunteers to share their responses to the first two open-ended questions. You will capture their responses on the board or screen and ask them to demonstrate by show of hands their agreement with the statement. For a quick overview of information to share when framing the GIFT, see Table 9.2.

TABLE 9.2: Checklist for Introducing the GIFT to Students

- Ensure anonymity of responses.
- Positively frame the experience as voluntary for the instructor and an opportunity to provide feedback that can improve the course for current students.
- Read or summarize a bias statement to help students focus on teaching behaviors rather than static traits.
- Outline how you will use your time with them.
  - 5–7 minutes individual survey response
  - 13–15 minutes facilitated discussion of open-ended questions
- Display the digital survey access information and/or distribute paper surveys.

Once you have framed the experience for students, provide them digital or paper access to the form and allow them time to complete the survey. To avoid "outing" students who may not have access to technology, you can ask if anyone would prefer a paper copy. While they complete the survey, notice whether students seem to be finishing early or need more time. You may want to check around the 5-minute mark to see how many students need more time and decide whether they need the full 7 minutes. Give a 1-minute warning before transitioning to the discussion so students have adequate time to complete their responses and submit the survey.

As you transition into the facilitated conversation, invite students to share first what works well for their learning in the course. Starting with what works helps students approach the discussion from a positive perspective and puts them in a formative feedback mindset rather than focusing attention on the negative aspects of the course. In your role as the facilitator, strive to remain as neutral as possible while still probing students for more information when necessary. For instance, students might say something about how much they enjoy the activities they do in class or that the instructor is approachable. Student comments often begin broad and vague, so these moments present excellent opportunities for a consultant to respond, "Can you tell me more about that?" or "What does that look like?" or "What does that mean to you?" Asking these kinds of probing questions can help the facilitator drill down to the behaviors a teacher engages in that help or hinder student learning, which makes it possible to provide more specific, actionable feedback to the instructor. During this debrief conversation, you should not try to change student opinions, demonstrate solidarity with their experiences, or explain aspects of the instructor's teaching that students may have misunderstood. Consider yourself the gatherer of information rather than the intermediary between the students and instructor.

Keep an eye on the time to ensure that you leave ample time to cover what is making it difficult for students to learn in the course. When facilitating this portion of the discussion, focus student attention on positive change by asking things like "What could your instructor do to improve x?" or "What suggestions do you have for doing y differently?" or "What do you think would help you learn better in this scenario?" These follow-up questions once again shift student attention to actions the instructor can take to improve the learning experience and help to maintain a positive tone to the session. Sometimes the session ends early because students do not have much to say; other times, you will need to limit student responses in one or both categories to ensure that the session ends within the specified timeframe. Before leaving, thank students for their time and feedback. Notify the instructor that they may return to the room or, if you conducted the session at the end of class, dismiss the students. The "Steps for Leading a Student Feedback Session" in Table 9.3 provide a handy overview of these steps for future reference.

TABLE 9.3: Steps for Leading a Student Feedback Session

- If using electronic surveys, provide a paper option as well.
- Monitor student progress to estimate how much more time they need.
- Give a 1-minute warning before moving into the facilitated debrief.
- Maintain a neutral, information-gathering approach to facilitating the debrief.
- Ask probing questions to better get a deeper understanding of student comments.
- Start with what helps students learn to set a positive tone for the conversation.
- Record student responses somewhere, preferably visibly on a board or screen.
- Invite a vote of agreement by show of hands after each response.
- Encourage students to give suggestions for improvement along with their observations of what is not working.
- Thank students for speaking candidly with you about their learning experience.
- Invite the instructor back into the room or dismiss the class.

Report Form

If you did not already schedule a debrief meeting with the instructor, you will want to do so as soon as possible upon completing the GIFT session. Be sure to allow yourself sufficient time to write the report before the meeting. Compiling the report is not a time-consuming endeavor once you have some experience doing so, but because these sessions necessarily fall at midterm, one of the busiest times of year, you may find it easy to put off as you deal with competing priorities. Setting a debrief date can help ensure that you prioritize completing the report within a reasonable timeframe. Guidance on the appropriate window for a debrief often idealistically recommends returning the report to the instructor before their next class period. In practice, we find that such a tight turnaround is rarely possible, either because the instructor teaches the course three days a week or because scheduling conflicts prohibit you from finding a meeting time that works before the next class period. For the feedback to be most effective, however, you do want to return it to the instructor as soon as possible so they can discuss it with their students. We find that a meeting time somewhere within a week of the GIFT session usually gives us enough time to write the report and allows us to find a meeting time that fits busy schedules while still returning the feedback soon enough for the instructor to be able to meaningfully discuss it with their students.

Before you begin the report, fill in the relevant information at the top of the form, making sure to update the number of students who participated in the survey. Depending on how you prefer to work, you may start the report either with the qualitative or quantitative sections. We find a slight advantage to starting with the quantitative data because it can help us identify big picture themes across CTB categories that makes it easier to sort and interpret the qualitative feedback. Collecting feedback through an electronic form makes it especially easy to complete the quantitative section as whatever platform you use should provide data on the total number of votes as well as a breakdown of the number of votes at each level in each category. Paper surveys will require a manual count. Once you have completed the Likert-scale table, calculate the average score for each question. Seeing the average scores for each question and each category helps you identify clear areas of strength, both in terms of individual actions and overall categories, as well as potential for

growth. Keeping these insights in mind can prepare you to identify themes as you shift your attention to the qualitative feedback.

Rather than reporting all the raw qualitative data, we recommend that you instead analyze comments for themes and create a curated overview of major themes and representative student comments for the final report. We do this for practical reasons. Because each student fills out the report individually, including every student comment in the report can quickly become overwhelming and repetitive for the instructor to read. Filtering the qualitative data in this manner can also make it easier for the instructor to digest the report and focus on the most relevant information rather than getting distracted by the red herring comment of one disgruntled student, as sometimes happens; as a result, it will also be easier to identify and discuss concrete action items in response to the student feedback received. To create the thematic report, we recommend that you first identify major CTB themes that emerged in the qualitative data and create subheadings with a tag for each major theme—for example, "Engage" or, if feedback straddles categories, "Engage/Include." Under each thematic heading, start a new bullet point for a comment that emerged in the facilitated debrief and summarize what students said based on your notes. Include the number or estimated percentage of students who agreed with the comment. In subbullets, provide a few (three to five) representative statements from the individual surveys to add additional depth and evidence for each major point, if possible. Often, a number of students will make similar comments, and there is no need to repeat the same feedback over and over. Sometimes, a single student might make a comment that does not fit into a recurring theme and was not addressed in the classroom. It can be important for the instructor to hear this individual voice even though their concern may not be shared by other students (e.g., comments about accessibility of course materials, experiences of toxic classroom interactions, etc.). We recommend you evaluate whether one-off comments should be included in the report and debrief conversation on a case-by-case basis. Aside from organizing feedback thematically, stick to reporting what students said in the debrief and in their surveys. Resist interpreting the data or adding suggestions for improvement. As much as possible, quote directly from the classroom conversation as well as student surveys. Doing so ensures that you let the students speak for themselves rather than putting words in their mouths. To view a sample student feedback report and get a better sense of what a completed report might look like, visit https:// criticalteachingbehaviors.com.

Debrief

Although you should refrain from including your interpretations in the written report, prepare for the debrief conversation by making notes on what you would like to cover with the instructor. These notes might include additional information about the atmosphere in the room during different points in the discussion (e.g., students became very animated and excited when talking about how you engage them in debates during class, which underscores their feedback on how much they enjoy this aspect of the class). You will certainly want to include concrete suggestions for growth. Students will likely provide a few useful suggestions for how the instructor can improve the learning experience. You can build on these suggestions and add others based on your own expertise and insight. If you do not feel comfortable making those suggestions just yet, consider the CTB categories in which you would like to prompt the instructor to grow; turn to the relevant chapter in this book for behaviors you can suggest the instructor implement to help them improve.

Midterm feedback debriefs should be conversations between the instructor and the consultant and, to the extent possible, should be led by the instructor rather than the consultant. To foster discussion and allow the instructor time to process your feedback before the meeting, consider providing the completed report as early as the morning of the consultation. We find that providing the report any earlier may lead some instructors to cancel their consultation, thinking they no longer need to discuss the report. If you prefer, you may wait to provide the report until the meeting, but allowing the instructor advance time to process the data and prepare questions can lead to a more productive, instructor-led conversation. Begin the discussion by asking the instructor something along the lines of "What questions, thoughts, or insights do you have after reviewing your report?" Allow the instructor to explore and reflect throughout the debrief. Ask probing questions, validate insights, and make suggestions as necessary. If your notes match your report, you will likely find that organic opportunities emerge for you

to share additional information and make suggestions. However, if you feel the instructor has overlooked something important that you wanted to discuss as you near the end of the meeting, you should feel free to bring it to their attention.

As you near the end of the conversation, you will want to discuss the instructor's plan for debriefing the feedback with their students. Remind the instructor that they should close the loop by discussing the outcomes of this consultation with students. They will not have time to address all the feedback they received, so this is an opportunity to help them consider what is most important to report back to students. Thank them for their feedback, and express appreciation for any positive feedback they provided. We need to know what to keep doing just as much as we need to know what to change. Regarding suggestions for change, there are three main types of responses an instructor can give: "I hear what you said about *x*, and consequently, I will do *y*," "I cannot or will not do *x* for *y* reasons," or "I hear what you said about *x*, but I will have to wait until next semester to make *y* changes." The first response identifies something the instructor can and will do now to improve the learning experience based on student feedback. When responding in this manner, the instructor should identify concrete changes they will make or actions they will take in response to student comments. If students said the instructor is not responsive to their emails, the instructor might respond by making a policy that says students can expect a response within 48 to 72 hours, for example. Making this type of policy is not enough; follow-through is important for conveying true value for student feedback. As a consultant, probe the instructor to discover what they are genuinely willing and able to commit to doing and remind them that failure to follow through could result in lower SETs. Opening the student debrief with a positive affirmation of what will change based on their suggestions makes them feel heard.

Sometimes we must tell our students we cannot do something they have urged us to do. Students assume that we as teachers have complete control over every aspect of our courses, which is not always true. Other times, they make suggestions for improvement that run counter to good teaching and learning practices. In these cases, the instructor needs to clarify why something is being done the way it is. For instance, students may commonly complain about the textbook in a course, but the instructor may have no control over which textbook is used. Students may also ask for study guides or practice tests that mirror the actual test so closely that success depends on memorization rather than true learning. When an instructor receives this type of feedback, they should plan to explain to their students the rationale behind current practice or behind their resistance to making a much-requested change. If students are requesting something that runs contrary to good teaching and learning practice, explaining the research related to that request can eliminate frustrations and dispel misunderstandings before they turn into negative SETs. This moment can also generate a compromise response along the lines of "I cannot or will not do *x* for *y* reasons, but I can meet you in the middle and do *z*."

Finally, students often provide valid insights for changes that simply cannot be implemented once the course is already up and running. They may suggest more formative assessments or a different grade distribution, to name a few of the more common requests. While this feedback can significantly improve the learning experience, these types of changes usually need to wait until the course can be redesigned after the current semester ends. Letting students know that we have heard their requests and will act on them to improve the learning experience in the future fosters a sense of trust, especially when paired with something we can do immediately in response to their feedback.

The role of the consultant is to help the instructor identify what feedback they would like to address with students and how they will frame their response to that feedback. When possible, it is best to strike a balance among the three responses. Focusing exclusively on what they will not do sends the message that the instructor does not really value student feedback, and while stating what they will do in the future conveys value, it does not benefit current students, which is one of the advantages of midterm feedback over SETs. In some instances, students only give feedback that cannot be addressed until later or cannot be addressed at all, but this should be the exception rather than the rule in terms of debriefing with the instructor. Work with the instructor to find something they can do in the present semester to improve the learning experience. Before concluding the debrief, ask the instructor to share their plans for growth and debrief with you so you can add them to the reflection box. This final step

is important for ensuring that the report captures the instructor's voice as well as the students'.

How Can You Adapt the CTB GIFT to Meet Your Needs?

This chapter provides a guide to using CTB materials to gather midterm student feedback through the GIFT method, but there is no "right" way to implement this method. Every context and set of needs is different and may require modifications to this process. The CTB student feedback survey and report are Creative Commons licensed to allow you the freedom to adapt these materials in ways that best meet your needs. The research provided earlier in the chapter indicates a few best practices to keep in mind as you do so.

One adaptation adopted by faculty in the College of Engineering at the Embry-Riddle Aeronautical University Daytona Beach campus is the omission of the guided discussion in the classroom. This adaptation was made in response to a common faculty concern regarding the amount of class time dedicated to conducting the GIFT. Already feeling pressed for time, instructors resisted giving up 20 minutes of their time to the full GIFT process. In response to this concern, teaching center staff offered two alternative options that increased faculty willingness to include midterm feedback into their teaching routine:

1. A consultant visits the classroom and facilitates the survey without the discussion; this only takes approximately 5 minutes of class time.
2. A consultant sets up the survey electronically and shares the link as well as general instructions for students with the instructor. The instructor then makes the survey available to students through the course LMS, and students are asked to complete it asynchronously by a predetermined deadline.

With each of these options the consultant still receives and analyzes responses to create a report and meets with the faculty for a debrief to discuss insights and next steps. We offer this as only one example of how you can adapt the CTB student feedback protocol to suit your context. We invite you to share your story and adaptations with us at criticalteachingbehaviors@

gmail.com so we can create a collaborative repository of options.

Chapter Takeaways

Midterm student feedback helps us incorporate the student perspective into our reflection on, plans for, and narrative of teaching effectiveness. Whether you have a peer or consultant you can ask to facilitate this process for you, we encourage you to use the CTB student feedback form to check in with your students. You might even offer to lead such a session for a trusted colleague in exchange for the same favor, as you are now the expert on the following:

- the benefits of collecting midterm student feedback, especially through the GIFT method
- the instructor benefits behind the design of the CTB student feedback survey and report form
- the process for conducting a CTB student feedback session

As we proceed to our last chapter on creating your narrative, we remind you that midterm student feedback is only one piece of documentation you can collect on your teaching. When paired with an observation report, a midterm feedback report can help you appreciate the "gift" of student feedback by prompting you to reflect with greater purpose and depth on your teaching, resulting in a more well-rounded narrative showcasing your teaching effectiveness.

Notes

1. The most significant difference between the GIFT and SGID methods is that SGIDs ask students to complete the survey collaboratively rather than individually.

2. A separate research study (in progress) indicates that there is little to no correlation between instructor ratings using the CTB tool and demographic factors. Additionally, statistically minded readers may want to know that initial validity and reliability analysis of the CTB midterm feedback survey were conducted on a data set of n=3044 student responses. Chronbach's alpha was employed as an initial step to establish interitem reliability and the dimensionality of the present survey. Completion of an omnibus test (using all 10 survey items) resulted in a Chronbach's alpha value of .891, which indicates good interitem reliability for the survey overall.

References

Abbott, R. D., Wulff, D. H., Nyquist, J. D., Ropp, V. A., & Hess, C. W. (1990). Satisfaction with processes of collecting student opinions about instruction: The student perspective. *Journal of Educational Psychology, 82*(2), 201–206. https://doi.org/10.1037/0022-066.82.2.201

Blue, J., Wentzell, G. W., & Evins, M. J. (2014). What do students want? Small group instructional diagnoses of STEM faculty. In P. V. Engelhardt, A. D. Churukian, & D. L. Jones (Eds.), *2014 PERC Proceedings* (pp. 43–46). American Association of Physics Teachers. http://doi.org/10.1119/perc.2014.pr.007

Boring, A. (2017). Gender biases in student evaluations of teaching. *Journal of Public Economics, 145,* 27–41.

Clark, D. J., & Redmond, M. V. (1982). *Small group instructional diagnosis: Final report* [ED217954]. ERIC. https://filed.eric.ed.gov/fulltext/ED217954.pdf

Cohen, P. A. (1980). Effectiveness of student-rating feedback for improving college instruction: A meta-analysis of findings. *Research in Higher Education, 13*(4), 321–341. https://doi.org/10.1007/BF00976252

Cook-Sather, A. (2009). From traditional accountability to shared responsibility: The benefits and challenges of student consultations gathering midcourse feedback in college classrooms. *Assessment & Evaluation in Higher Education, 34*(2), 231–241. https://doi.org/10/1080/02602930801956042

Diamond, M. R. (2004). The usefulness of structured midterm feedback as a catalyst for change in higher education classes. *Active Learning in Higher Education, 5*(3), 217–231. https:doi.org/10.1177/1469787404046845

Finelli, C. J., Ott, M., Gottfried, A. C., Hershock, C., O'Neal, C., & Kaplan, M. (2008). Utilizing instructional consultations to enhance the teaching performance of engineering faculty. *Journal of Engineering Education, 97*(4), 397–411. http://doi.org/10.1002/j.2168-9830.2008.tb00909.x

Finelli, C. J., Pinder-Grover, T., & Wright, M. C. (2011). Consultations on teaching. Using student feedback for instructional improvement. In C. E. Cook & M. L. Kaplan (Eds.), *Advancing the culture of teaching at a research university: How a teaching center can make a difference* (pp. 65–79). Stylus.

Hunt, N. (2003). Does mid-semester feedback make a difference? *The Journal of Scholarship of Teaching and Learning, 3*(2), 13–20.

Hurney, C. A., Harris, N. L., Bates Prins, S. C. & Kruck, S. E. (2014). The impact of a learner-centered, mid-semester course evaluation on students. *Journal of Faculty Development, 28*(3), 55–62.

Hurney, C. A., Rener, C. M., & Troisi, J. D. (2022). *Mid-course correction for the college classroom: Putting small group instructional diagnosis to work*. Stylus.

Kreitzer, R. J., & Sweet-Cushman, J. (2021, February 9). Evaluating student evaluations of teaching: A review of measurement and equity bias in SETs and recommendations for ethical reform. *Journal of Academic Ethics*. Advance online publication. https://doi.org/10.1007/s10805-021-09400-w

Lammers, W. J., Gillaspy, J. A., Jr., & Hancock, F. (2017). Predicting academic success with early, middle, and late semester assessment of student-instructor rapport. *Teaching of Psychology, 44*(2), 145–149. https://doi.org/10.1177/0098628317692618

Lewis, K. G. (2001). Using midsemester student feedback and responding to it. In K. G. Lewis (Ed.), *Techniques and Strategies for Interpreting Student Evaluations* (New Directions for Teaching and Learning, no. 87, pp. 33–44). Jossey-Bass.

Mauger, D. (2010). *Small group instructional feedback: A student perspective of its impact on the teaching and learning environment* (Publication No. 3407167) [Doctoral dissertation, George Fox University]. ProQuest Dissertations & Theses Global.

McDonnell, G. P., & Dodd, M. D. (2017). Should students have the power to change course structure? *Teaching of Psychology, 44*(2), 91–99. https://doi.org/10.1177/0098628317692604

McGowan, W. R. (2009). *Faculty and student perceptions of the effects of mid-course evaluations on learning and teaching* (Publication No. 3376925) [Doctoral dissertation, Brigham Young University]. ProQuest Dissertations & Theses Global.

Mitchell, K. M. W., & Martin, J. (2018) Gender bias in student evaluations. *Political Science and Politics, 51*(3), 648–652. https://doi.org/10.1017/S104909651800001X

Newby, T., Sherman, M., & Coffman, S. J. (1991, April 1). *Instructional diagnosis: Effective open-ended faculty evaluation* [Conference session]. The Annual Meeting of the American Educational Research Association, Chicago, IL, United States.

Penny, A. R., & Coe, R. (2004). Effectiveness of consultation on student ratings feedback: A meta-analysis. *Review of Educational Research, 74*(2), 215–253. https://doi.org/10.3102/00346543074002215

Piccinin, S. (1999). How individual consultation affects teaching. In C. G. Knapper & S. Piccinin (Eds.), *Taking Small Group Learning Online: Best Practices for Team-Based Learning* (New Directions for Teaching and Learning, no. 70, pp. 71–83). Jossey-Bass.

Richardson, J. T. E. (2005). Instruments for obtaining student feedback: A review of the literature. *Assessment & Evaluation in Higher Education, 30*(4), 387–415. https://doi.org/10.1080/ 02602930500099193

Sherry, A. C., Fulford, C. P., & Zhang, S. (1998). Assessing distance learners' satisfaction with instruction: A quantitative and qualitative measure. *The American Journal of Distance Education, 12*(3), 4–28. https://doi.org/10.1080/08923649809527002

Snooks, M. K., Neeley, S. E., & Williamson, K. M. (2004). From GIFT and GIFT to BBQ: Streamlining midterm student evaluations to improve teaching and learning. *To Improve the Academy, 22*(1), 110–124. https://doi.org//10/1007/s10956-017-9703-3

Sozer, E. M., Zeybekoglu, Z., & Kaya, M. (2019). Using mid-semester course evaluation as a feedback tool for improving learning and teaching in higher education. *Assessment & Evaluation in Higher Education, 44*(7), 1003–1016. http://doi.org//10/1080/02602938.2018.1 564810

Svinicki, M. (2001). Encouraging your students to give feedback. In K. G. Lewis (Ed.), *Techniques and Strategies for Interpreting Student Feedback* (New Directions for Teaching and Learning, no. 87, pp. 17–24). Jossey-Bass. https://onlinelibrary.wiley.com/toc/15360768/2001/2001/87

Veeck, A., O'Reilly, K., MacMillan, A., & Yu, H. (2016). The use of collaborative midterm student evaluations to provide actionable results. *Journal of Marketing Education, 38*(3), 157–169. https://doi.org/10.1177/0273475315619652

Wickramasinghe, S. R., & Timpson, W. M. (2006). Mid-semester student feedback enhances student learning. *Education for Chemical Engineers, 1*(1), 126–133. http://doi.org//10/1205/ece06012

Wulff, D. H., Stanton-Spicer, A. Q., Hess, C. W., & Nyquist, J. D. (1985). The student perspective on evaluating teaching effectiveness. *ACA Bulletin, 53*, 39–47.

CHAPTER 10

Creating a Narrative of Teaching Effectiveness

THE PREVIOUS CHAPTERS IN this "Applications" portion of the book have focused on individual perspectives on your teaching: your own, as framed by your core value and your reflections on reports; your peers, captured in observation reports; and your students, solicited through midterm feedback. While each of these perspectives plays an important role in documenting your teaching, they do not in and of themselves constitute an effective teaching narrative. In this final chapter, we will focus on the bigger picture of how you can use the CTB framework to tie together each of these perspectives, as well as other relevant materials, into a coherent, persuasive narrative of teaching effectiveness. This process starts by articulating the values you bring to the learning space. Defining the underlying values that inform how you teach and interact with students allows you to purposefully select and frame materials consistent with who you are as an instructor. For this reason, we strongly recommend that you complete the "Identifying Your Core Value" exercise in the introduction to Part Two (chapter 7) if you have not done so already. Having a core value category and statement will be essential to making the most of this chapter.

We will synthesize the content of the previous chapters by focusing on the documentation of teaching effectiveness in this final chapter with the goal of answering the following questions:

- Why do we document teaching effectiveness?
- How do we document teaching effectiveness?
- How can the CTB framework help you document teaching effectiveness?

We dedicate the majority of this chapter to the last question. Rather than guiding you through the entire process of creating your narrative, we focus on helping you lay the groundwork necessary to create a persuasive narrative and provide guidance to help you use the CTB to create coherence across your narrative and supporting documents.

Why Do We Document Teaching Effectiveness?

This may seem like a simple question with perhaps a self-evident answer for you personally but understanding your purpose for engaging in the documentation process and the audience for whom you are producing the documentation will help you craft a narrative and select materials more appropriately targeted to that audience. There are many reasons why you might want or need to document your teaching effectiveness, but we find they fall into three broad categories: reflection on our development, identification of areas for growth, and showcasing of our achievements. Each of these different purposes can have a variety of different audiences as well: reviewers, peers, students, and even yourself. For instance, you might need to create a portfolio of accomplishments to submit to reviewers on an award committee, but you might also decide to adapt this portfolio as something to share on a website where students and colleagues can learn more about you. Or you might capture your reflection on teaching to share with a faculty learning community, teaching circle, or other professional development support group, which may lead you to more formally present or publish on your teaching. Although you may start documenting your teaching for specific reasons and a narrow audience, your purposes and audiences may shift even as you are developing your materials. Regardless of purpose or intended audience, we are also an audience for our own teaching effectiveness narratives. Collecting and reflecting on concrete evidence of development and the impact of instructional changes can give us needed encouragement on difficult teaching days while also helping us identify ways we would like to continue growing as an instructor. It can keep teaching from feeling stale or boring by allowing us to see opportunities for innovation and experimentation. Documenting our teaching can ultimately reinvigorate our instructional lives as well as the lives of interested peers and students.

While there are a variety of reasons to document teaching and a wide range of audiences for whom you might prepare such documentation, we recognize that showcasing achievement is likely the most significant motivator. Application, promotion, tenure, annual review, grant, and award packages often require evidence of teaching effectiveness, and for many of us, these requirements spark the realization that we need to gather documentation of our teaching. Ideally, we plan ahead and consider the types of materials we will want to include in such a package so we have time to design, refine, and collect them in advance, but more realistically, we may not consider the need to document our teaching until we must begin assembling our packages. In such cases, the time crunch can pressure us to choose materials haphazardly and without much thought to the larger narrative they work together to create. Because the audience for such a package may include experts from your field, reviewers from other disciplines, seasoned teachers, administrators with limited teaching experience, and everything in between, a clear guiding narrative with strong supporting evidence is essential to creating an intelligible, compelling case for your teaching effectiveness. We encourage you to reflect on your motivation for documenting your teaching and make notes about your intended audience to help frame your thoughts as we move forward. Remember that the sooner you begin documenting your teaching, the easier it will be to craft a persuasive set of materials when the time comes to showcase your achievements. Long-standing documentation of your teaching can help you more readily identify how you have grown throughout your career as well as how your perspective and goals have changed, thereby allowing you to create a more holistic narrative of teaching development over time.

How Do We Document Teaching Effectiveness?

In higher education, we most commonly document teaching effectiveness through teaching portfolios, the foundation of which is the teaching statement. Typically, teaching portfolios and statements serve as persuasive documents designed to do one thing: prove to your readers that you are an effective instructor. The ability of your documents to make this argument successfully can help determine the outcomes of hiring, tenure, promotion, annual review, or award committee decisions in your favor. While this is not a chapter on assembling your teaching portfolio or writing your teaching philosophy statement, the instruction we provide on using the CTB to create a narrative of teaching effectiveness is integrally tied to both of these documents. To establish a common understanding of these materials, we offer a brief overview of teaching statements and portfolios in the following before we move forward with our discussion of how you can use the CTB framework to shape your teaching narrative.

Peter Seldin (1997) describes the teaching portfolio as

a factual description of a professor's teaching strengths and accomplishments. It includes documents and materials which collectively suggest the scope and quality of a professor's teaching performance. It is to teaching what lists of publications, grants, and honors are to research and scholarship. (p. 2)

Teaching portfolios typically feature a range of your most exemplary teaching materials, including but not limited to a teaching philosophy statement; representative course syllabi; sample assessments; student evaluations of teaching; unsolicited student feedback; samples of student work; peer observation reports; teaching honors, awards, presentations, and publications; and teaching-related professional development activities. Depending on your purpose and any specific guidelines, you may create a hard copy or a digital portfolio. Digital portfolios range from PDFs to files uploaded through a specific platform to websites. Websites can be especially useful for instructors who want more creativity and flexibility in the presentation of their portfolios. They also allow you to create a "living" record of and reflection on your teaching (as long as you remember to update the site) that is accessible to peers and students.

Regardless of format, a teaching portfolio should be more than a CV of teaching accomplishments followed by an appendix of unexplained evidence; instead,

> a good portfolio is woven together by narrative commentary from the faculty member that describes the context for the documentation and presents reflections on the teaching itself. It presents multiple sources of evidence, chronicles the development of the instructor and learning of students, and projects a future vision. (Chism, 2007, p. 168)

A sensemaking narrative provides the guiding logic for an effective teaching portfolio, yet all too often, instructors neglect the narrative either out of unawareness or a desire to present unbiased evidence that allows readers to draw their own conclusions. However, without a narrative that explains the evidence you have selected and where readers should focus their attention when reviewing artifacts, busy readers may skim over what you consider to be a crucial example of your teaching effectiveness without even noticing important features, or worse, they might misunderstand your evidence or its impact on students and interpret it as poor teaching practice. A planned, intentional narrative, on the other hand, helps you select artifacts and highlight important features of those artifacts that bolster your claims about your teaching beliefs and practices.

Of course, your narrative and the artifacts you select should showcase teaching-related achievements, but a narrative limited to accomplishments may in fact damage your credibility with your audience and therefore your ability to persuade. Faculty members who have served on tenure and promotion committees note that a narrative deficient of teaching struggles and subsequent growth can signal red flags for readers. Anyone who has taught knows that teaching is not a single, unbroken chain of successes. For this reason, a narrative that demonstrates growth by making comparisons between early and revised versions of artifacts or by otherwise showcasing changes in beliefs and practice throughout

your teaching career can be helpful for establishing yourself as a reflective practitioner. Consider the portfolio narrative a record of your efforts to grow as an instructor. While you certainly want to include your achievements, you may also want to look back on your career by reflecting on struggles, feedback, and improvement efforts as well as look forward by identifying areas for future growth as evidence of a continued commitment to effective instruction. Framing your narrative in this manner will allow you to highlight accomplishments while also proactively accounting for any anomalous data (student ratings, peer evaluations, etc.) by directly addressing a teaching struggle you faced and what you did or will do to overcome this struggle.

A strong teaching philosophy establishes the narrative that will carry the reader through your portfolio artifacts. When we hear the phrase *teaching philosophy*, many of us in higher ed tend to get, well, philosophical in our approach to writing these statements. After all, is that not what the name tells us to do? Vanderbilt's Center for Teaching (n.d.) explains that the

> Teaching Statement is a purposeful and reflective essay about the author's teaching beliefs and practices. . . . At its best, a Teaching Statement gives a clear and unique portrait of the author as a teacher, avoiding generic or empty philosophical statements about teaching. (p. 1)

Your teaching philosophy should, in part, explain your approach to and beliefs about teaching and learning, but if it never goes beyond philosophy to concrete examples that show readers how you act upon those beliefs to reach specific goals, your statement will have missed an important opportunity to show your readers what your teaching looks like in action. Aligning your portfolio components with the beliefs and examples expressed in your philosophy (and regularly guiding your readers by pointing out that alignment) builds narrative coherence that makes your materials more persuasive, but the process of reflecting upon and explaining evidence from the classroom that demonstrates how you enact your pedagogical beliefs also helps keep you accountable. If you say, for instance, that you value student engagement but struggle to think of anything you do to engage students, it may be time to evaluate what you can do differently to better align your teaching with those beliefs. The more genuine and intentional the alignment between your teaching values, behaviors, and documentation, the more effective your narrative will be because it will capture a holistic picture of you as a teacher.

Teaching philosophies reflect the instructor who wrote them. The intensely personal nature of these statements makes it difficult to provide definitive guidance on what they should include or how they should be written. The following are a few general content items to include:

- values and belief about teaching and learning (why you teach the way you teach)
- goals for student learning (the purpose for your teaching)
- teaching methods (how you teach)
- how you know your teaching methods are reaching your goals for student learning (assessment methods and evidence of effectiveness)
- reflection for growth and self-assessment

The teaching philosophy statement is typically the first item in a teaching portfolio, and as such, it should clearly articulate the primary message that will move the portfolio forward and unify the appended artifacts. The exercises in the "Identifying Your Core Value" chapter are designed not only to help you identify a value category that you can use to reflect on your observation and student feedback reports but also to help you formulate statements or ideas that you can use to begin your teaching philosophy. In the remainder of this chapter, we will discuss how you can use your core value category to help you identify and frame evidence of teaching effectiveness to create a coherent, persuasive narrative.

How Can the CTB Help You Document Teaching Effectiveness?

As we bring this book to a close, we return to the CTB framework itself to discuss how it can assist you in documenting your teaching by guiding you in the following ways:

- connect your core value to teaching behaviors
- select evidence that captures these behaviors
- create an aligned narrative that connects core values, behaviors, and evidence to showcase your effectiveness as a teacher

The following exercises are designed to help you reach these goals. As with all exercises in this book, you may wish to revisit them periodically and compare your answers over time to reflect on growth throughout your teaching career.

Connecting Core Value to Teaching Behaviors

Recall the core value category and statement you generated through the "Identifying Your Core Value" exercises in chapter 7. We will use your core value category to take inventory of your teaching behaviors. To do this, you may refer to the framework for an overview of behaviors listed in your value category, but behaviors in the framework itself are written to be both brief and broad for the sake of space. For a more comprehensive list of behaviors, we recommend that you review the "What Do We Do?" box at the end of your value category's chapter. Mark behaviors as follows or create and complete a four-column list with the following headers:

- (✓) Behaviors You Know You Exhibit
- (+) Behaviors You Plan to Implement Soon
- (−) Behaviors You Do Not Yet Exhibit
- (?) Behaviors You Are Uncertain You Exhibit

Remember that being a good teacher does not mean checking every behavior listed. Not every behavior is right for every instructor, discipline, or classroom context. The value of this exercise lies in honest self-assessment of what you do well, what you could do better, what you intend to do, and what you intentionally choose not to do. If you do not know whether you exhibit a particular behavior, ask. Areas of uncertainty can be especially interesting to pursue through peer or student feedback because they can lead to valuable conversations and insights about our teaching that prompt further reflection.

CTB categories are artificially neat, and behaviors in one category may be relevant in another category if framed properly. For this reason, you may wish to repeat the process with each of the other categories through the lens of your core value. Rather than digging into each category chapter in depth, however, you might start by reviewing the framework overview behaviors instead and thinking about them within the context of your value category. Lauren, for instance, identifies her core value as "Include." When reviewing the "Engage" behaviors, she might think about how she "establishes open and regular communication" or "encourages participation of all students by using varied instructional strategies" for the purposes of creating a more inclusive classroom environment. She can then look more closely at the unpacked list of behaviors for those items in the "Engage" chapter if she desires to identify more specific behaviors that could relate to her core value category.

Select Evidence That Captures Behaviors

Behaviors compiled through the previous activity prepare you to make informed choices about the evidence you collect to support your core value statement. This next step also prompts you to look beyond what happens in the classroom to consider the myriad training, preparations, reflections, revisions, and so on you engage in to improve your teaching as sources of documentation. Often, student evaluations, syllabi, assignment prompts, and examples of student work form the bulk of evidence collected to showcase teaching effectiveness. While these artifacts should certainly be included in a portfolio and may even be required components, they focus attention primarily on what happens within the classroom. However, most instructors can easily agree that time spent in the classroom represents only the tip of the iceberg of effective instruction; the bulk of the work necessary to design and deliver quality learning experiences happens outside the classroom and consequently remains hidden below the surface of what can be seen. By proposing sources of documentation, the CTB framework helps you align your evidence with your behaviors and encourages you to think beyond the tip of the iceberg in terms of what you document and showcase.

The purpose of this activity is to help you intentionally select evidence that showcases your behaviors and advances a coherent narrative aligned with your core value. Mirroring the outlined process, start by reviewing the "potential sources of documentation" column for your value category on the CTB framework (Appendix A). You may complete this activity by creating lists with the following headers or by marking the framework as follows:

- (✔) Evidence You Already Have
- (+) Evidence You Can Easily Start Collecting or Can Develop a Plan to Collect

- (-) Evidence You Do Not Have or Do Not Find Relevant
- (?) Evidence Items You Need Further Explained

Should you need more information about any of the evidence listed, the "What Do We Show" section at the end of the category chapters elaborates on each piece of evidence and provides a brief explanation of how it can demonstrate a particular behavior. By completing this activity, you inventory available evidence for alignment with your core value and may even identify evidence you had not previously considered using. Artifacts, like behaviors, do not fall neatly into a single category, so you may wish to repeat this process with the other categories on the framework. Just be sure to use your core value category to evaluate the usefulness of potential evidence. For example, you may have excellent rubrics that you would like to include in your portfolio; however, unless you frame these rubrics in a way that aligns with and advances your core value narrative, they will become an unnecessary distraction for readers. If you have a strict page limit, they may waste valuable space you could use to showcase artifacts better aligned with your narrative. Depending on your purpose for documenting your teaching, there may be items you must include in the portfolio. Beyond those requirements, you likely have some freedom of choice as to what else to include. Engaging in the process of aligning artifacts with behaviors and core values encourages you to select only the evidence that will contribute to the narrative cohesion of your portfolio.

Creating an Aligned Narrative

This last step prompts you to tie the behaviors and evidence you selected to your core value by explaining the logic behind your selections. If you have completed the exercises thus far, you should have a set of behaviors and evidence that align nicely with your core value category and statement. Remember, however, that evidence does not speak for itself. Unless you make this alignment explicit for your readers, they may not readily see the connections that seem obvious to you. As the author, your job is to explain the evidence you provide in a way that helps your readers understand why you included it and how it connects to the bigger picture narrative you have constructed about your teaching effectiveness. Depending on your disciplinary writing conventions, this task may be more or less difficult. The uniqueness of teaching portfolios means we cannot provide you a cookie-cutter template for constructing a persuasive narrative that ties all your materials together, nor would we want to do so. What we can provide are template statements that can give you a place to start when constructing a cohesive narrative. Refer to Table 10.1 for sample statements you can use to connect your values, behaviors, and evidence when explaining your current teaching practices and rationale for them, as well as reflections on your growth over time and plans for future growth. Keep in mind that these statements are only starter templates to help you translate your connecting logic into explanations that make sense to an external audience. You can and should adapt, edit, and revise them as you develop your materials.

The most important aspect of these narrative-starting mad libs are the explanations they prompt you to provide. Although you may need to keep them brief, explanations will likely need more than the simple fill-in-the-blank space indicated in these templates. Your explanations should unpack the relationship between the evidence being highlighted and the larger core value narrative. To help you better understand what this unpacking might look like, consider the example in Table 10.2 based on Lauren's materials.

In response to the first prompt, she merely fills in the blanks with her core value category, the action she took, and the purpose of that action in relation to her value. Her response to the second prompt names the evidence to which she wants to call the reader's attention before launching more specifically into details the reader should notice about that evidence, in this case the syllabus headers and space for students to cocreate engagement guidelines. She then calls attention to additional evidence (e.g., student feedback) that indicates the impact of her intervention. Students say they feel like a member of a community where the instructor cares about their success and is there to support them. This feedback aligns with her original goal of "creating a sense of community from Day 1" and therefore suggests that her teaching changes have been effective. Syllabi are typically lengthy documents; busy reviewers do not have time to carefully read through even one, no less more than one, syllabus. Rather than simply appending her revised syllabus and leaving to chance whether the reader happens to see and correctly interpret the inclusive features she worked hard to incorporate, she directly draws attention to the aspects of the syllabus she wants the reader to see before moving on to additional evidence that demonstrates the success of her

---

TABLE 10.1: Prompts for Starting Your Narrative

To Explain What You Do as an Instructor and Why

- Because I value [*insert your core value category or some version of your statement*], I have implemented [*name the particular behavior you want to showcase (e.g., active learning, aligned assessment, ADA-compliant materials, etc.)*] that allows me to better [*explain briefly the relationship between your behavior and your value*].
- I have collected the following evidence to assess and demonstrate my efforts. The appended [*name evidence item (e.g., active learning strategy, TiLTed assignment, ADA-compliant video, etc.)*] shows [*explain how the evidence supplied demonstrates your values and behaviors stated previously*].

To Explain How You Have Grown as an Instructor

- I have completed [*list relevant professional development, information gathering, data analysis, self-assessment, etc.*] to grow as a teacher in [*name a CTB category*].
- This experience has led me to make [*name an intervention you have made as a result of your experience*] changes to my teaching. The impact of these changes was [*explain the relevance of your intervention*], as demonstrated by [*indicate supporting evidence*].

To Explain How You Plan to Grow as an Instructor

- I have identified [*name a CTB category or behavior*] as a potential growth opportunity.
- To develop in this area, I plan to [*explain the professional development, information gathering, data analysis, self-assessment, etc. you will engage in*].

TABLE 10.2: Example—Explaining What You Do as an Instructor and Why

- Because I value inclusive teaching, I have significantly revised my course syllabus to create a sense of community more effectively from Day 1 of my course.
- I have collected the following evidence to assess and demonstrate my efforts. The appended syllabi show the evolution of my syllabus design. Notice that the first syllabus conforms to the standard "syllabus-as-contract" model, as seen in section headers like "Course Policies" and "Assignments and Grading." In the revised version of the syllabus, these headers become "How We'll Engage With Each Other" and "How to Succeed in This Course," changes made based on research I did into inclusive syllabi creation. My revised syllabus also contains a blank space entitled "Respectful Engagement in This Course Means . . ." where students cocreate the guidelines for engagement in the course. The attached student feedback indicates that these changes make students feel like members of a community and inspire confidence in my desire for them to succeed. Unsolicited feedback additionally reveals that these language choices make me seem more approachable before they even meet me. Overall, the changes I have made to my course syllabus demonstrate my commitment to growing as an inclusive instructor while student feedback indicates that these changes have been effective for helping me create stronger relationships and trust with my students.

---

changes. The explanations she provides make review of her materials quick and easy for readers while also ensuring that they take away the intended message showcasing her teaching effectiveness.

Before we close out this section on creating your narrative, we want to address once more the importance of framing your narrative from one primary categorical perspective. You may recall from the "Identifying Your Core Value" exercise that we encouraged you to choose one value category even if you find your value statement could fit in multiple categories. Our purpose for making this recommendation was to prepare you to write a more coherent, persuasive narrative. If you try to frame your evidence and explanations from too many categorical perspectives, you will end up with a jumbled mosaic of artifacts that does not advance any particular teaching value. We encourage you to take a moment to revisit the "Core Value Reflection Example" in Appendix B one more time as we examine how Lauren reflects on her teaching motivations to determine which category best represents her value. Lauren realizes that her core value could easily fit into both the Include and Engage categories, and she can think of concrete examples of what she does because of her value that could also fall into either category. However, she makes a deliberate decision to frame her narrative through the Include category after examining the underlying beliefs and motivations that lead her to engage in specific teaching

behaviors. As she explains, she exhibits several behaviors from the Engage category, but her motivation for doing so relates more to her desire to create an inclusive, supportive classroom space where students feel like she cares about their success and belonging than a push to get students to "take responsibility for their intellectual development."

Her decision to frame her artifacts from the Include lens does not preclude her from selecting evidence beyond that category. Lauren mentions student feedback several times throughout her reflection, and consequently, she might provide examples of her feedback on student assignments in her portfolio. While feedback on assignments is listed as evidence for the Assess category, her presentation of the assignment feedback might include a description of how it provides timely and differentiated support necessary for creating a learning experience that scaffolds students to reach their own definitions of success as she mentions in her reflection. Her framing of the evidence advances the narrative she created around her core teaching value category—Include. As these examples indicate, you can and should use CTB categories as lenses through which you interpret evidence that can demonstrate successful behaviors in all categories to ensure that you portray yourself as a well-rounded instructor; however, to create a cohesive narrative, remember to frame all evidence in such a way as to support your core teaching value.

Conclusion

To practice what we preach about alignment, we conclude by returning to the outcomes listed in the introduction. If you have read and completed exercises along the way, you should now be able to do the following:

- identify behaviors consistent with good teaching
- reflect upon the teaching behaviors you already exhibit
- implement research-based, effective teaching behaviors across each of the six CTB categories
- document your teaching behaviors
- articulate a core value statement that motivates your approach to teaching
- conduct and/or reflect on a peer observation
- collect and/or reflect on midterm student feedback
- use your core value statement to purposefully select and frame evidence of effectiveness in a coherent teaching narrative

Our ultimate goals for you in reaching these outcomes are listed in the subtitle of this book ("Defining, Documenting, and Discussing Good Teaching"). We hope that you feel better equipped to define what good teaching looks like in practice, document your teaching effectiveness, and discuss teaching more

meaningfully with your colleagues. For administrators reading this book, we hope you feel more prepared to provide guidance to instructors on what good teaching looks like and how to document it. As a final thought, we reiterate that there is no "one-size-fits-all" method of good teaching. What works for some instructors may not work the same way for others. We offer the CTB framework as a guide to help you develop your own teaching style and objectively identify effective teaching behaviors in yourself and others. The conversation about what good teaching is should not end now that you have reached the conclusion of this book; rather, we hope that the end of this book is the beginning of more fruitful, research-based conversations about good teaching for all of higher ed.

References

Chism, N. V. N. (1997–1998). Developing a philosophy of teaching statement. *Essays on Teaching Excellence: Toward the Best in the Academy, 9*(3). http://podnetwork.org/content/uploads/V9-N3-Chism.pdf

Chism, N. V. N. (2007). *Peer review of teaching: A sourcebook.* Anker.

Seldin, P. (1997). *The teaching portfolio: A practical guide to improved performance and promotion/tenure decisions.* Anker.

Vanderbilt Center for Teaching. (n.d.). *Teaching statements.* https://cft.vanderbilt.edu/guides-sub-pages/teaching-statements/

Appendix Note

To view the full appendices, use the URL or scan the QR code.
https://www.routledge.com/Critical-Teaching-Behaviors-Defining-Documenting-and-Discussing-Good/
Barbeau-Cornejo-Happel/p/book/9781642673692

Appendix A

Critical Teaching Behaviors Framework

Categories and Definitions	What Are Representative Behaviors in This Category? (Examples listed are not exhaustive)	What Are Potential Sources of Documentation in This Category? (Examples listed are not exhaustive)
Align Instructors who align components of learning experiences start with clear learning goals. Measurable outcomes, teaching and learning activities, assessment tasks, and feedback build on each other to support student progress toward these goals.	AL.1 Connect course outcomes to program, department, and/or institutional outcomes and accreditation standards as applicable AL.2 Define actionable, learner-centered outcomes for learning units (module, lesson, etc.) and assignments AL.3 Align content, assessments, and activities with outcomes AL.4 Communicate course, module, lesson, and/or assignment outcome(s) at each stage of learning AL.5 Emphasize connections of course concepts and skills across lessons, learning units, and courses AL.6 Present content and activities at multiple, appropriate levels of engagement and challenge	• course map • course materials and assignments that explicitly show alignment across course components • learning outcomes at course, module, lesson, and assignment levels • lesson plan • peer feedback and/or observation • student feedback • syllabus • test blueprints
Include Instructors who create an inclusive learning environment promote equity by using accessibility standards and learner-centered strategies when designing and delivering content. They cultivate an atmosphere in which students see themselves positively represented and experience a sense of belonging conducive to emotional well-being for learning.	IN.1 Build community and relational trust between students–instructor and students–students IN.2 Decode pathways to success and connect students with resources IN.3 Use learner-centered strategies in course design and delivery IN.4 Select content and activities that honor and integrate diverse voices, perspectives, and experiences IN.5 Remove barriers to success by designing activities and materials with equitable access and representation in mind IN.6 Assess personal biases and mitigate their potential impact on student learning and success	• ground rules for interaction in the learning space • instructor-created accessible digital materials • learning materials cocreated with students • lesson plan • mentorship agreement and products of mentorship • peer feedback and/or observation • student feedback • syllabus • teaching statement and/or diversity statement

(*Continues*)

(*Continued*)

Engage	EN.1 Establish regular and open communication	• activity instructions/prompts
Instructors who engage students purposefully select research-based techniques to ensure that students actively participate in the learning process and take responsibility for their intellectual development.	EN.2 Design course activities to intentionally promote student–instructor, student–content, and student–student engagement EN.3 Encourage participation of all students by using varied instructional strategies EN.4 Foster self-regulated learning EN.5 Relate course content to relevant examples and applications EN.6 Incorporate current research in the field to stimulate discipline-specific critical thinking and promote student participation in disciplinary research	• communications to students • lesson plan • online module • peer feedback and/or observation • presentation slides for interactive lectures • student feedback • student work samples • syllabus • video recording of classroom teaching/video lecture
Assess	AS.1 Schedule a range of regular summative assessments to measure student progress toward learning outcomes	• assessments, including instructions, prompts, or questions
Instructors who assess learning develop and facilitate transparent, meaningful tasks to provide students with timely feedback on their learning and to measure achievement of learning outcomes. They frequently review data to improve instruction.	AS.2 Embed formative assessments and opportunities for self-assessment in instruction AS.3 Scaffold assessments AS.4 Communicate purpose, task, and criteria for assessments AS.5 Provide timely, constructive feedback to students AS.6 Review assessment data to make informed decisions about course content, structure, and activities	• lesson plan • peer feedback and/or observation • representative examples of feedback to students • rubrics/grading criteria • student data demonstrating achievement of learning outcomes • student feedback • student work samples • syllabus
Integrate Technology	IT.1 Select limited technologies from available options to enhance student learning and meet outcomes	• activity or task instructions or prompt
Instructors who integrate technology responsibly use tools to design accessible, high-quality instructional materials and engaging learning opportunities beyond traditional barriers of place and time.	IT.2 Leverage technology to increase access, facilitate ease of use, and optimize the student learning experience IT.3 Use technology effectively and efficiently IT.4 Train students to use instructional technology and provide support IT.5 Ensure materials and tools meet legal requirements IT.6 Consider pedagogical needs relevant to instructional modality	• examples or screenshots of activities conducted through technology • instructional units focused on the development of technology and/or digital literacy skill • instructor-created media (text, video, audio, etc.) or online learning units • lesson plan • peer feedback and/or observation • student feedback • syllabus

| **Reflect**

Instructors who reflect gather feedback on their teaching from self-assessment, peers, and students to regularly identify opportunities for growth. They pursue improvements to their instruction through engagement with professional development and scholarship. | RE.1 Assess personal growth
RE.2 Invite feedback on teaching from colleagues
RE.3 Solicit student feedback
RE.4 Engage with scholarship and professional development related to teaching
RE.5 Plan for personal growth by identifying categories for development and setting goals
RE.6 Conduct research on teaching and learning | • course journal
• participation in teaching-related professional development
• presentations led on teaching topics
• SoTL/DBER work and/or recognition
• teaching awards or recognition
• teaching statement
• written reflection on peer feedback and/or observation
• written reflection on student feedback |

Appendix B

Core Value Reflection Worksheet and Example

Core Value Blank Worksheet

Prompts	*Responses*
Articulating Your Core Value	
What motivates your approach to teaching?	
What is the one thing you believe an effective instructor *must* do or believe to promote student learning?	
What are your immediate and future (10+ years) goals for students when teaching your subject?	
What do you believe is the foundation of good teaching?	
Which CTB category definition and/or behaviors resonate most with your approach to teaching? Why?	
Identifying Your Core Value Category	
Into which category does your value statement best fit?	
Why do you think your statement fits into this category?	
Does it surprise you that your core value fits best in this category? Why or why not?	
Is there another category into which your core value might fit? If so, which of the two (or more) categories would you choose to represent your core teaching value and why?	
Do you have a secondary value that falls into a different category?	
What connection do you see between your primary and secondary values if you had more than one?	

Core Value Reflection Example

	Sample Responses
Articulating Your Core Value	*Selected prompt: What motivates your approach to teaching?* My approach to teaching is motivated by a deeply held belief that instructors must adapt their teaching, feedback, and student support strategies to meet students where they are in their learning journeys.
	Selected prompt: What do you believe an effective instructor must *do to promote student learning?*
	I recognize that students come into my classroom with a wide range of backgrounds, experiences, and preparation for success, but I fundamentally believe that all of them *can* be successful in my courses. I want them to believe this about themselves and to see me as a supportive coach toward that success. I also understand that success will mean something different for each of my students; it is not limited to getting an "A." As a writing teacher, I see many students who come into my classroom with a fixed mindset about their writing skills: They either are or aren't good writers. Being an effective writing instructor means helping students develop a growth mindset toward writing. Regardless of our starting point, we can all continuously improve our writing skills.
	Selected prompt: What are your immediate and future (10+ years) goals for students when teaching your subject?
	Many semesters, my greatest sense of achievement comes from seeing some of my students with the most fixed mindsets realize that writing is a skill they can develop with sufficient practice. Beyond realizing that they can become strong writers, I want them to see the value in doing so. In our modern world, a significant amount of our communication, regardless of field, is carried out in writing. Strong writing skills can unlock opportunities throughout their careers. It pays to develop some proficiency in writing.
Identifying Your Core Value Category	Include—The behaviors in the Include category best fit with my own teaching strategies. I value using learner-centered strategies, like encouraging a growth mindset through scaffolding, feedback, and reflection, to develop self-regulation. Through the feedback I give and peer workshopping opportunities, I hope to develop trust relationships with and among students that "cultivate an atmosphere in which students experience a sense of belonging." When students feel like they belong in a classroom, I believe the barriers to success are lowered. In this case, belonging might mean coming to see themselves as writers or as members of a writing community.
	Engage—Encouraging a growth mindset does help "ensure that students actively participate in the learning process and take responsibility for their intellectual development." I try to facilitate adaptive learning experiences through the feedback I provide on student writing and student choice in writing assignments. While there is a certain amount of content I have to cover in class, individualized feedback allows me to focus on areas of growth particular to each student. Allowing students to choose what they write about hopefully encourages interest and passion in their topics. I'm heavily invested in helping students see the value and relevance of developing their writing skills in relation to their own interests, passions, and career paths, so I do see how Engage might be a core value for me.

Draft a statement about your teaching that summarizes your core value.	I believe that being an effective instructor in my discipline means fostering a growth mindset attitude toward writing by helping students see themselves as writers and experience a sense of belonging to a classroom writing community.
Into which category does your value statement best fit?	Include
Why do you think your statement fits into this category?	Even though my value statement could fit into the Engage category, I chose Include because I think I'm most motivated by helping students think of themselves as writers, which for me translates into cultivating a sense of belonging in my classroom. We all belong there because we are all writers, and we are all engaged in improving, regardless of where we start.
Does it surprise you that your core value fits best in this category? Why or why not?	Not entirely. I hadn't considered my value through such a lens before. Reviewing the definitions on the framework helped me understand something fundamental to the way I approach teaching. I'm not sure I would have phrased it this way myself, but now that I've reviewed the framework, I have a much clearer sense of the kinds of behaviors I engage in that demonstrate my commitment to creating an inclusive learning environment and how I can document those behaviors to build this narrative.
Is there another category into which your core value might fit? If so, which of the two (or more) categories would you choose to represent your core teaching value and why?	I do think my value overlaps with elements of the Engage category because I try to incorporate adaptive learning experiences into my course through feedback and student choice in assignments. Expressing genuine concern for learning serves to engage and motivate students, but I think my primary concern for their learning stems more from the perspective of letting them know that I care about them as individuals and helping them feel like they're part of the classroom community of writers. While the behaviors might overlap the Include and Engage categories, my underlying motivations for these behaviors fall more into the Include category.

Appendix C

Teaching Observation Instructor Worksheet

Prior to the scheduled observation, answer the following questions and share this sheet with the observer along with a copy of your course syllabus and calendar.

Faculty Name:	
Course Title:	
Observation Date, Time, and Location or Unit/Module:	
Students Enrolled:	
Course Overview • How many times have you taught this course? • How has it evolved? • What are you particularly happy with? • What would you change and why?	
Lesson/Module Overview • What are the outcomes for the lesson/module I will observe? • What are your plans for achieving these outcomes? • What should students have done to prepare for this lesson?	
Requests Do you have specific questions for the observer (i.e., request for feedback on specific activities, interactions, content delivery)?	
Materials Attached Attach a copy of your syllabus and other relevant course materials.	

Appendix D

Observation Report

Faculty Observed: Course/Date/Time/Module:

Observer/Consultant: Number of Students:

At the initiative of the instructor, the consultant conducted this classroom observation. This report is based on the consultant's review of course materials provided by the instructor (e.g., syllabus, assessments, lesson plans, etc.), observations during the class period, and points raised during the debrief with the instructor.

Note for observer: Take notes on what is happening in the classroom. After the observation, review your notes and instructor-provided course materials and write summary comments on each of the CTB categories in the report form. Note that there are a range of behaviors listed in each category; not all will be identifiable in a single observation. Be sure to note CTB categories in which the instructor demonstrates particular strength as well as categories for potential growth. Schedule a meeting with your colleague to discuss the observation.

Note for observed faculty: To promote reflective practice and assist in the creation of professional development narratives, faculty should complete the "Faculty Reflection" column after the observation and before the debrief consultation. Be sure to share these reflections with your consultant.

Reflect: Instructors who reflect gather feedback on their teaching from self-assessment, students, and peers to regularly identify opportunities for growth. They pursue improvements to their instruction through professional development and research activities.

Observer Summary Comments on Strengths and Areas for Improvement

List strengths and suggestions for growth. Note categories in which the instructor demonstrates strengths or on which the instructor might focus for improvement.

Instructor Summary

After reviewing your reflections and making notes on individual CTB categories, summarize your reflection. Note categories in which you demonstrated strengths and areas on which you might focus for improvement. Indicate what steps you will take to grow in the future.

Critical Teaching Behaviors	*Instructor Reflection*	*Observer Notes*
Categories and Definitions	*Narrative Examples and Evidence of Behaviors and Strategies*	*Examples and Evidence of Instructor Behaviors and Student Responses*
1. Align: Instructors who align components of learning experiences start with clear learning goals. Measurable outcomes, teaching and learning activities, assessment tasks, and feedback build on each other to support student progress toward these goals.		
1.1. Aligns content, assessments, and activities with outcomes 1.2. Communicates course, module, lesson, and/or assignment outcome(s) at each stage of learning 1.3. Emphasizes connections of course concepts and skills across lessons, learning units, and courses 1.4. Presents content and activities at multiple, appropriate levels of engagement and challenge 1.5. Activates prior knowledge 1.6. Uses time effectively and efficiently toward achievement of outcomes 1.7. Communicates course policies and expectations (e.g., states policies in the syllabus, posts introduction video, etc.)		
2. Include: Instructors who create an inclusive learning environment promote equity by using accessibility standards and learner-centered strategies when designing and delivering content. They cultivate an atmosphere in which students see themselves positively represented and experience a sense of belonging conducive to emotional well-being for learning.		
2.1. Removes barriers to success by designing activities and materials with equitable access and representation in mind (e.g., posts mobile-friendly materials, makes online activities available for asynchronous learning, adopts low- or no-cost materials, provides alternate options for activities, etc.) 2.2. Recognizes and accommodates diversity of student needs and circumstances 2.3. Selects activities, examples, and materials with respect for all students and viewpoints 2.4. Builds student–instructor and student–student relationships and trust (e.g., posts instructor welcome video and/or bio and asks students to do the same, uses student names, makes time to be available, cultivates approachable persona, etc.) 2.5. Invites student questions, examples, and experiences and listens carefully when students speak 2.6. Uses learner-centered strategies in course design and delivery to promote student agency and self-regulation 2.7. Connects students with campus and learning support resources		

Critical Teaching Behaviors	Instructor Reflection	Observer Notes
3. Engage: Instructors who engage students purposefully select research-based techniques to ensure that students actively participate in the learning process and take responsibility for their intellectual development.		
3.1. Establishes regular and open communication 3.2. Encourages participation of all students by using varied active learning strategies (e.g., asks questions and allows appropriate wait time; uses group work, writing activities, discussions, problem-solving, etc.) 3.3. Explains content with examples, demonstrations, visual aids, anecdotes from personal and student experiences, etc. 3.4. Incorporates current research in the field to stimulate discipline-specific critical thinking 3.5. Designs course activities to intentionally promote student–instructor, student–content, and student–student engagement 3.6. Shows enthusiasm for course content and clarifies its relevance and importance 3.7. Speaks clearly and varies tone to emphasize important material and maintain interest		
4. Assess: Instructors who assess learning develop and facilitate transparent, meaningful tasks to provide students with timely feedback on their learning and to measure achievement of learning outcomes. They frequently review data to improve instruction.		
4.1. Includes assessment and grading policies in syllabus 4.2. Schedules regular summative assessments to measure student progress toward outcomes 4.3. Embeds formative assessments and opportunities for self-assessment in instruction 4.4. Assigns a range of assessments to allow students to authentically demonstrate learning 4.5. Communicates purpose, task, and criteria for assessments 4.6. Scaffolds assessments (e.g., breaks large or complex assignments into smaller tasks, provides opportunities for practice with feedback, etc.) 4.7. Provides timely, constructive feedback to students		

(Continues)

(Continued)

Critical Teaching Behaviors	Instructor Reflection	Observer Notes
5. Integrate Technology: Instructors who integrate technology responsibly use tools to design accessible, high-quality instructional materials and engaging learning opportunities beyond traditional barriers of place and time.		
5.1. Integrates limited technologies to enhance student learning (e.g., uses polls, audio-visuals, collaborative tools, reactions and chat features, etc.)		
5.2. Organizes online course materials transparently (e.g., logically organizes materials into units, designs content and tasks to be easily accessible, posts video showing organization of online materials, demonstrates where to find relevant materials, etc.)		
5.3. Designs synchronous and asynchronous course components to complement each other		
5.4. Ensures materials and tools meet requirements of ADA, FERPA, and other regulations		
5.5. Creates multimodal course media including text, visuals, audio, and video		
5.6. Uses technology effectively and efficiently (e.g., operates technology knowledgeably, creates visuals and presentation materials that are easily readable, etc.)		
5.7. Trains students to use instructional technology and provides support		

Appendix E

CTB Observation Process Introduction and Overview

What Is the Critical Teaching Behaviors Framework?

- The CTB framework *synthesizes research on teaching in higher education* into six categories of evidence-based instructor behaviors proven effective in increasing student learning gains and retention.
- A focus on *observable behaviors and strategies* allows instructors and observers to identify concrete strengths and areas for improvement in course delivery and design.
- The CTB framework provides faculty, staff, and administrators with a foundation for *determining shared expectations* for good teaching and *using a common language* to showcase, discuss, and evaluate teaching effectiveness.

How Can I Use the CTB Observation Worksheet?

The observation worksheet provides an overview of the six categories of critical teaching behaviors and lists select examples of concrete instructor actions in each category.

- *Strategies listed in each category are intended to provide examples rather than serve as an exhaustive list.* Observers will likely identify other strategies that can serve as evidence of achievement in the six critical teaching behaviors.
- *It is not expected that instructors demonstrate all strategies listed in every single class.* However, it is important that behaviors from most, if not all, categories are present in the class period/module observed and that they are well integrated into the outcomes and flow of the class/module.
- In addition to feedback from others, *the process of critical self-reflection can lead to improved teaching.* To encourage this behavior, the worksheet is designed to serve as a conversation starter between colleagues that considers both the observer's notes from the classroom and the instructor's reflections on the class observed.
- Teaching observations are an important source of data for evaluating effective teaching; however, *documentation of teaching quality should be comprehensively based on multiple sources of data.*

Recommended Peer Observations Process

Recommendations for the Observer
- *Prior to observation.* Ask the instructor to share their course syllabus and complete a reflection on the course (see Appendix C, "Teaching Observation Instructor Worksheet"). Review their notes. Be familiar with the CTB categories and possible strategies in each area.
- *During the observation.* Take notes on what is happening in the classroom. Consider bringing a copy of the CTB observation form to prompt your note-taking.
  - How is the instructor presenting information?
  - Are students engaged in learning? Are they attentive?

○ What do the instructor's and students' behaviors indicate about the learning environment in this course? How does the environment feel?

○ How does the instructor use technology?

○ How do class structure and activities support each other and prepare students to perform desired tasks?

○ How does the instructor know students achieved the learning outcomes for the lesson (assessment)?

○ Jot down any questions you want to ask the instructor—what additional information do you need?

• *For online observations.* Review the Course Orientation, Welcome, or Introduction module and the module indicated for review on the instructor worksheet. Use the CTB observation form to take notes on the structure, presentation, and content of modules as well as student–student and student–instructor interactions.

• *After the observation.* Review your notes and write organized comments on each of the CTB categories in the report form. Be sure to note CTB categories in which the instructor demonstrates particular strength as well as categories for potential growth. Schedule a meeting with your colleague to discuss the observation.

Recommendations for the Instructor

• *Prior to the observation.* Share a copy of your syllabus and your reflection on the course (see Appendix C, "Teaching Observation Instructor Worksheet") with the observer and any additional materials you would like your observer to have (i.e., lesson plan, student worksheets, etc.). Familiarize yourself with the CTB categories and strategies in each area.

• *During the observation.* Relax! Teach the class as you would normally to ensure a realistic observation.

• *For online observations.* Record your reflections on the Course Orientation, Welcome, or Introduction module as well as the module selected for review. What are you proud of? What would you do differently in the future?

• *After the observation.* Reflect on the class. What went well? What would you do differently in the future? Write reflective comments for each of the CTB categories.

Follow-Up Discussion

• Allow time for both instructor and observer to share their thoughts on the observation. Address any questions.

• Discuss a professional development plan based on both the strength and improvement areas. Determine two to five concrete action steps; these may include ideas for relevant professional development options, strategies to incorporate in future classes, recommendations for strategies to continue using, and so on.

• Observer should update the last box on the report form based on the discussion and share a final version with the instructor. The instructor may choose to include the observation worksheet in their portfolio as one component toward documenting effective teaching.

Notes on Evaluative Observations

• For evaluative observations it is especially important to use common standards and expectations to increase the fairness of reviews, for which the CTB framework provides such a tool.

• When using the CTB framework for evaluative purposes, we recommend following the same observation process already outlined to ensure that instructors have a chance to self-assess, receive feedback, and reflect on appropriate professional development goals to promote growth.

• The final report of an evaluative observation will likely emphasize the summary of observed strengths and weaknesses more heavily than specific observations and instructor reflections to increase its readability for an audience beyond the instructor and observer.

Appendix F

Midterm Student Feedback Survey (GIFT)

Instructor:

Course Title:

This survey will take approximately 5 minutes to complete.

This student feedback survey is conducted at the request of your instructor. Please take time to provide your honest and specific feedback on the following questions. If possible, include examples and explanations of your comments. Make sure to keep comments professional and constructive.

Your feedback allows faculty members to reflect on their teaching, learning activities, and course structure. This reflection provides an opportunity to resolve miscommunications and/or make changes to positively affect learning.

1. What's working well in this class? What are the strengths of the class and which aspects are having a positive impact on your learning?

2. What's not working so well in this class? What specific changes could be made to improve your learning experience in this class?

How often does the instructor exhibit the following behaviors? Please read each statement carefully and select the rating that best represents your experience.

1 = Never   2 = Rarely   3 = Sometimes   4 = Frequently   5 = Always

The instructor:

Explains how assignments, lessons, and course activities help you develop knowledge and skills related to course goals	1	2	3	4	5
Gives exams and assignments that reflect course readings, lectures, and class activities	1	2	3	4	5
Shares course materials on the online learning platform in a way that makes it easy to find and access them	1	2	3	4	5
Uses technologies and/or apps that enhance your learning and experience in the course (e.g., list some of your campus technologies, including LMS)	1	2	3	4	5
Makes you feel like an important and valued member of the class community	1	2	3	4	5
Conducts activities with respect for all students and viewpoints	1	2	3	4	5
Encourages participation from all students by incorporating a range of activities such as time for questions, meaningful individual activities, small-group activities, and/or discussions	1	2	3	4	5
Connects content to current research in the field and/or real-life applications/examples	1	2	3	4	5
Provides regular opportunities to help you assess your learning (quizzes, homework, discussions, project drafts, etc.)	1	2	3	4	5
Gives timely and specific feedback that helps you improve on future assignments	1	2	3	4	5

Provide any necessary clarifications in the open response fields on the previous page.

Appendix G

Midterm Student Feedback Report

Instructor: Students attending:

Course/Date/Time: Consultant:

At the initiative of the instructor, the consultant conducted this midsemester student feedback. A total of [X] students participated.

Feedback Process

Students responded individually to the open-ended and Likert-scale questions indicated in the "Feedback Summary."

The consultant then conducted a whole-class debrief where students shared feedback. The consultant asked clarification questions as appropriate and requested all students in the class demonstrate their agreement or disagreement with statements by a show of hands. General comments were recorded and included in this report.

Individual student responses to survey questions are summarized in the following and representative comments are included verbatim.

Feedback Summary

1. What's working well in this class? What are the strengths of the class and which aspects are having a positive impact on your learning?

2. What's not working so well in this class? What specific changes could be made to improve your learning experience in this class?

Frequency of Teaching Behaviors

In this portion of the feedback session, students used the following scale to give feedback on the frequency with which the instructor exhibits the following teaching behaviors:

1 = Never   2 = Rarely   3 = Sometimes   4 = Frequently   5 = Always

The table indicates the average frequency each rating was selected on the scale, and total number of responses for each item.

Item	1	2	3	4	5	Number	Average
Align							
Instructors who align components of learning experiences start with clearly defined learning outcomes. Teaching and learning activities, assessment tasks, and feedback build on each other to support student progress toward these outcomes.							
Explains how assignments, lessons, and course activities help you develop knowledge and skills related to course goals							
Gives exams and assignments that reflect course readings, lectures, and class activities							
Integrate Technology							
Instructors who integrate technology responsibly use tools to provide access to high-quality instructional materials and accessible, engaging learning opportunities beyond traditional barriers of place and time.							
Shares course materials on the online learning platform in a way that makes it easy to find and access them							
Uses technologies and/or apps that enhance your learning and experience in the course (e.g., list some of your campus technologies, including LMS)							
Include							
Instructors who create an inclusive learning environment plan for student diversity by utilizing accessibility standards when designing and delivering content. They cultivate an atmosphere in which students experience a sense of belonging conducive to emotional well-being for learning.							
Makes you feel like an important and valued member of the class community							
Conducts activities with respect for all students and viewpoints							
Engage							
Instructors who engage students purposefully select research-based techniques to ensure that students actively participate in the learning process and take responsibility for their intellectual development.							
Encourages participation from all students by incorporating a range of activities such as time for questions, meaningful individual activities, small-group activities, and/or discussions							
Connects content to current research in the field and/or real-life applications/examples							

Assess							
Instructors who integrate assessment into their teaching develop and facilitate transparent, meaningful assessment tasks to provide students with timely feedback on their learning and measure achievement of learning outcomes. They regularly review data to improve instruction.							
Provides regular opportunities to help you assess your learning (quizzes, homework, discussions, project drafts, etc.)							
Gives timely and specific feedback that helps you improve on future assignments							

Reflect
Instructors who reflect regularly gather feedback on their teaching from self-assessment, students, and peers to identify opportunities for growth. They pursue improvements to their instruction through professional development and research activities.
Professional Development Plan
Based on feedback from students and the debrief conversation, how will you follow up with students about the insights provided? What steps do you plan to take to enhance teaching strengths and address areas for improvement?

Appendix H

Peer Observation Email Templates

These email templates are intended to help observers communicate the CTB process to faculty requesting peer observations. They may be used as written or adapted as you see fit.

Preobservation Email

Dear [insert name],

Thank you for your interest in a teaching observation. This email provides an overview of the observation process.

Your voice is a critical component of a teaching observation. As such, the steps in the following ask that you complete a preobservation worksheet. After the observation, you will be asked to complete a reflection for me to include in the final report. I rely on the information you provide to gain a holistic perspective on your teaching and write a more complete report.

Please review the following steps and associated documents. Let me know if you have any questions.

Familiarize yourself with the CTB Peer Teaching Observation Instructions *(include link to instructions or attach)*.

Complete and share the brief Instructor Worksheet *(include link to worksheet or attach)* by making an editable copy of the doc.

Review the CTB Observation report form and (optional) identify one or two categories in which you would like to receive targeted feedback.

Share your syllabus and any other course materials relevant to the observation.

If you prefer to discuss your responses to the worksheet in person, I'm happy to meet before the observation.

Postobservation Email With Instructions for CTB Reflection

Dear [insert name],

Thank you for inviting me to observe your class. As I mentioned in my previous email, your voice is a critical component of the observation process. In the next 2 days, please share the following information with me:

- your responses in the reflection column of the peer observation report form *(include link to report or attach)*
- summarized strengths, potential growth areas, and any plans for professional development related to your teaching in the "Reflect" box
- a few times in the next week that work for a debrief conversation

I will begin writing my report only after you share your reflections with me. The insights you share in your reflection allow me to get a more complete picture of your teaching, affirm your own impressions of your teaching, and share resources relevant to your areas of interest and growth.

When you share your reflection document, please also provide a few meeting options to allow us to schedule a time to debrief your report.

Best,

Appendix I

Midterm Feedback (GIFT) Email Templates

Like the Peer Observation templates, the information in the following may be used as is or adapted to meet your personal preferences.

Pre-GIFT Email

Dear [insert name],

I'm following up on your interest in a midterm student feedback session. To get your session scheduled, please confirm the following information:

- course title and number
- preferred date(s) for the session
- course start and end time
- preferred timing for my visit (beginning or end of class)
- meeting location
- number of students
- preferred dates/times for a debrief conversation

If you would like feedback on some specific aspect of the course, please include that in your response as well.

Budget about 20 minutes to allow sufficient time for students to discuss their responses. Courses of more than 40 students may take closer to 25 minutes. In the following, I provide a brief overview of what will occur during the session.

After introducing me, you will leave the room to ensure anonymity of responses.

I will explain that you have voluntarily requested feedback to help improve the student experience in your course and let students know that the process is completely anonymous on their end.

For the first 5 to 7 minutes, students will work individually to complete the feedback survey provided. The survey asks a few quantitative questions about the frequency of teaching behaviors as well as the following qualitative questions:

- What's working well in this class? What are the strengths of the class and which aspects are having a positive impact on your learning?
- What's not working so well in this class? What specific changes could be made to improve your learning experience in this class?

With our remaining time, I will invite students to share their responses to the qualitative questions and record them on the board. After each statement, I will ask students to demonstrate, by show of hands, how many of them agree.

I will thank them for their time and either invite you back into the room or dismiss them.

If you have any questions about this process or would like me to gather input on something specific, please let me know. I'm happy to discuss further by email or a short meeting.

Sample GIFT Bias Statement

To reduce biases in feedback, we recommend sharing some version of the following statement with students before administering the GIFT survey (adapted from the University of Georgia's Center for Teaching and Learning).

Student evaluations of teaching play an important role in the review of teaching and learning. Research shows student evaluations of teaching are often influenced by unconscious and unintentional biases about the race and gender of the instructor. Women and instructors of color are systematically rated lower in their teaching evaluations than white men, even when there are no actual differences in the instruction or in what students have learned. To help reduce the effect of bias in your feedback, please focus on the content and delivery of the course (assignments, readings, in-class teaching strategies, online materials, sense of belonging, instructor availability and responsiveness) rather than the static factors the instructor cannot control (identity, appearance, personality, location of origin).

About the Authors

Lauren Barbeau is the assistant director for learning and technology initiatives at the Georgia Institute of Technology Center for Teaching and Learning. She earned her PhD in English, specializing in 19th-century American literature with a certificate in American culture studies, from Washington University in St. Louis. Before becoming an educational developer, she taught writing and literature courses. She began her educational development career at Georgia Southern University, and subsequently served as the assistant director for faculty development and SoTL at the University of Georgia. Her research interests include teaching with technology as well as documenting and assessing teaching.

Claudia Cornejo Happel is an associate director of the Center for Teaching and Learning Excellence at Embry-Riddle Aeronautical University, Daytona Beach, Florida. She earned her PhD in Spanish, specializing in colonial Latin American art, literature, and culture, from the Ohio State University and an educational specialist (EdS) degree from Georgia Southern University. Claudia has previously held positions in the University Center for the Advancement of Teaching at Ohio State—an opportunity that was instrumental in shaping her interest in educational development—and the Center for Teaching Excellence at Georgia Southern University. Her research interests include documenting and assessing teaching, SoTL, as well as inclusive instructional practices.

Index